ASEAN and India
The Way Forward

ASEAN and India
The Way Forward

Editors

Tommy Koh
Ambassador-at-Large, Singapore

Hernaikh Singh
Institute of South Asian Studies, National University of Singapore, Singapore

Moe Thuzar
ISEAS-Yusof Ishak Institute, Singapore

World Scientific

NEW JERSEY • LONDON • SINGAPORE • BEIJING • SHANGHAI • HONG KONG • TAIPEI • CHENNAI • TOKYO

Published by

World Scientific Publishing Co. Pte. Ltd.
5 Toh Tuck Link, Singapore 596224
USA office: 27 Warren Street, Suite 401-402, Hackensack, NJ 07601
UK office: 57 Shelton Street, Covent Garden, London WC2H 9HE

National Library Board, Singapore Cataloguing in Publication Data
Name(s): Koh, Tommy T. B. (Tommy Thong Bee), 1937– editor. |
   Singh, Hernaikh, editor. | Moe Thuzar, editor.
Title: ASEAN and India : the way forward / editors, Tommy Koh, Hernaikh Singh, Moe Thuzar.
Description: Singapore : World Scientific Publishing Co. Pte. Ltd., [2023]
Identifier(s): ISBN 978-981-12-6289-0 (hardcover) | ISBN 978-981-12-6351-4 (paperback) |
   ISBN 978-981-12-6290-6 (ebook for institutions) |
   ISBN 978-981-12-6291-3 (ebook for individuals)
Subject(s): LCSH: Southeast Asia--Foreign relations--India. | India--Foreign relations--
   Southeast Asia. | Southeast Asia--Foreign economic relations--India. |
   India--Foreign economic relations--Southeast Asia.
Classification: DDC 327.59054--dc23

British Library Cataloguing-in-Publication Data
A catalogue record for this book is available from the British Library.

Copyright © 2023 by World Scientific Publishing Co. Pte. Ltd.

All rights reserved. This book, or parts thereof, may not be reproduced in any form or by any means, electronic or mechanical, including photocopying, recording or any information storage and retrieval system now known or to be invented, without written permission from the publisher.

For photocopying of material in this volume, please pay a copying fee through the Copyright Clearance Center, Inc., 222 Rosewood Drive, Danvers, MA 01923, USA. In this case permission to photocopy is not required from the publisher.

For any available supplementary material, please visit
https://www.worldscientific.com/worldscibooks/10.1142/13041#t=suppl

Desk Editor: Jiang Yulin

Typeset by Stallion Press
Email: enquiries@stallionpress.com

Foreword

Three decades ago, India and the Association of Southeast Asian Nations (ASEAN) took a momentous decision to upgrade their relationship. At that time, neither could have really foreseen the transformational consequences of their action. There are today more than 30 mechanisms between the two, including an annual summit and seven ministerial dialogues. But more than the intensity of their contacts, what it brought about was a profound shift in their respective perceptions of each other as well as of their larger geo-political circumstances.

For India, the 'Look East' policy, as it was initially known, was a rebalancing that took into account the benefits that more successful Asian nations could offer. It was not only a geographical re-prioritisation but also a change in its economic strategy and its trade outlook. The rebalancing led to a number of Free Trade Agreements and additional avenues of connectivity. Indian talent now accessed a broader arena for its activities and achievements. In due course, initiatives were undertaken to build physical connections between South Asia and Southeast Asia. As political comfort increased, the ASEAN member nations and India also entered into defence and security partnerships of some significance. The graduation to an 'Act East' policy signified how far this relationship has come.

For ASEAN, closer ties with India provided access to an economy where reform was driving a market enlargement. Trade and commerce were buttressed by additional opportunities of financial investment and projects. The flow of skills from India contributed to the competitiveness of ASEAN and, in some cases, to greater entrepreneurship and creativity. As the benefits of reform in India grew, so did the Indian investment footprint in the ASEAN region. The growth of tourism in this period was also impressive.

The strategic reflection of this enhanced relationship should also be recognised. India's participation in ASEAN-led forums may have served its foreign policy interests. But they certainly contributed to giving these mechanisms a larger coverage and a higher profile. By bridging the Asia-Pacific and the Indian Ocean regions, this partnership has contributed to the emergence of the Indo-Pacific today. For that reason, we must also pay due regard to the centrality of ASEAN in this context.

India's growing ties with ASEAN were the prerequisite for it to reach out to partners beyond. Ties with Japan and South Korea were energised as a result. Economic contacts with China expanded steadily. And the remarkable upswing in India-Australia relations that includes a recently concluded Free Trade Agreement is its latest corollary. Even as this happens, bilateral cooperation with the individual ASEAN member states has intensified. Sub-regional mechanisms like the Mekong-Ganga Cooperation have also developed.

Looking back, the tryst that India made with ASEAN has had four profound implications. One, it spurred the re-globalisation of India that is now gathering momentum. Two, it enhanced Indian awareness of its maritime interests. Three, it introduced economic and governance practices that drew from experiences to its East. And four, it re-connected an extended neighbourhood that had been distanced by post-war developments. These are the key trends that will contribute to the emergence of the New India.

Dr S Jaishankar
Minister of External Affairs
Republic of India

Foreword

Southeast Asia and India have sustained deep cultural, linguistic, religious, commercial, scientific and political relations for over more than two millennia. It is worth bearing these long-term historical currents in mind as we contemplate how the Association of Southeast Asian Nations (ASEAN) and India developed a dynamic, substantive and mutually beneficial relationship over the past five decades. ASEAN and India share strategic interests in developing our economies synergistically and seeking regional peace and prosperity. All of us subscribe to an open, inclusive regional architecture. Singapore has always been a staunch supporter of India's engagement with ASEAN. India was a Sectoral Dialogue Partner of ASEAN in 1992 and then became a full Dialogue Partner just three years later in 1995. The inaugural annual ASEAN-India Summit was held in 2002. Relations were further upgraded to a Strategic Partnership in 2012. In 2018, all 10 ASEAN leaders were the chief guests to witness India's 69th Republic Day Parade in conjunction with the ASEAN-India Commemorative Summit.

As Singapore commenced our three-year coordinatorship of ASEAN-India dialogue relations in August 2021, we hope to work more closely with India to elevate ASEAN-India relations to new heights as we emerge from the COVID-19 pandemic. I thank the editors of the book, Tommy Koh, Hernaikh Singh and Moe Thuzar, for their timely and ambitious undertaking. Through their extensive research, Tommy, Hernaikh and Moe have gathered essays on a comprehensive range of topics. Singapore is keen to pursue many of these areas. In particular, there is great potential for cooperation in emerging areas such as post COVID-19 recovery, technology, digital economy and climate change. We note that there are synergies between the ASEAN Smart Cities Network and India's Smart Cities Mission. With India's expertise in cybersecurity, we would also be keen to work with India on regional capacity building, such as through the ASEAN-Singapore Cybersecurity Centre of Excellence. There is scope for both sides to explore how we can build on some of the interesting initiatives which India has piloted on this front, such as the ASEAN-India Hackathon and the ASEAN-India Track 1.5 Dialogue on Cyber Issues. There are also many avenues for cooperation in the circular economy and waste management. There has been good cooperation at the ASEAN Working Group on Climate Change in past years, and we hope to rejuvenate these meaningful initiatives. We also hope to make further progress in the implementation of the ASEAN-India Free Trade Area.

The editors have provided room for diversity in perspectives. This recognises the unique political, economic and socio-cultural contexts and challenges facing both ASEAN and India. For example, ASEAN understandably would have preferred that India be part of the Regional Comprehensive Economic Partnership (RCEP) as India's participation would make the RCEP truly 'comprehensive'. Nevertheless, the door will always remain open for India to join the pact when it is ready to do so. I am also glad to see that the book addresses the Indo-Pacific concept. Both ASEAN and India have similar visions for an open and inclusive regional architecture with an emphasis on ASEAN centrality and the rules-based world order.

This book sets out both the rich history and great potential of the ASEAN-India partnership as we collectively chart a path towards enduring collaboration, resilience and prosperity.

Dr Vivian Balakrishnan
Minister for Foreign Affairs
Republic of Singapore

Foreword

It bears reminding that as we celebrate the 30th anniversary of the relations between the Association of Southeast Asian Nations (ASEAN) and India in 2022, we must appreciate that the region's ties with India are not measured in terms of decades but in centuries. Before the Indo-Pacific concept came into the mainstream diplomatic and strategic circles, Southeast Asia was — and continues to be — the bridge between the East and West. As early as the 13th century, Indian traders brought goods and wares from the Indian subcontinent, the Arab world and Europe to the region, and shared with Southeast Asia their languages, cultures and religions. It is this legacy that forms part of the cornerstone of ASEAN's rich and diverse living cultural heritage.

Thus, as we mark three decades of dynamic and mutually beneficial relations between ASEAN and India, it is apt that both partners have dedicated 2022 as the 'ASEAN-India Friendship Year' to honour our enduring historic and contemporary relationship, which is multifaceted and underpinned by robust trade, socio-cultural and political ties.

India is ASEAN's fifth largest trade partner. Spurred by the entry into force of the ASEAN-India Trade in Goods Agreement (AITGA) on 1 January 2010, bilateral trade increased by 36 percent in the past decade, from US$56.7 billion in 2010 to US$77.1 billion in 2019. However, bilateral trade suffered due the COVID-19 pandemic and declined to US$63.8 billion in 2020. Nevertheless, the overall forward momentum is expected to continue with the agreement of the ASEAN and Indian Economic Ministers in August 2020 to commence discussions on a scoping paper to review the AITGA to ensure that it will be more user-friendly, simple and trade facilitative for businesses.

Cooperation in the economic sphere spans from trade and investment, energy, finance, science, technology and innovation, and information and communication technology to the blue economy and the digital economy. The ASEAN-India connectivity partnership to enhance physical and digital connectivity, including exploring synergies between the Master Plan for ASEAN Connectivity 2025 and India's connectivity strategies under its 'Act East' policy in line with the 'Connecting the Connectivities' approach, will provide additional impetus to broaden and upscale bilateral economic ties. Within the region, India has supported sub-regional cooperation through the Mekong-Ganga Cooperation and the Bengal Initiative for Multisectoral Technical and Economic Cooperation.

Socio-cultural ties remain one of the most enduring and important facets of ASEAN-India relations. Leveraging on the dense network of people-to-people ties, ASEAN and India have enhanced mutual understanding and appreciation of each other's culture, arts and history. Efforts to engage the youth through the ASEAN-India Youth Summit, which was inaugurated in 2017, should be further encouraged to ensure that the ASEAN-India partnership is sustained across all generations of our respective communities.

Similarly, the ASEAN-India Students Exchange Programme, ASEAN-India Media Exchange Programme, ASEAN-India Collaborative R&D Scheme and other collaborative ventures in disaster management, public health, sustainable development, biodiversity conservation, smart cities, and technical and vocational education and training would provide additional avenues to strengthen people-to-people relations.

On the political front, India has been a staunch supporter — in words and deeds — of ASEAN centrality. This support is evident in India's affirmation of the ASEAN Outlook on the Indo-Pacific which is manifested through the ASEAN-India Joint Statement on Cooperation on the ASEAN Outlook on the Indo-Pacific for Peace, Stability, and Prosperity in the Region which was adopted at the 18th ASEAN-India Summit on 28 October 2021. In addition, India has actively participated in and contributed positively to ASEAN-led mechanisms, including the East Asia Summit, ASEAN Regional Forum, ASEAN Defence Ministers' Meeting-Plus and the Expanded ASEAN Maritime Forum. In addition, India is currently co-chairing with Indonesia the Experts Working Group (EWG) on Humanitarian Assistance and Disaster Relief and has previously co-chaired the EWGs on Humanitarian Mine Action and Military Medicine.

This commemorative anniversary is an opportune moment for ASEAN and India to take stock of the progress of their bilateral partnership as well as to collectively reflect on the journey ahead. The ASEAN-India partnership is full of potential and both parties need to realise these opportunities for the betterment of their peoples. Beyond the polemics of revisioning the regional architecture, ASEAN and India need to take tangible steps towards the gradual integration of their respective economies. The potential upgrading of the AITGA is a good starting point and the return of India into the Regional Comprehensive Economic Partnership fold would be a momentous turning point in the region's economic growth and development. Accordingly, the Plan of Action to Implement the ASEAN-India Partnership for Peace, Progress and Shared Prosperity (2021–2025) would elevate ASEAN-India ties to greater heights.

I strongly commend the initiative of Professor Tommy Koh, Mr Hernaikh Singh and Ms Moe Thuzar to lead this effort to commemorate the 30 years of ASEAN-India relations and, through this volume, help us to consider new pathways and modalities to solidify this important relationship. I also thank the contributors for their insightful analyses and thoughts and express my appreciation to Singapore as the country coordinator for shepherding the ASEAN-India Dialogue Relations for 2021–2024.

Dato Lim Jock Hoi
Secretary-General
ASEAN

Introduction

Relations between India and Southeast Asia go back a thousand years. For most of that period, the relationship was peaceful. Indian religions — Hinduism and Buddhism — were adopted by many Southeast Asians. India was a source of inspiration to Southeast Asia in many fields, including state rituals, culture, cuisine and language. India's cultural influence in Southeast Asia continues to this day. For example, it is remarkable that the great Indian epic, *Ramayana*, is performed in nine of the 10 member states of the Association of Southeast Asian Nations (ASEAN). That historical, cultural connection, and the enduring relevance of the epic's main themes, particularly that of leadership in addressing pressing problems and issues, inspired ASEAN to adapt the performance into a contemporary dance production. With the participation of prominent performing artistes from the different ASEAN member states, the production, 'Realising Rama', was performed for audiences in various cities across the 10 ASEAN member states and in New Delhi.

Bilateral interactions notwithstanding, ASEAN and India 'reconnected' in 1992 when India became a Sectoral Dialogue Partner of ASEAN. India became a full Dialogue Partner in 1995. The first ASEAN-India Summit was held in 2002. In 2012, the relationship was elevated to a strategic partnership. ASEAN and India have designated 2022 as the 'Friendship Year' to commemorate the 30th anniversary of the ASEAN-India formal relationship and the 20th anniversary of the strategic partnership.

In this 'Friendship Year' of ASEAN-India relations, we decided to invite a diverse group of scholars and practitioners to contribute to this book for three reasons.

First, Singapore began its three-year tenure as the country coordinator for ASEAN's relations with India in August 2021. We hope that the book will offer new ideas to thought leaders in both India and the ASEAN member states to further enrich, refresh and elevate the relationship.

Second, we are true believers in ASEAN. We believe that ASEAN will overcome its many challenges, including the crisis in Myanmar. We believe that ASEAN will continue to make rapid economic progress and will become the world's fifth largest economy in the not-too-distant future. We believe that a united and neutral ASEAN can continue to play a central role in the affairs of the region. At the same time, we believe in India and in its future. Like ASEAN, India is faced with many challenges. We believe that India will overcome its challenges. We believe that India will become the world's third largest economy by the middle of the century.

Third, we believe that the relationship between ASEAN and India is a very important one. It is a relationship between the 1.3 billion people of India and the 650 million people of ASEAN. It is a relationship between two vibrant economies. It is a relationship which is relatively free of problems. There is, therefore, a high degree of comfort and trust in the relationship. However, the truth is that the relationship is far below its potential. ASEAN is underperforming in India and India is underperforming in ASEAN. The ASEAN-India relationship is a pale shadow of the ASEAN-China relationship. We want to change that. This book is dedicated to the objective of raising the ASEAN-India relationship to the same level as the ASEAN-China relationship.

We are very grateful to the 42 Indians and Southeast Asians who have offered their perspectives on a wide range of issues in the

ASEAN-India relationship. We are particularly grateful to India's Minister of External Affairs, Dr S Jaishankar; Singapore's Foreign Minister, Dr Vivian Balakrishnan; and ASEAN's Secretary-General, Dato Lim Jock Hoi, for their enlightening and instructive forewords for the book. A similar note of appreciation also goes to Ambassador Ong Keng Yong and High Commissioner P Kumaran for sharing their thoughts in the book's concluding section.

We also thank Ms Wini Fred Gurung at the Institute of South Asian Studies in the National University of Singapore for her administrative assistance to the publication. Finally, we are grateful to our publisher, World Scientific Publishing, our editor, Jiang Yulin, and the designer, Ng Chin Choon, for bringing out this publication.

Tommy Koh
Hernaikh Singh
Moe Thuzar

Contents

Foreword by Dr S Jaishankar   v
Foreword by Dr Vivian Balakrishnan   vii
Foreword by Dato Lim Jock Hoi   ix
Introduction   xiii

SECTION I   HISTORY   1

Chapter 1   Mapping Myths: Some Traces of South Asian Pre-modern Connections with Southeast Asia   3

Nalina Gopal

Chapter 2   India and ASEAN: Evolving, Intense and Differentiated Engagement   9

S D Muni

SECTION II   AREAS OF CONVERGENCE   15

Trade Relations   17

Chapter 3   ASEAN-India Trade Relations: Evolution and Prospects   19

Manu Bhaskaran

Chapter 4 Trade Relations between ASEAN and India: Reviewing the Last Decade	27
Amitendu Palit	

Investment Relations — 33

Chapter 5 ASEAN-India Trade and Investment Relations: Perspectives from the Philippines	35
Francis Mark A Quimba	
Chapter 6 ASEAN-India Investment Relations: Opportunities for a Strategic Partnership in a Post COVID-19 World	43
Rahul Sen	

Business Ties — 53

Chapter 7 ASEAN-India Business Relationship: Perspectives of a Singaporean Indian Business Leader	55
Karan Singh Thakral	
Chapter 8 Business Linkages between India and ASEAN	63
Naushad Forbes	

Political and Security Relations — 71

Chapter 9 Relations between India and ASEAN: The 'ASEAN Way' and the Indo-Pacific Way	73
Sinderpal Singh	
Chapter 10 India and ASEAN: Strong Base but Headwinds Ahead	79
T C A Raghavan	

Connectivity   85

Chapter 11 ASEAN-India Connectivity: Progress and Challenges   87

Myo Thant

Chapter 12 Thirty Years of ASEAN-India Connectivity   95

Prabir De

Cultural Ties   103

Chapter 13 Cultural Linkages between ASEAN and India: The Past to Post COVID-19   105

Sophana Srichampa

Chapter 14 ASEAN-India Rhapsody of Cultural Exchanges   111

Rajeev Ranjan Chaturvedy

People-to-people Ties   119

Chapter 15 ASEAN-India: Strengthening People-to-people Ties   121

Tan Ming Hui and Nazia Hussain

Chapter 16 People-centred: Advancing India-ASEAN Ties through People-to-people Contacts   129

Shankari Sundararaman

SECTION III   AREAS OF DIFFERENCES   137

The Regional Comprehensive Economic Partnership   139

Chapter 17 The Regional Comprehensive Economic Partnership: The Journey   141

Sulaimah Mahmood

Chapter 18 Withdrawal from the Regional Comprehensive Economic Partnership — Where Does It Take India?   149

Sudhir T Devare

Attitude towards China   **155**

Chapter 19 ASEAN and India's Relations with China: Perceptions and Priorities   157

Kavi Chongkittavorn and Moe Thuzar

Chapter 20 How India and China View Each Other   163

Shivshankar Menon

The Asia-Pacific Versus the Indo-Pacific   **171**

Chapter 21 India and ASEAN's Visions of the Indo-Pacific: Same Dream, Different Beds   173

Hoang Thi Ha

Chapter 22 The Asia-Pacific or the Indo-Pacific: Changing Geo-political Priorities   181

C Raja Mohan

SECTION IV LOOKING TO THE FUTURE   **187**

Smart Cities   **189**

Chapter 23 From a Smart to a Learning City: The Singapore Model for ASEAN and India   191

Limin Hee and Aaron Maniam

Chapter 24 Indian Smart Cities: The Challenges Ahead   199

Pushpa Pathak and Marie-Hélène Zérah

Digital Economy and E-commerce — 207

Chapter 25 Race towards a Digital Future: The Case for Greater ASEAN-India Cooperation — 209

Jayant Menon

Chapter 26 India and ASEAN: Enhancing Collaboration in the Digital Economy and E-commerce — 217

Arpita Mukherjee

Environment and Sustainability — 225

Chapter 27 Untapped Potential in the ASEAN-India Relationship: Climate Change and Green Recovery — 227

Sharon Seah

Chapter 28 Build Resilience and Tap Opportunities for a Greener Future — 235

Arunabha Ghosh and Sanjana Chhabra

Open Skies — 243

Chapter 29 ASEAN-India Air Connectivity: Time for a More Liberal Open Skies Policy — 245

Ridha Aditya Nugraha

Chapter 30 Open Skies: Pathway to Enhanced India-ASEAN Economic Ties — 251

Deeparghya Mukherjee

Human Security — 257

Chapter 31 Human Security: The ASEAN Perspective — 259

Kasira Cheeppensook

Chapter 32 Foundations of Good Governance: Enduring
Relevance of Human Security   265

D P K Pillay

SECTION V   CONCLUSION   271

Chapter 33 Dynamics of ASEAN-India Relations   273

Ong Keng Yong

Chapter 34 India and ASEAN: The Past and the Future   279

P Kumaran

About the Editors   287
About the Authors   289
Index   301

1

Mapping Myths: Some Traces of South Asian Pre-modern Connections with Southeast Asia

Nalina Gopal

South and Southeast Asia have had interactions at least since the early centuries of the Common Era (CE), and these interactions have left a deep impact on the socio-cultural fabric of both regions. While it is important to free the understanding of indigenous Southeast Asian cultures of external agency, it is also true that no culture evolves in isolation. These cultures were connected, not distanced by the waters that lay in between, and so were its people.

The pre-modern maritime fame of the Straits of Malacca was unparalleled; the waterway was perhaps the most important thoroughfare connecting the Indian Ocean with the South China Sea, and the East with the West. Embedded in shared mythologies and literary traditions of the regions lie traces of these centuries of cultural interplay and reciprocity. Buried in the library of the Sri Thendayuthapani Temple, Singapore, is a copy of *Manimekalai*, a 6th century CE Buddhist epic set in the Chola town of Kaveripumpattinam. In it unfolds a tale that reveals Tamil familiarity with Cavakam (Java) in pre-modern times. Its heroine is named after the Buddhist goddess of the sea, Manimekhala (meaning girdle of gems). She appears across Southeast Asian regional art, literature and cosmologies as Nang Mekhala in Thailand and Laos, Mani Maykhala in Myanmar and Moni Mekhala in Cambodia, and she even features in local versions of the *Ramayana*, unlike any Indian version of the epic. She first appears in the Pali *Sankha* and *Mahajanaka Jatakas* (dating to around the 4th century BCE) and, in the latter, saves the future Buddha when he is stranded at sea.

Interestingly, we also find reference to *Suvarnabhumi* or the Land of Gold, long associated with Southeast Asia, in this pair of Jataka stories concerning the goddess. In these stories, the two protagonists, Sankha and Janaka, sail in search of fortune to *Suvarnabhumi*, or *Chryse Chersonesos*, as the Greeks knew it.

> "…The city's protectress, the goddess Manimekhala, lost patience and allowed the curse to be accomplished. The furious ocean swelled up and the magnificent city of Puhar was swallowed by its flood."
>
> An extract from Cattanar's *Manimekalai*,
> one of the five ancient Tamil classics,
> as translated by Alan Daniélou

The *Manimekalai* speaks of a curse the goddess casts, angered by the fact that the Chola king did not celebrate a festival dedicated to the god Indra, and causes the town of Puhar to be submerged by a deluge. The epic gives us a plausible explanation for the disappearance of the ancient port town of Puhar by alluding to the tidal wave or tsunami, as we might know it today, that had drowned the coastal epicentre of Chola maritime activity.

Over a series of underwater excavations conducted between the 1960s and 1990s, Indian archaeologists have discovered the remnants of wharves in what they have confirmed was part of the famed old port. An early Chola capital, Puhar's virtues are extolled in the *Pattinapalai* and the *Silapadikaram*, Tamil literature of the Sangam era; the former classic is well-known for noting the wares of *Kazhagam* or Kedah and Sri Lanka flooding the markets of Puhar. But beyond the knowledge of the Southeast Asian kingdoms, the treatise also provides us an inkling as to how the Buddhist world was mapped in Tamil literary imagination, extending from Tamil country to Southeast Asia, from Kanchi through Cape Comorin to Java, which emerged as an important centre of Mahayana Buddhism. The goddess Manimekhala appears ensconced in fantastical seascapes. She is a symbol of shared cultures, a celestial figure who has been accorded a place in several regional variations. While Sheldon Pollock's Sanskrit Cosmopolis (that he dates between the 4th and 14th centuries CE) maps interconnections between South and Southeast Asia through the use of Sanskrit as a political instrument by regional polities, Anne Monius has suggested that texts such as the *Manimekalai* serve as discrete reminders of a cultural or literary region extending from South India to Southeast Asia. Indeed, episodes, as recounted in the *Manimekalai*, even inspired retellings in the Malay world, as seen in the *Hikayat Raja Muda*.

Tamil legends have even found place in the *Hikayat Hang Tuah* and the Malay Annals or *Sejarah Melayu*. A thorough perusal of the 17th century text *Sejarah Melayu*, otherwise known as the *Sulalat al-salāṭīn*, displays the Malay world's familiarity with the legends of the Cholas for several centuries. This literary feat contains perhaps the earliest citation of the term *Keling* or *Kling* in the context of Malacca and Singapore, used favourably to refer to a kingdom of glory, and one that had long-sustained commercial, political and even marital alliances with the Malay Archipelago. Kalinga was an important port, and it was following its conquest, and with the strength of Kalinga's fleet that the Chola king, Rajendra Chola I, acquired success in his siege against Kedah in 1025 CE.

Sejarah Melayu also perhaps holds the key to the mystery surrounding the Singapore Stone, a pre-modern inscription and the oldest epigraphic evidence found on the island. It provides the legend of the creation and installation of the Singapore Stone. It recounts the story of Sang Nila Utama, the founder of the kingdom of Singapura who is said to have stood in front of the ancient will and testament of Raja Chulan (identified by scholars as Rajendra Chola I) in the form of the inscribed Singapore Stone. The popular tale of Badang, a local strongman is celebrated after his defeat of a *Kling* rival, and it is in his chronicle that the location of the Stone at the mouth of the Singapore River, where it was rediscovered in the 19th century, is indicated.

Yet another trans-regional mythic motif is Varuna or Baruna, as he is known in the Malay world. The *Tolkappiyam* assigns Varuna as the patron deity of *Neytal* or the sandy, coastal region. The *Pattinapalai* makes reference to the coastal communities worshipping the fierce and sacred power residing in the ocean, perhaps indicative of the absorption of the Vedic God Varuna into the Tamil pantheon. Varuna appears in the *Hikayat Sang Boma*, the Malay version of the old Javanese text, *Bhaumakavya*, in which he, the god of the sea, emerges from the sea, accompanied by celestial sprites to aid the protagonist of the tale, Boma. Varuna is the oceanic deity Dewa Baruna in Bali, who rides a creature of the sea — *makara*, and has a number of sea temples dedicated to him.

These are but some instances of shared mythologies associated with the seascapes of the South and Southeast Asian societies revealing the voracious appetite littoral communities in these regions had for stories of fantastic maritime adventures. They are also a timely reminder of the need to revisit the importance of waterbodies in Asian societies, and to relook at them not as periphery but the epicentre, not as the means but as the end, as control over the waters meant control over the commercial networks. After all, control over such a powerful natural element has, since time immemorial, been an ancient human quest.

The recent discovery of a shipwreck dating back to around 600 years near Pedra Branca at the eastern entrance to the Straits of Singapore could shed some light on a crucial waterway whose maritime past still remains relatively unknown. One hopes that advances in historical and archaeological research would aid in identifying missing jigsaw pieces to unfold a *longue durée* narrative of pre-modern contact between South and Southeast Asia. These missing pieces, if found, could well fuel the trans-regional myths and legends of the future.

2

India and ASEAN: Evolving, Intense and Differentiated Engagement

S D Muni

India has deep and extensive civilisational bonds with the Association of Southeast Asian Nations (ASEAN) region, going back centuries. India's economic prosperity and security have historically depended on the depth and spread of its engagement with this region. This will continue to be so, especially in the context of the changing growth dynamics and shifting strategic balance in the region.

Seeking Membership

When ASEAN was being formed in 1967, India appeared keen to explore the possibility of joining it and to ensure that it remained outside the then prevailing Cold War rivalries while becoming a bulwark of peace and prosperity in the region. Prime Minister Indira Gandhi sent Minister for External Affairs Mohammadali Carim Chagla to Malaysia and Singapore in May 1967. Welcoming the idea of a cooperative developmental grouping in the region, he said in Singapore:

"...if Singapore chooses to join any regional cooperation, we will be happy to join such a grouping, if other members want India to do so. If others want to have a small grouping, India will be very happy to remain outside and help such a grouping...India does not want to dominate any regional grouping."

However, the then prevailing strategic context of the Cold War and deepening United States (US) war in Vietnam did not welcome India in ASEAN. In India's perception, ASEAN was being conceived and supported by the US to cope with the ideological and strategic consequences of the US' difficulties in its Vietnam War. Initially, only the non-communist countries of the region were invited to be ASEAN members. In the perception of the ASEAN member states, India was a communist supporter, being strategically closer to the then Soviet Union as well as Vietnam. There were ASEAN member states like Indonesia that were strategically uncomfortable with India because of the Pakistan influence (recall Pakistan's war with India in 1965). Regional economic cooperation for development, the ostensible purpose of establishing ASEAN, did not seem to be a priority.

These perceptions were moderated and revised with the exchange of visits between India and the ASEAN member states against the background of ASEAN's gradual emergence, leading to its first summit in 1976. In 1973, India endorsed ASEAN's November 1971 Declaration of constituting itself as a Zone of Peace, Freedom and Neutrality (ZOPFAN). ASEAN, as a nuclear weapons free zone, was an essential component of ZOPFAN. This had strong synergy with India's support for the Sri Lankan move in 1974 to make the Indian Ocean a nuclear weapons free zone. India submitted a formal request to join ASEAN as a Dialogue Partner in December 1976. Pursuance of this request by the new non-Congress government in New Delhi (1977–1980) underlined the bipartisan (Congress–non-Congress) support in India for the association with ASEAN. In response to this, an exploratory ASEAN mission, led by its Secretary-General Datuk Ali bin Abdullah, visited New Delhi in November 1978. When Singapore's strongman, Prime Minister Lee Kuan

Yew, visited India in December 1978, New Delhi pleaded with him for closer economic cooperation with the ASEAN member states. ASEAN accepted, in principle, India as a Dialogue Partner and invited it to a senior official-level meeting of ASEAN in Kuala Lumpur in May 1980. India's status was to be firmed up at the ministerial meeting scheduled for July 1980 but this did not happen. India's Minister for External Affairs Narasimha Rao skipped this meeting in the face of ASEAN displeasure with India's recognition of the Vietnam-backed Heng Samrin regime in Cambodia. ASEAN also did not call India for subsequent meetings, underlining the fact that strategic considerations weighed heavier than regional cooperation on both sides. Malaysian leader, Prime Minister Mahathir Mohamad, tried to revive the idea of India's dialogue partnership in January 1982 but it did not work. Perhaps, the other ASEAN member states were not ready for India's association as yet.

Institutional Integration

The process of India's smooth institutional integration with ASEAN started with the beginning of India's 'Look East' policy, initiated by Rao as Prime Minister in the early 1990s. The Cold War had then come to an end, the Cambodian conflict was inching towards resolution, and the former Soviet Union disintegrated, creating a strategic void for India. Moreover, China was steadily rising and India had set out to open its economy. In this changing strategic context, ASEAN accepted India as a Sectoral Dialogue Partner in January 1992. This, in a way, was a demotion because more than a decade earlier in 1980, as noted previously, ASEAN was prepared to welcome India as a full Dialogue Partner.

In November 1995, India was upgraded from the Sectoral to the Full Dialogue Partner status by ASEAN. This decision was, however, not very smooth. ASEAN had granted the Sectoral Dialogue Partner status to India along with Pakistan in 1992 and some members like Malaysia and Indonesia wanted Pakistan to also be elevated to the full Dialogue Partner status together with India. However, Singapore's persuasive and sustained diplomatic efforts succeeded in mellowing the reservations of Malaysia and Indonesia on according the status only to India. New Delhi's keen interest in enhancing its economic engagement with ASEAN and the latter's strategic imperatives to have India in the group for its fast-changing regional balance, facilitated Singapore's role. India's then Foreign Minister I K Gujral publicly thanked Singapore for this and promised that India would work hard to meet ASEAN's expectations.

India's full Dialogue Partner status enabled it to become a member of the ASEAN Regional Forum, established in 1995 to address security-related issues. India was also keen to secure the membership of two other ASEAN forums — the Asia-Europe Meeting, established in March 1996; and ASEAN+3 (ASEAN plus China, Japan and Korea) Summit, initiated in 1997. However, it did not succeed in doing so. Instead, India was accommodated by ASEAN as a separate Summit partner with the institutionalisation of the India-ASEAN summit in 2002. India acceded to one of the basic ASEAN documents — the Treaty of Amity and Cooperation in October 2003. India also joined the East Asia Summit, established by an ASEAN initiative in 2005, and it was invited to participate in the ASEAN Defence Ministers' Meeting Plus, which was conceived in 2010, as a forum for the exchange of views and consultations on the region's security-related issues. India also became a member of the Expanded ASEAN Maritime Forum (EAMF) in October 2012. In December 2012, India hosted a Commemorative Summit with ASEAN to mark 20 years of its association. At this Summit, India and ASEAN adopted a 'Vision Statement' for their future relations and raised the status of their status to Strategic Partnership.

India's complete institutional integration with the ASEAN structures necessitated the posting of a full-time diplomatic mission to ASEAN in Jakarta in 2014. India also established the ASEAN-India Centre in New Delhi to "strengthen its strategic partnership across three pillars of security, economic and socio-cultural cooperation" and help facilitate the realisation of the ASEAN Community. India's redefining of its 'Look East' policy as an 'Act East' policy in 2014 reinforced the seriousness of its commitment to the region's peace and prosperity. There are now more than 30 different dialogue mechanisms, ranging from summits and ministerial meetings to the meetings of senior officials and Tracks 1.5 and 2.0 conferences and consultations. India and ASEAN held their 18th Summit in October 2021 and the year 2022 is celebrated as the 'ASEAN-India Friendship Year' to mark 30 years of their partnership. Through such an extensive engagement, diverse areas of cooperation like security, connectivity, trade and investments, space technology and counter-terrorism, maritime security and defence collaboration, and pandemic and climate change, are explored, planned and executed. The strategic contours of the Asia-Pacific region have been recast into the new strategic entity of the Indo-Pacific. The recognition of the underlying connectivity of the Indian and Pacific Oceans has enhanced India's significance in ASEAN's regional affairs. India has been strongly reiterating the centrality of ASEAN in its approach to the Indo-Pacific and both sides are working to enhance convergence between India's Indo-Pacific Oceans Initiative and the ASEAN Outlook on the Indo-Pacific.

Emerging Challenges

India began with a differentiated approach to the ASEAN member states. Development cooperation was emphasised in relation to the relatively underdeveloped and new members like Cambodia, Laos, Myanmar and Vietnam. For strategic and trade and investments, Singapore has always remained a major partner. To cope with the changing dynamics of the Indo-Pacific region, increasing strategic importance is also placed by India on Vietnam, Indonesia and Thailand. There is a creeping sense of discomfort in ASEAN about India's slow implementation of connectivity and development cooperation projects. Initial slowdown in the COVID-19 vaccine exports had also irritated many countries. India's 'Act East' policy has tried to respond to this, but it has yet to cover considerable distance, as was evident in its decision to opt out of the world's biggest free trade arrangement — the Regional Comprehensive Economic Partnership. Although the ASEAN region is one of the largest trading partners of India, trade and investment targets between the two have often remained unfulfilled.

India remains committed to keeping ASEAN central to its 'Act East' policy and Indo-Pacific approach. However, the changing dynamics of the region are pushing India into strategic equations beyond ASEAN, such as in the Quadrilateral Security Dialogue. There are also growing concerns in India about the fragility of cohesion among the ASEAN member states on complex issues like the South China Sea territorial/maritime disputes and Chinese assertion against other countries in the region like Vietnam, Philippines, Japan and India. Singapore's Prime Minister Lee Hsien Loong's candid statement in this respect delivered in a lecture on 13 March 2018 may be recalled. He said:

> "One area where [the] ASEAN [member] countries do not have a unified stance and for fundamental reasons, is our strategic outlook…. Looking ahead, ASEAN must continue working hard to remain an effective and central player in the region…. The 21st century is a different world…. We have to adjust to a strategic balance which is shifting both globally and in the region. New powers are growing in strength and influence, especially China and India."

Voicing his concern on ASEAN's cohesiveness, India's Prime Minister Narendra Modi, while emphasising ASEAN centrality in India's 'Act East' policy at the 17th India-ASEAN Summit in November 2020, said, "…a *cohesive, responsive* and prosperous ASEAN is central to [the] Indo-Pacific vision" (italics added). Recent developments of democratic distress in some of the ASEAN member states like Myanmar and Thailand also tend to have an adverse spill-over on ASEAN's cohesion and responsiveness. The emerging geo-strategic and geo-economic imperatives of the Indo-Pacific region are, however, such that they will keep the India and ASEAN relationship resilient and strong. In mutual cooperation and coordination, both sides will be able to effectively address the challenges of shifting strategic equations, redefining supply chains of trade and investments, expansive conduct of existing and aspiring regional hegemons, and unpredictable pandemics and natural disasters.

Section II
AREAS OF CONVERGENCE

TRADE RELATIONS

3

ASEAN-India Trade Relations: Evolution and Prospects

Manu Bhaskaran

After China, the two great economic development phenomena of the 21st century are likely to be the Association of Southeast Asian Nations (ASEAN) and India, two neighbouring regions with much in common and little in dispute. India has close to 1.4 billion people and soon will be the world's most populous country as China's population growth slows. ASEAN, with around 650 million people, is smaller — but not that much smaller. Each of the two regions has a total economic output of around US$3 trillion.

The past two decades of deepening high-level ties have demonstrated that there is so much the two can gain through a close economic partnership. Yet, that expansion has not met the high expectations that many had. This chapter looks at the trends in the economic engagement between the two regions and offers an explanation as to how and why these trends evolved. It concludes with a plea for the two regions to step up cooperation so as to jointly face what is likely to be a difficult external environment.

Characterising the ASEAN-India Relationship

The evolving ASEAN-India relationship can be summarised according to the following themes.

First, there are good reasons why India and ASEAN should enjoy an extensive economic relationship. There are deep historical roots to this relationship, After all, the Southeast Asian region neighbours on India and so there has been multifaceted engagement between the two regions for hundreds of years. These include trade ties and flows of people which have resulted in deep religious and cultural engagements that spanned centuries. The result is that there are many linguistic, cultural and religious ties that bind the two together. Moreover, there is a large Indian diaspora residing in many parts of Southeast Asia as well. All these suggest a strong potential for a very substantial economic relationship.

Second, there was considerable effort made to leverage off these foundations to build a substantial economic relationship. Thus, as ASEAN and India opened up their economies over time, there emerged a strong desire on both sides for a substantial economic relationship.

India became a Sectoral Dialogue Partner of ASEAN in 1992. From 2002 onwards, the two have held annual summit meetings of their leaders. In 2010, an ASEAN-India Free Trade Agreement (AIFTA) came into effect. In 2012, the relationship was further upgraded to that of a strategic partnership. In 2015, the ASEAN-India Trade in Services and Investment Agreement was signed. There are up to 30 separate dialogue mechanisms that bring the two sides together in regular engagement. In addition, there are many bilateral agreements between individual ASEAN member states and India. The most successful of these is the India-Singapore Comprehensive Economic Cooperation Agreement.

Third, while these efforts produced expanded economic ties, the results were not commensurate with the effort put in and the potential of the relationship. Figure 3.1 shows how growth in trade in goods between the two accelerated in the decade of the 2000s as India's economy enjoyed rapid growth and as India began liberalising trade,

Figure 3.1: India's trade flows to ASEAN as a whole, 2000–2019
Source: India's Ministry of Commerce and Industry.

mainly by reducing tariff barriers. This growth was given further impetus when the AIFTA came into effect and indeed the value of two-trade did grow, but only for a couple of years before it flattened out until 2019 when it grew again. The fact of the matter is that the AIFTA did not bring in the rapid growth that might have been expected.

A similar pattern is evident in direct investment flows between the two regions. As Figure 3.2 shows, direct investment flows between the two expanded exuberantly from around 2007 but then reached a plateau around 2012 and stagnated thereafter.

Figure 3.3 shows the growth of tourist flows between the two regions. ASEAN enjoyed a strong and rapidly growing inflow of Indian tourists. ASEAN tourist arrivals in India did grow as well but the numbers were well short of Indian visitors to ASEAN.

Fourth, the economic relationship was characterised by several imbalances. As Figure 3.1 shows, India has experienced a large and growing deficit in goods trade with ASEAN. In similar vein, Figure 3.2 shows that there was more Indian direct investment flowing into ASEAN than the other way. This has led to many in India feeling that the gains from opening up to trade, including trade and investment with ASEAN, were limited.

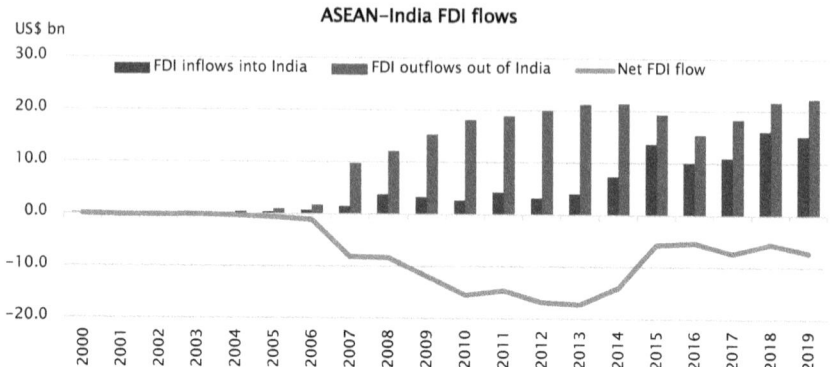

Figure 3.2: India's foreign direct investment flows to ASEAN as a whole, 2000-2019
Note: Due to data discrepancies, ASEAN here refers to Singapore, Malaysia, Thailand, Vietnam and the Philippines where data was available.
Source: CEIC.

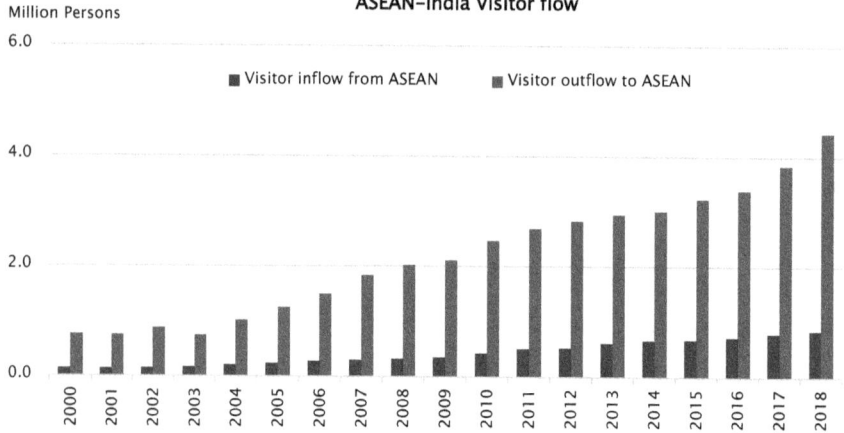

Figure 3.3: Tourist flows between ASEAN nations and India
Note: Due to data difficulties, the ASEAN nations refer to Singapore, Thailand, Malaysia, Indonesia, Myanmar and the Philippines where data was obtainable.
Source: CEIC.

Moreover, while the aggregate data showed considerable growth in ASEAN-India economic engagement, it would seem that much of the substance of the relationship seemed to be skewed to just a few countries, particularly Singapore. Figure 3.4 brings this out when we look at the total combined goods trade between India and ASEAN.

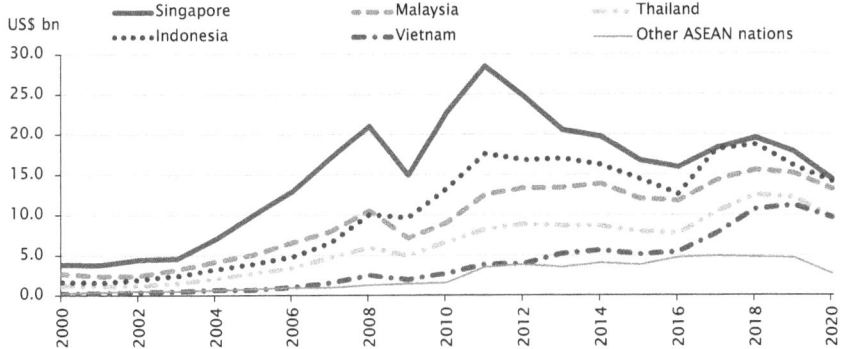

Figure 3.4: Combined total goods trade between India and ASEAN
Note: The total combined goods trade is calculated by summing total exports and imports with India. Other ASEAN nations refer to the aggregate total trade of the Philippines, Laos, Myanmar, Cambodia and Brunei.
Source: CEIC.

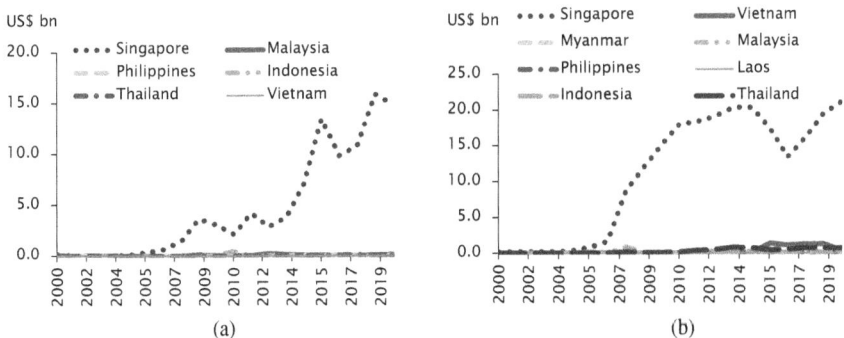

Figure 3.5: (a) FDI inflows from ASEAN; (b) FDI outflows to ASEAN
Source: CEIC.

The skew in the relationship is most evident in foreign direct investment flows which are shown in Figures 3.5(a) and 3.5(b).

Another imbalance also hung over the ASEAN-India relationship. With China's extraordinary economic surge, China became such a massive market for goods and services and such a large source of investment and finance that it tended to dominate ASEAN's economic policy thinking. India was important but paled in significance to China. Table 3.1 brings this out more clearly.

Table 3.1: Comparing India and China's flows to ASEAN

	2010	2015	2019
Imports of goods from ASEAN (US$ bn)			
China	112.6	145.3	202.5
India	37.1	40.6	48.3
FDI net outflows to ASEAN (US$ bn)			
China	3.6	6.6	9.1
India	4.4	1.5	2.1
Visitor outflows to ASEAN (million persons)			
China	5.4	18.6	32.3
India	2.5	3.3	5.3

Source: ASEAN Secretariat.

Fifth, this less than satisfactory outcome has deep roots and will not be easily overcome. There appears to have been a general disappointment within the Indian political and business establishment over the gains from opening up to the rest of the world. India has suffered a massive trade deficit with China and ASEAN. This has led to a shift in the policy thinking on trade liberalisation and an increasing wariness. Indian policymakers may feel that under current circumstances, India is not in a position to extract proportionate benefits from trade opening. Partly, as a result, India pulled out of the Regional Comprehensive Economic Partnership after many years of negotiations, leaving its trading partners, including ASEAN, severely disappointed.

Why did this come about?

The reasons for this unhappy outcome are complex. The earlier opening up of the Chinese and ASEAN economies could have allowed these economies to develop a high degree of manufacturing competitiveness ahead of India. India began opening up its economy in stages — very tepidly in the 1980s and more vigorously after 1991 — a decade or more after China and ASEAN had done so. Consequently, the ASEAN economies were well-positioned to enjoy the massive relocation of production activity from Japan, South Korea and Taiwan that occurred after the Plaza Accords in 1985. As a result, there grew clusters of globally competitive manufacturing in Thailand, Malaysia and Indonesia.

Consequently, manufacturing activity in these countries became integrated into the global value chains of the large multinational companies. In 2001, when China entered the World Trade Organization (WTO), there was another substantial shift in global manufacturing towards establishing value chains straddling China and ASEAN. ASEAN became a large supplier of components to China and the two together prospered, competing with as well as complementing each other.

That competition spurred efficiency gains which allowed both to greatly improve their global competitiveness — in terms of unit costs of production, quality factors and speed of delivery. India might have been late in the game and missed out on these dynamic gains; so when it opened up, its manufacturing sector struggled to compete outside some segments such as two-wheelers, pharmaceuticals and engineering goods.

Finally, there are good reasons why the two regions should make another push to deepen their economic engagement. The coming years will be years of considerable opportunity but also manifold dislocations.

Geo-political challenges are growing as a rising China rubs up against the incumbent superpower, the United States (US). The South China Sea and the Indian Ocean regions could become major arenas of big power contestation, placing both India and ASEAN at risk. A related risk is that of greater protectionism, as seen in the signs of a trade war between the US and China. As the US and China create contending technological standards, the danger of technological bifurcation could lead to a world divided into two technological camps.

A second set of dislocations may arise from the multiple technological revolutions underway. While these promise huge new opportunities for growth, there is also the possibility of considerable dislocation. The structure of competitive advantage could change. For example, new technologies such as robots, artificial intelligence and 3D printing could make manufacturing in high-wage developed economies competitive again in some areas, leading to a re-shoring of production back to those richer countries at the expense of the developing economies. Automation could also replace labour, leading to considerable unemployment.

Third, a process of supply chain reconfiguration is underway. China is moving up the value chain which is resulting in some manufacturing activity moving out of the country, quite often to economies such as Vietnam, Cambodia and Bangladesh. However, as China moves up the value chain, it is also becoming more proficient in fabricating intermediate goods that others such as ASEAN had once excelled in.

Finally, India and ASEAN face common global challenges such as climate change and the need to prepare for the next pandemic.

Sadly, the multilateral mechanisms for global collaboration to confront these very real challenges have weakened. The WTO, for example, has struggled to produce any major global-scaled multilateral trade agreement.

The next best option is for large regions such as India and ASEAN to work together. It would make sense for these two big regions to collaborate so as to face this new world. After all, there is strength in numbers and, together, both regions can shape the global discourse more to suit their interests than if each operated separately.

4

Trade Relations between ASEAN and India: Reviewing the Last Decade

Amitendu Palit

Several reasons were responsible for the robust expectations of India's bilateral trade with the Association of Southeast Asian Nations (ASEAN) scaling new heights during the last decade.

First, India's 'Look East' policy, announced in 1994 and focused on expanding India's economic relations with ASEAN, had come a long way. After more than a decade of its promulgation, the 'Look East' policy was envisaged to have created enough ground for the fast acceleration of trade between India and Southeast Asia. With businesses from both sides gaining greater familiarity with each other through various business-to-business channels, economic complementarities between India and Southeast Asia were ripe for exploitation and for generating large increases in bilateral trade.

Second, trade was also expected to expand manifold through the comprehensive economic cooperation agreements (CECA) entered into by India and Southeast Asia. India became a part of the ASEAN+1 free trade agreement (FTA) network through its CECA with ASEAN in both goods and services. These agreements provided India and ASEAN institutional rules-based frameworks to engage in trade in goods and services, facilitate cross-border investments and encourage the movement of people. In addition to the CECA with ASEAN being formalised before the beginning of the last decade, India entered into bilateral CECA with two of the largest ASEAN economies — Singapore and Malaysia. Both these agreements were to add further impetus to the India-ASEAN CECA by enabling deeper economic integration of India and Southeast Asia.

Third, strategic engagement between India and ASEAN increased at a fast pace during the first decade of the current century and into the last decade. This culminated in India-ASEAN relations being upgraded to that of a strategic partnership in 2012. India also became a part of the ASEAN Regional Forum and joined ASEAN in the East Asia Summit. Furthermore, from 2012, India joined ASEAN and its FTA partners — Australia, China, Korea, Japan, New Zealand — in negotiating the Regional Comprehensive Economic Partnership (RCEP). India's enhanced collaboration with ASEAN and rising prominence in the ASEAN-centric regional architecture were complemented by the Narendra Modi government's decision to upgrade the 'Look East' policy to the 'Act East' policy in 2014.

Deeper political, security and strategic ties between India and Southeast Asia reflected a steady growth in mutual trust and faith and more engagement. The latter manifested in various institutional dialogue and consultation mechanisms (for example, the annual Delhi Dialogue and ASEAN-India regional think tank meetings) between India and ASEAN. All these mechanisms focused strongly on trade, investment, connectivity and economic engagements.

Have the expectations of bilateral trade reaching new heights materialised?

Trade statistics from the Export Import Data Bank of India's Ministry of Commerce and Industry indicate a significant increase in bilateral trade during the last decade. India's goods exports to ASEAN increased from US$18.1 billion in 2009–2010 to US$31.5 billion in 2019–2020. During the same period, India's imports from ASEAN increased from US$25.8 billion to US$55.4 billion. Taken together, bilateral trade rose from US$43.9 billion in 2009–2010 to US$86.9 billion in 2019–2020, reflecting an almost doubling of trade between the two sides.

Besides the absolute values, it is important to look at India-ASEAN trade in a relative sense. The share of India's exports to ASEAN in its total exports remained unchanged at 10.1 percent between 2009 and 2010 and between 2019 and 2020. The share of imports, on the other hand, increased from 8.9 percent to 11.7 percent during the same period. As a result, the share of India's overall trade with ASEAN in its overall external trade, based on the author's computations, increased from 9.5 percent in 2009–2010 to 10.9 percent in 2019–2020. With the share of India's exports to ASEAN remaining unchanged during the decade, the increase in overall trade has almost entirely been driven by India's consumption of greater imports from ASEAN.

Singapore remains the largest market for Indian exports to the region. However, its share in India's total exports to ASEAN reduced from 41.9 percent in 2009–2010 to 28.3 percent in 2019–2020. Similarly, Indonesia's share of India's total exports to ASEAN declined from 16.9 percent to 13.1 percent in the same period. However, Malaysia's share in India's exports increased from 15.6 percent to 20.2 percent in the same period; Thailand's share in India's exports also increased from 9.6 percent to 13.6 percent, as did Vietnam's from 10.1 percent to 16.0 percent. At the end of the last decade, Vietnam became the third largest market for Indian exports to Southeast Asia, after Singapore and Malaysia, overtaking Indonesia and Thailand. India's exports to other ASEAN member states are much less. While the Philippines accounts for less than five percent of Indian exports to ASEAN, the shares of Brunei, Cambodia, Laos and Myanmar are marginal.

Indonesia continues to remain the largest source of India's imports from ASEAN despite its share reducing from 33.6 percent in 2009–2010 to 27.2 percent in 2019–2020. Singapore, the second largest source of India's imports, saw its share in total imports rise from 25 percent to 26.6 percent. Like Indonesia, Malaysia's share in Indian imports also dropped from 20.1 percent to 17.7 percent. Vietnam's importance as a source of Indian imports increased greatly during the last decade. From only two percent of Indian imports in 2009–2010, Vietnam's share has increased to 13.2 percent, which is higher than that of Thailand at 12.2 percent. Myanmar, which in 2009–2010, accounted for around five percent of Indian imports to ASEAN, accounted for only one percent in 2019–2020.

The shares of the individual ASEAN member states in India's exports and imports point to India's trade with the region being dominated by the larger economies. Singapore, Malaysia and Indonesia dominate ASEAN's trade with India. However, during the last decade, Vietnam emerged as a major trade partner for India from the region — both in exports and imports — displacing Thailand. This is indeed a notable feature as India's similar trade engagements with the other CLMV countries — Cambodia, Laos and Myanmar — have hardly flourished, while those with Brunei and the Philippines have remained stagnant.

Several Indian experts have expressed disappointment over Indian exports to the ASEAN markets not having increased as much as its imports from ASEAN. The fact that an increase in bilateral trade — as noted before — has almost entirely been due to an increase in India's imports from ASEAN — has been a cause for consternation in India. This has led to concerns over the India-ASEAN CECA in goods being 'imbalanced', in the sense of it having given more market access to ASEAN's exports to India as opposed to Indian exports to ASEAN. These concerns are largely misplaced.

India's imports from Southeast Asia are high because of the region's ability to supply a large number of essential imports to India — resource-based exports such as coal, agricultural products like vegetable oils, and a large number of capital goods such as machinery and machine components — at cheaper rates than those available in

India. Nevertheless, concerns over cheap imports 'injuring' domestic producers has made the India-ASEAN CECA being looked at skeptically.

India's concerns over its exports not getting enough market access in Southeast Asia have also been influenced by the lack of progress on the India-ASEAN services in the CECA. The agreement has been hampered by difficulties in concluding mutual recognition agreements to enable the movement of professionals between India and Southeast Asia. India's obvious interest in this regard has been in the movement of its skilled professionals — in information technology, finance and other technical services — to Southeast Asia. Such ambitions have remained unfulfilled.

One of the major setbacks in the India-ASEAN trade relations in the last decade was India's withdrawal from the RCEP in November 2019. The RCEP, which came into effect in January 2022, is a mega-FTA involving ASEAN and its FTA partners. After staying committed to the RCEP process since its beginning, India withdrew when the negotiations were being concluded. Domestic reasons, primarily political sensitivities involved in allowing greater market access to imports in several areas, were cited as the main reasons.

In most manufacturing industries, India continues to remain less competitive than Southeast Asia and the other RCEP members. Indian exports from these industries would have found it difficult to penetrate into the ASEAN markets, whereas ASEAN's exports to India would have increased further from concessions given by the RCEP. By staying out of the RCEP, however, India lost a great opportunity of attracting export-oriented foreign investments from the region, which could have facilitated India's entry in regional supply chains. Furthermore, India's withdrawal was inconsistent with the rising trajectory of its strategic bonhomie with ASEAN, which had increased significantly during the last decade.

India's trade with ASEAN can be much higher than what it is right now. However, the character of the trade might need to change for that. Great benefits can materialise for India and Southeast Asia from digital trade. Securing these benefits requires greater integration of digital trade platforms and cross-border payment systems between India and ASEAN. India has made significant progress in imbibing digital trade facilitation mechanisms. In ASEAN, the comparable progress is limited to the frontrunners of technological competence such as Singapore, Malaysia and Indonesia. At the same time, bilateral services trade can flourish through greater movement of students, tourists and business visitors. However, again, the synergies with India in this regard are not uniform across the region.

Countries with which India's trade ties are strong right now, such as Singapore, Malaysia, Indonesia, Thailand and Vietnam, are the countries of ASEAN that are expected to remain and further grow in stature as India's major trade partners in services as well. On the goods trade, the circumstances created by the COVID-19 pandemic underline the strong trade possibilities that exist between ASEAN and India in the fields of healthcare products, including vaccines.

The emergence of new and far-reaching possibilities of trade creation between India and Southeast Asia can curb, to a large extent, the disappointment that currently exists between both sides on trade: India's grievances over limited gains from its CECAs with ASEAN and ASEAN's frustration over India backing out of the RCEP. The new areas can script a new story for India-ASEAN trade in the current decade.

INVESTMENT
RELATIONS

5

ASEAN-India Trade and Investment Relations: Perspectives from the Philippines

Francis Mark A Quimba

Despite not being party to the Regional Comprehensive Economic Partnership, India remains a key partner of the Association of Southeast Asian Nations (ASEAN) in general and for the Philippines in particular. This partnership can be seen in trade (goods and services) and investment flows between ASEAN and India. Trade in goods and services is directly correlated with investment as studies have shown that the influx of foreign direct investment (FDI) to a host country often results in an increase in exports of the country of origin. Trade agreements between the individual ASEAN economies, namely, Singapore and Malaysia (negotiations have been launched between India and Thailand and India and Indonesia), and with ASEAN, are an indication of the strong ties that exist between India and the region.

India remains a key partner of ASEAN in terms of trade of goods and services and investments.

From 2010 to 2019, Singapore and Indonesia were the main ASEAN exporters to India. The two countries had a combined share of around

50 to 60 percent of total ASEAN exports to India. Malaysia also posted considerable figures during the period — around 17 to 22 percent of total ASEAN exports to India. Meanwhile, the share of the Philippines' exports to India fluctuated during the decade, ranging between 0.7 percent and 1.3 percent only.

In terms of ASEAN imports, Singapore was the main importer of Indian goods. During the 2010–2012 period, its share of total ASEAN imports from India ranged from 46 to 50 percent. However, its share gradually decreased in the succeeding years to 22.5 percent in 2019. On the other hand, Thailand and Vietnam emerged as important markets for India in the region. From 20.3 percent in 2010, the combined share of the two countries increased to 31.3 percent in 2019.

In terms of services, from 2010 to 2019, Singapore was consistently the main trading partner, as the country accounted for around half of total ASEAN services trade with India. Indonesia, Malaysia and Thailand were also important services trade partners in the region — their combined shares in ASEAN services trade with India ranged between 30 percent and 40 percent during the 2010s.

Singapore has been the main recipient of Indian investments since the late 2000s. On average, the country has been receiving FDI inflows greater than US$1 billion. During the last few years, Indonesia and Vietnam have emerged as new recipients of Indian FDI; in 2020, Indonesia reported the highest annual inflows from India at US$303.5 million.

While the Philippines has not registered stronger ties with India in terms of trade and services, and investment, there remain areas in which ASEAN and India can cooperate.

In the context of ASEAN-India trade, the Philippines has not accounted for substantial shares in goods trade. As mentioned earlier, the Philippines' share of exports to India averaged one percent between 2010 and 2019. However, it accounted for a larger share in ASEAN's goods imports from India. Meanwhile, the services sector accounted for the highest share in the Philippines' services exports to India —

around 20 percent to 42 percent — in the same period. Wholesale and retail trade services were also an integral component of services exports to India, although a decreasing trend has been observed throughout the period — from 18.8 percent in 2001–2005, its average share dwindled to 10.7 percent in the 2016–2018 period. Meanwhile, computer programming, consultancy and information technology (IT) services slowly emerged as an important service group in exports — its average share since the late 2000s ranged from 15 percent to 18 percent, remarkably higher than the 7.1 percent average share in the early 2000s.

The Philippines' services imports from India comprised mainly computer programming, consultancy and IT activities. During the 2000s and 2010s, this services group accounted for around one-third of Philippines' services imports from India. Wholesale and retail trade, accommodation and food services, and administrative and support services have also been major imported services from India during the last two decades. On average, the combined share of the three services groups made up another third of the total services imports from India.

Relative to other ASEAN member states, the Philippines' investment relations with India have been modest in the previous two decades. During the period 2005–2010, FDI net inflows from India were negative in 2009 and zero for three other years. The FDI figures improved in the succeeding decade, as annual net inflows greater than US$1 million were observed in four years — the highest being US$8.8 million in 2017. Reports on Indian FDI outflows reveal that most of Indian investment in the Philippines were in financial and insurance activities. Since 2008, the sector has generally accounted for 70 to 98 percent of Indian FDI outflows to the Philippines.

Despite the modest trade and investment relations between the Philippines and India, especially in comparison with India's relation with ASEAN, notable improvements in trade and FDI figures could still be observed during the 2010s. With important trade and investment policies such as the ASEAN-India FTA potentially stimulating these improvements, it is crucial to maintain the momentum and further strengthen the relationship between the two countries.

The Philippines can capitalise on the ASEAN-India trade and investment relations in several sectors.

During the virtual courtesy call by India's Ambassador to the Philippines Shambhu Kumaran on 5 April 2021, Philippine Department of Trade and Industry Secretary Ramon Lopez noted that the Philippines could be India's partner in the production of active pharmaceutical ingredients, vaccines, essential medicines and biologicals as well as data centres and other related IT infrastructure. On the side of India, possible industries for cooperation include jeepney and electronic manufacturing, and geothermal energy. These industries supplement those that were identified during the 13th Philippines-India Joint Working Group on Trade and Investments in September 2020, which include agribusiness, electronics, infrastructure, renewable energy and manufacturing.

The two countries started negotiations on a bilateral investment treaty in October 2020. The agreement has been in the pipeline for years, after India proposed a new treaty based on the model text for the Indian bilateral investment treaty. The following sectors have had considerable progress in terms of facilitating trade and investments between the Philippines and India, and further cooperation in these sectors would be integral in strengthening the relationship of the two countries:

i. IT — non-voice sectors: medical, financial and legal services, game development, engineering design in manufacturing and software development — Collaboration in the business process outsourcing (BPO) sector has grown exponentially in the last few years. Several Indian IT companies have already set up BPO operations in the Philippines and these include WIPRO, TCS, L&T Infotech, Innodata, IL&FS Genpact, Infosys, HIGS (Hindujas) and Tech Mahindra. This close partnership in IT and BPO has become a win-win situation for both countries.

ii. Pharmaceuticals: generics, medical equipment, vaccines, over the counter, oncology and high-end medicines, herbal medicines — Currently, Indian pharmaceutical companies have established a strong presence in pharmaceuticals (generics) where major firms like Dabur Pharma, Lupin, Torrent, ZydusCadilla and Claris Life Sciences have set up liaison offices to promote their products. Lupin has also acquired a stake in a local company.

iii. Infrastructure — Building on the rapidly expanding infrastructure demands of the Philippines, Indian companies have a slate of ongoing and prospective projects in aviation and airports, railways, maritime and shipbuilding and road transport for potential involvement. Indian construction companies have become increasingly active in the Philippines in recent years. The GMR Group has established a strong presence, as evidenced by the completion of the Clark Airport construction project. The group is also credited for the operation of the Mactan-Cebu Airport.

Aside from physical infrastructure, the Philippines can also cooperate with India in improving its digital infrastructure and supporting its banking and finance sector. In a virtual meeting with the Philippine Secretary of Finance in March 2021, Ambassador Kumaran mentioned that India can lend its expertise to the Philippines in setting up its national broadband network as well as its national identity system. Another area for Indian companies to participate in is the rolling out of a shared cyber-defence plan for Philippine state-run banks and their subsidiaries.

iv. Manufacturing: electronics, shipbuilding, tools and dyes, furniture, garments, power and transport and automotive — Tata Motors and Mahindra have made their presence felt in the automobile sector in the Philippines. Tata Motors, globally renowned for manufacturing commercial vehicles, together with its partner Pilipinas Taj Autogroup Inc., distributes Tata Motors commercial vehicles in the country which includes the newly unveiled Prima heavy truck platform, an entire range of heavy intermediate and light commercial vehicles, mini trucks, pickups and buses. As the Philippine partner of Tata Motors is focused mainly on sales, an area for further cooperation would be for Tata Motors to explore the feasibility of transferring automotive manufacturing segments to the country.

Meanwhile, Mahindra Motors is already an active player to the Jeepney Modernization Programme of the Philippines Department of Transportation through the supply of modern jeeps in the local market as the common mode of transportation for Filipinos.

v. Renewable energy — The Philippines and India are keen on cooperating in renewable energy as both countries have targets in this area. To pursue this cooperation, the Philippines and India have pursued a memorandum of understanding (MOU) on energy cooperation which is expected to provide the platform to discuss policies and programmes on harnessing renewable sources between the two countries. As of July 2021, the document was still being reviewed by the Philippines Department of Foreign Affairs.

vi. Agribusiness — A bilateral collaboration between the two countries in agricultural and financial technologies has been proposed. It is aimed at improving the operations of small farmers and addressing constraints in the country's agriculture value chains and access to finance.

vii. Tourism — In 2019, the Philippine Department of Tourism and the Indian Ministry of Tourism signed an MOU to expand bilateral cooperation in the areas of the tourism, trade, and hospitality sectors. Among others, the five-year agreement entails initiatives on mutual visits; exchange of promotion, marketing, destination, development and management experiences; exchange of official standards and certification practices; development of tour packages; cooperation between the two countries' respective public and private sectors; research and statistical exchange; and training.

The new and modernised air services agreement between the Philippines and India could also facilitate tourism growth and strengthen cultural ties. The 1949 Philippines-India Agreement on Air Services was amended in 2018; further changes were then proposed in 2020, and the new agreement was signed in September 2021. The said agreement aims to promote international air services, advance a quality international aviation system and ensure air safety between the two countries.

viii. Logistics — The Philippines and India signed the MOU on defence industry and logistics cooperation during the visit by India's Prime Minister Narendra Modi to the Philippines in November 2017. The MOU includes a framework to enhance cooperation in logistics support and services as well as in the development, production and procurement of defence materials.

Conclusion

The economically advanced countries in ASEAN have achieved significant success in engaging India in trade and investments. However, several ASEAN member states, including the Philippines, have not sufficiently capitalised on the opportunities provided by the relationship. There is the possibility for greater cooperation and collaboration between the Philippines and India, as highlighted above. Many of these areas in fact also provide similar opportunities for the other smaller ASEAN economies to engage India, moving forward.

6

ASEAN-India Investment Relations: Opportunities for a Strategic Partnership in a Post COVID-19 World

Rahul Sen

Introduction

Economic relations between the Association of Southeast Asian Nations (ASEAN) and India have intensified in strength and dimensions over the past two decades since India launched its 'Look East' policy in 1991. From being a dialogue to a summit level partner and, thereafter, to a strategic partner in 2012, the trade and investment relations have gathered further momentum with the signing of two important bilateral agreements over the past decade. First, the ASEAN-India Trade in Goods Agreement, in effect since 2010 and, more recently, the ASEAN-India Trade in Services and Investment Agreements (AITSIA) since July 2015. Post-free trade agreements, trade between ASEAN and India increased from US$37 billion in 2009 to US$78.9 billion in 2020–2021.

According to a July 2021 report by the Strategic Investment Research Unit (SIRU) of the National Investment Promotion and Facilitation Agency, India, its 'Act East' policy, launched in 2014, has given a new direction to further strengthening the bilateral economic relations between India and ASEAN. While the 'Look East' policy was focused on trade and economic agreements with ASEAN as an organisation and with selected ASEAN member states such as Singapore, the 'Act East' policy has a broader economic and geo-strategic engagement vision involving the wider Indo-Pacific region that comprises countries bordering the Indian and Pacific oceans, including ASEAN. From the investment perspective, a key factor driving India's 'Act East' policy is connectivity in its physical, digital, cultural and human aspects, with India's northeast region being developed as key gateway and nodal point for India's 'Act East' policy.

Data Trends and Overview

India and the ASEAN member states collectively account for a combined population of about two billion and a combined current gross domestic product of US$5.7 trillion as of 2021. According to the Indian Ministry of Commerce and Industry's latest data, the top three trade and investment partners from ASEAN are Singapore (bilateral trade worth US$22 billion, 3.2 percent of India's total), Indonesia (bilateral trade worth US$17.5 billion, 2.5 percent of India's total) and Malaysia (bilateral trade worth US$14.4 billion, 2.1 percent of India's total). Their digital economies are also projected to grow rapidly by 2025 to about US$1 trillion in India and US$300 billion in ASEAN, driven by 735 million internet users in India and about 416 million in ASEAN.

In the wake of the COVID-19 pandemic, another key driver has been the introduction of investor-friendly policies to encourage businesses to partner in the long-term development of the Indian economy through the recently announced *Atmanirbhar Bharat* (Self-reliant India) policies that includes the Production Linked Incentives (PLI), announced in 2022, for specific manufacturing sectors. The aim is to encourage foreign investors to partner with local companies to create a global export platform for manufacturing from India.

ASEAN's Investments into India

Over the period April 2000 to September 2021, the ASEAN member states' foreign direct investment (FDI) equity inflows into India were valued at US$126.4 billion, constituting 22.5 percent of the total (Table 6.1). Singapore was the leading foreign investor in India among the ASEAN member states, investing US$123 billion in the same period, followed by about US$1 billion each by Malaysia and Thailand. Six other ASEAN member states collectively invested another US$1 billion in the Indian economy during this period.

Since the AITSIA was signed, ASEAN's investments in India have been growing (Figure 6.1) with an expected downturn in 2019–2020 with the onset of the COVID-19 pandemic. Over 2020–21, despite the ongoing pandemic, ASEAN's investments in India grew by 19 percent to about US$17.7 billion, with about US$5 billion worth of this investment from Singapore between January and June 2021. This was consistent with the global trend of India attracting the highest ever FDI worth US$81.72 billion over 2020–2021, 10 percent higher than the previous financial year.

Table 6.1: Country-wise ASEAN FDI equity inflows to India (April 2000 to September 2021)

Rank as FDI Source	Country	FDI Inflows (US$ Billion)	Share in Total
2	Singapore	123.15	21.96
26	Malaysia	1.13	0.20
27	Thailand	1.11	0.20
31	Indonesia	0.64	0.11
42	Philippines	0.34	0.06
60	Cambodia	0.05	0.01
81	Brunei Darussalam	0.015	0.00
95	Myanmar	0.009	0.00
101	Vietnam	0.005	0.00
	ASEAN	126.44	22.54

Source: Computed from *FDI Newsletter*, Government of India.

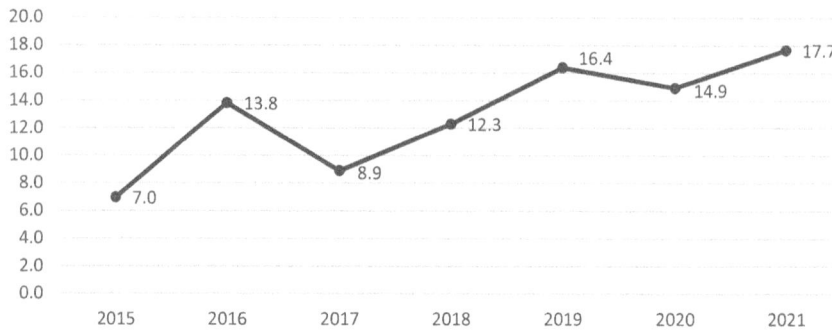

Figure 6.1: FDI equity inflow from ASEAN to India 2015–2021 (in US$ billion)
Source: Government of India.

Table 6.2: Sectoral distribution of FDI inflows from ASEAN to India, 2021

Industries	US$ Billion	Share in Total (%)
Others (Agri-business, food processing, mining, etc.)	30.17	29.0
Services sector (including financial/non-financial and other business services)	18.79	18.0
Trading	14.9	14.0
Computer software and hardware	17.29	16.0
Constructive infrastructure activities	10.38	10.0
Telecommunications	6.51	6.0
Drug and pharmaceuticals	3.76	4.0
Power	3.21	3.0

Source: SIRU Report July 2021, Government of India.

Seventy-two percent of the total cumulative inflows of ASEAN FDI equity inflows into India over the past two decades (worth US$91 billion) were between 2015 and 2021, suggestive of the AITSIA being an important driver. The investment component of the AITSIA provides investment protection on a mutual basis to ensure fair and equitable treatment for investors from both ASEAN and India.

The overall sectoral distribution of ASEAN's FDI inflows into India (Table 6.2) suggests that as of 2021, the services sector, trading, computer software and information and communication technology (ICT), pharmaceuticals, power and others (likely to include agriculture, allied activities and specific manufacturing industries) constituted the key areas of bilateral investments. The ASEAN member states have been investing in some key areas of developmental significance to the Indian economy. These include the rapidly growing ICT, digital and financial technology sectors in the wake of the COVID-19 pandemic, from which the Indian economy is poised to emerge as one of the rapidly growing economies in the world and is expected to grow at nine percent in 2022 and 7.1 percent in 2023, according to the International Monetary Fund. Such high growth grates, coupled with business-friendly policies and a push to infrastructural development, are likely to generate a huge potential for private investment opportunities in India. Its stock market equity capitalisation is now the sixth highest in the world worth US$3.4 trillion, catching up with the United Kingdom (US$3.6 trillion), suggesting a high degree of long-term investor confidence.

India's Investments in ASEAN

Despite the ongoing COVID-19 pandemic, ASEAN remains an attractive destination for FDI, with its share of global inflows increasing from 11.9 percent to 13.7 percent over 2019–2020. India's investments in ASEAN have been of a smaller magnitude but rising rapidly in recent years since the signing of the AITSIA. Indian FDI into the ASEAN member states was worth US$2.12 billion in 2020 (Figure 6.2). This accounted for 1.5 percent of the total FDI inflows into the ASEAN member states, compared to 0.9 per cent of the total in 2014. India was not among the top 10 source countries for FDI in ASEAN.

According to data from the ASEAN Secretariat data, nearly two-thirds of all investments from India to ASEAN were in wholesale and retail trade, the automobile industry and in financial and insurance services. However, investments were also in real estate, professional services as well as hospitality and ICT-led services, apart from transport, construction, and manufacturing. Most of these investments have been in Singapore and Indonesia, although increasingly, other ASEAN member states like Thailand, Malaysia, Vietnam and the

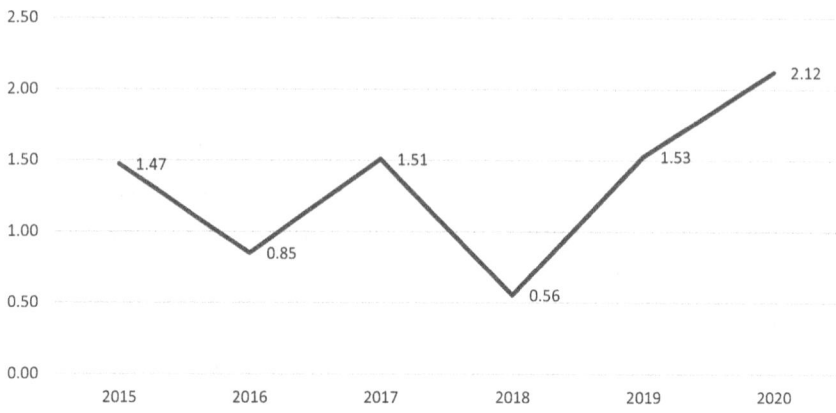

Figure 6.2: India's FDI inflows into ASEAN 2015–2020 (in US$ billion)
Source: ASEAN Statistical Yearbook 2021.

Table 6.3: Sectoral distribution of FDI inflows from India to ASEAN, 2015–2020

Industries	US$ Million	Share in Total (%)
Wholesale and retail trade; repair of motor vehicles and motorcycles	2,519.3	31.3
Financial and insurance activities	2,486.2	30.9
Real estate activities	1,407.8	17.5
Professional, scientific, and technical activities	524.6	6.5
Accommodation and food service activities	359.4	4.5
Information and communication	320.7	4.0
Other services activities	291.4	3.6
Transportation and storage	270.3	3.4
Construction	95	1.2
Manufacturing	90.6	1.1

Source: ASEAN Statistical Yearbook 2021.

Philippines have also been attracting outward investments from India in recent years.

Sectoral Opportunities for a Strategic Partnership

The SIRU report and the ASEAN Investment Report 2020–2021 provide examples of bilateral investments being drivers of the strategic partnership between India and ASEAN, and how several businesses are already leveraging on the opportunities to tap new niche opportunities in global markets. All these sectors are eligible under the PLI scheme.

Digital Technologies

Indian multinational enterprises (MNEs) active in IT, the digital economy and e-commerce with new investments or expansions in ASEAN since 2020 include Unicommerce India that opened offices in Singapore and Indonesia. Tata Communications provides cloud services in Malaysia and Vietnam as well as data centres in the Philippines and Thailand. Tech Mahindra (India) has data centres in Indonesia, Malaysia and Singapore that complement its IT consulting services and support its BPO operations in the region, including in the Philippines. Airtel India has invested in the Internet of Things (IoT) software solutions to the ASEAN member states during the post-pandemic period. Singapore was the point of presence for the top 50 Industrial IoT MNEs in ASEAN in 2021, with India being the fourth leading international funders of the top 50 ASEAN start-ups.

Among venture capital investments in new start-ups, Indian firms have featured in the top five among the top 50 start-ups in terms of headquarters in Singapore and Indonesia. This includes Sequoia Capital (India) that has partnered with over 50 financial technology start-ups across India and ASEAN.

The Blue Economy

The blue economy provides a big opportunity area for investors in India and ASEAN to create a strategic partnership. Both sides are part of the Indian Ocean Rim Association formed to improve economic cooperation in the Indian Ocean and wider Indo-Pacific region and share a huge amount of maritime resources whose economic utilisation are yet to be fully explored. Major investments in this area include research and development in marine biotechnology, marine ICT activities and the development of coastal tourism opportunities. The SIRU report suggests India has plans to invest nearly US$13 billion in its maritime infrastructure, including ports and shipping and ASEAN investors should see this as a strategic investment opportunity in the development of India's blue economy.

Pharmaceuticals, Healthcare and Other Manufacturing Activities

The current pandemic has demonstrated India's capability in developing pharmaceuticals and healthcare products globally and has now opened opportunities for strategic investments in and by India in a range of areas in the healthcare industry, including generic drug manufacturing, vaccine development, production to clinical trial market and bioinformatics. As a recent example of such a strategic investment, NephroPlus (India) secured its first overseas acquisition in 2020 by taking a majority stake in Royal Care Dialysis (Philippines), which owns six dialysis centres.

There are also opportunities to be tapped along the vaccine manufacturing supply chain between India and ASEAN as vaccine development becomes a crucial factor affecting the recovery of these economies from recurring outbreaks of COVID-19. The ASEAN member states are major producers of primary and secondary packaging and distribution products in the vaccine supply chain while India is competent in vaccine ingredients and its final manufacturing, complementing each other in this important area for mutual economic recovery.

Conclusion

ASEAN-India bilateral investment flows have been on an upward trend since the AITSIA, led primarily by Singapore and, to a lesser extent, Malaysia and Indonesia in ASEAN. This is likely to be sustained in the post-pandemic world, with India's 'Act East' policy, and now economic policies incorporating the Self-reliant India and PIL-linked incentives for foreign investment providing sectoral investment opportunities for long-term strategic partnership in key areas of health, education and infrastructure development harnessing the potential of the blue economy. Both have been resilient in their economic recovery efforts from the ongoing pandemic and have helped each other in these difficult times. The effort to reach out and strategically partner in each other's long-term development will be crucial for the future of ASEAN-India investment relations.

BUSINESS TIES

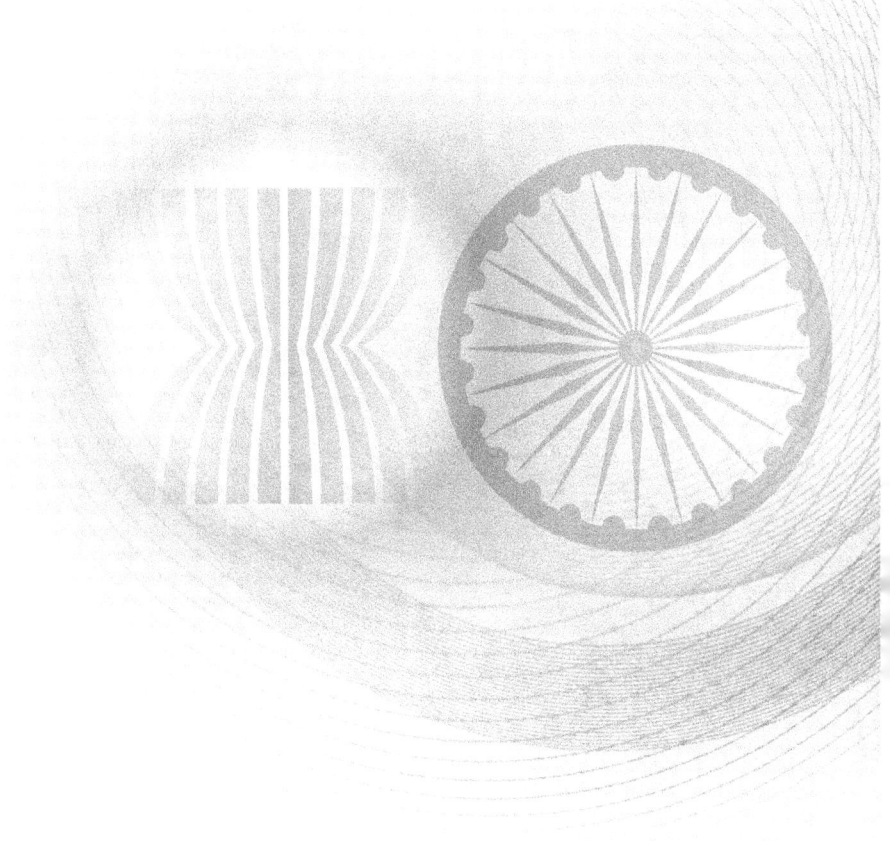

7

ASEAN-India Business Relationship: Perspectives of a Singaporean Indian Business Leader

Karan Singh Thakral

Introduction

The India-Association of Southeast Asian Nations (ASEAN) business story has been a professional and personal one for my family and me. Headquartered in Singapore, the Thakral Group has been actively investing and operating businesses in ASEAN for over a century and in India over the last five decades. It has been involved in many sectors, including garment manufacturing, real-estate development, consumer electronics distribution and retail, information technology services and venture capital. Over the last 30 years, I have led the Thakral Group's India operations and have effectively lived a third of my life — about 100 days each year — in India.

Like my family, many others in the region have also developed close business ties with India. I witnessed the blossoming of these ties first-hand as I led the South Asian Business Group of the Singapore Business Federation and as a board member of the ASEAN-India Business Council since 2004. I have also been an active member of business associations such as the Federation of Indian Chambers of Commerce and Industry and the Confederation of Indian Industry. These collective experiences have convinced me of the immense potential of the ASEAN-India business relationship.

Looking back and ahead, this chapter lays out some thoughts on the challenges and prospects for the relationship between the two sides.

ASEAN-India Business Ties: From the Past to the Present

India and Southeast Asia's relations are rooted in two millennia of history. Ties were borne out of trade, political, cultural and ancient religious connections. Vibrant commercial relations, driven by seaward trade, developed between the Indian and Southeast Asian empires. These ties were renewed in the 19th and 20th centuries. In Malaya, the British brought soldiers and rubber tappers with them, who are the ancestors of much of the Indian population in Singapore and Malaysia today. Even after the British left India in 1947 (and Malaya in 1957 and Singapore in 1963), many Indian families settled in the region, creating the foundation upon which early commerce began.

The first round of post-Independence business ties arguably began in the 1970s, as regional connectivity between India and Southeast Asia improved with flights between the two sides. Foreign airlines began flights from major Indian cities to Southeast Asia. Many long-haul flights from Southeast Asia to Europe chose India for a layover as well. During that time, consumers in the Southeast Asian countries sought Indian products. Over time, with the increase in disposable incomes in India, there was demand for foreign products, and Indians, in turn, sought non-Indian manufactured goods. This complementarity opened cross-border business opportunities. As a trading hub, with conducive taxes and duties and a world-class port, Singapore became a central node in the supply and transit of such goods. Elsewhere, other Southeast Asian countries also purchased Indian textiles and raw materials.

In the mid-1970s, large Indian industrial houses began to look at ASEAN as a potential market and set up manufacturing plants in sectors such as textiles and chemicals, among others. Among these houses, the Aditya Birla Group and the Tata Group were the most active. They were among the first Indian business houses to expand abroad. As they ventured into Southeast Asia, these two conglomerates were cognisant of the importance of working with local partners who had good knowledge and understanding of the domestic environment in each country. My father, Kartar Singh Thakral, along with several other regional businessmen, were enthusiastic about the ASEAN-India business opportunities. Given its many years of experience in the region, the Thakral Group was a natural partner for these Indian industrialists. Consequently, the Thakral Group partnered with Aditya Birla in many ventures. My father was also a board member of the Tata Group-Singapore. From my business trips to India in the 1980s, I saw first-hand the Indian consumers' appetite for electronic goods from Singapore, beginning with home appliances, calculators and digital watches, followed by televisions and videocassette recorder sets. Business ties were helped by events like the 1982 Asian Games, hosted by India in New Delhi, which opened the eyes of Southeast Asian businesses to the consumer power of India. India's relationship with the Soviet Union also played a role, as goods passed from Southeast Asia, Japan and South Korea to India, and then on to the Eastern bloc in Europe.

Despite the promise, trade with India from the 1970s to the early-1990s did not reach its full potential largely due to the 'Licence Raj' — a licence and regulatory system and its consequent red tape which hampered the operation of businesses in India. This changed in the early 1990s. India's Prime Minister Narasimha Rao decided that India needed to open its economy to the external world and that India should also 'Look East' to Southeast Asia. The drastic change in several business laws and removal of red tape during this period was a game-changer. This change in outlook galvanised ASEAN-India business ties and was welcomed by Southeast Asia, particularly by Singapore's leaders. Singapore's first Prime Minister, Lee Kuan Yew, greatly respected Rao and, as a demonstration of his commitment, Lee, then Senior Minister, personally led a delegation of Singaporean businessmen to India, which included my father and several other notable luminaries such as Sat Pal Khattar and Gopinath Pillai. This visit was a big boost for both the Singaporean and Indian business communities. Following the visit, Pillai, Khattar and my father came together to informally build a Singapore consortium that conducted projects jointly with Indian partners in sectors like real estate development and logistics. Many of these projects were successful and some continue even to this day. For example, in New Delhi, Khattar and my family are partners with Dr Vinay Bharat Ram and Sumant Bharat Ram (of the DCM family) in the joint development of Delhi's largest real estate project. Singapore's leaders, including Prime Minister Goh Chok Tong, pioneered a "mild Indian fever" in Singapore that sustained the interest in India. The rise in business relations was further fuelled by the global software boom in the 1990s. Given the Indian expertise in software engineering, there was a great respect for Indians, both in Southeast Asia and around the world.

In the three-decade cycle from 1991 to the present, India-ASEAN business ties have been on an overwhelmingly positive trajectory. The volume of trade and business has grown multifold and is among the best business growth stories in the world. From a meagre US$3 billion in bilateral trade in the early 1990s, India-ASEAN trade has grown exponentially to around US$80 billion annually in recent years. Today, both India and ASEAN are among the other's most important business partners. Together, they can drive not only mutual growth but also the growth of the world at large. As we move further into the 21st century, the ASEAN member states and businesses have come to realise that India will be a long-term partner and vice versa.

ASEAN-India Business: Challenges and Potential

The economies of ASEAN and India have both been on a strong upward trend for several years. Today, ASEAN has a similar gross domestic product to India. Some ASEAN member states have even better growth rates than that of India. The reality is that both India and China have played a key role in ASEAN's growth, as the "two wings" supporting the region.

However, the larger story is that more can and should be done between ASEAN and India. Together, ASEAN and India have a population of about two billion people and a combined US$6 trillion economy. Metaphorically speaking, if both sides think of one and one together not simply as two (1+1) but as an exponential eleven (1 and 1), there is a huge potential waiting to be tapped. However, for this to truly happen, further changes and reforms are necessary.

The relationship between India and ASEAN has long been like one of brothers. However, the expectation in India is often that ASEAN should look at India as the 'elder brother' on account of its size and historical connections. Keeping with this analogy, many Indian businesses still appear to hold the view that an 'elder brother' cannot learn from the 'younger sibling' or that the Indian company must always be the dominant and senior partner. This has been a hindrance to Indian companies. India should also look to ASEAN for lessons to adopt in business. For example, Singapore, with its commitment to developing human capital and emphasis on good and strong governance, is a model to follow. Other countries, such as Thailand and Malaysia, have strong tourism sectors which India can emulate.

Second, to further improve its competitiveness, India needs to continue to streamline its ease of doing business and continue to promote entrepreneurship and governance. Historically, the business landscape in India has proven to be challenging, due to red tape and legal complexities. For example, some laws in India are not yet streamlined, in part due to the federal system, resulting in delays.

The current government, under Prime Minister Narendra Modi's leadership, has identified many of these issues and, over the last eight years, has launched progressive initiatives, such as the Goods and Services Tax bill in 2017, 'Make in India' in 2014 and the Real Estate Regulation and Development Act in 2016, amongst others. These initiatives have resulted in a significant improvement in the business landscape, with further strong headroom for growth. Given the foundation that the government has created through these progressive initiatives, India is at an inflection point in terms of its growth journey.

With a huge population, a growing middle class and some of the brightest minds in the world — we have only seen the start of the Indian growth story. With the right leadership, India will continue to thrive and grow.

Moving forward, ASEAN and India can cooperate (bilaterally or multilaterally) particularly in the digital economy where both sides can leverage their respective strengths. India has a competitive advantage in its massive domestic supply of skilled digital professionals. Both ASEAN and India are also regional leaders in the size of their digital markets. Together, the two partners can collaborate in areas such as cross-border e-payments, financial technology and cutting-edge fields such as artificial intelligence. Progress is already underway in some of these areas. For example, in 2019, during Modi's visit to Singapore, the two governments announced that the Indian 'digital wallet' RuPay app would be usable in Singapore.

On the part of ASEAN, connectivity is the need of the hour. Many ASEAN member states are not as well-connected to India as they could and should be. Some ASEAN member states have yet to establish regular direct flight routes to India. When connectivity improves, it will be a catalyst for further economic ties between ASEAN and India. The ASEAN member states need to ramp up connectivity with India's major cities such as New Delhi, Mumbai, Bengaluru and Chennai. Only then can the ASEAN member states take advantage of India's potential, especially in sectors such as tourism.

Conclusion

Over the four and a half decades since my first trip to India in 1975, I have seen ASEAN-India ties on an upward trajectory, with small bumps along the way. Globally, there is an overwhelming optimism about both ASEAN and India. The possibilities of the two economies growing in tandem and in partnership are immense.

I have never been more convinced that this will be one of the defining partnerships of the 21st century. Linked by a shared history, our people-to-people ties will form the foundation of this partnership. Both India and Southeast Asia have industrious and hardworking populations and a growing middle class. With both economies growing rapidly, we will naturally look to each other to further our growth story.

8

Business Linkages between India and ASEAN

Naushad Forbes

Ties between India and the Association of Southeast Asian Nations (ASEAN) date back over a millennia and have grown stronger over time. The mode of trade has changed over the centuries, but the ties remain.

India's focus on a strengthened and multifaceted relationship with ASEAN is an outcome of the significant changes in the world's political and economic scenario since the early 1990s and India's own journey of economic liberalisation. India's search for economic space resulted in the 'Look East' policy which has today matured into a dynamic and action oriented 'Act East' policy.

Home to approximately two billion people, with an economic size of US$6 trillion, India and ASEAN share both land and maritime boundaries and a substantial proportion of world resources as well as strong consumer markets with a quarter of the world's middle-class consumers. It is also amongst the fastest growing regions of the world.

Together, we enjoy the largest working-age population, the right culture to foster entrepreneurship, dynamic industry sectors and geographical proximity of member states.

India's pre COVID-19 pandemic trade with ASEAN was around US$87 billion in 2019–2020. As a strategic partner to ASEAN, India has actively associated with ASEAN-led forums dealing with strategic and defence issues, including the East Asia Summit, ASEAN Regional Forum, ASEAN Defence Ministers Meeting-Plus, expanded ASEAN Maritime Forum, and the Indo-Pacific Oceans Initiative. Sub-regional cooperation is also underway through groupings such as the Bay of Bengal Initiative for Multi-Sectoral Technical and Economic Cooperation, Mekong Ganga Cooperation, Indian Ocean Rim Association and others.

India's 'Act East' policy is based on culture, commerce, connectivity and capacity building. It includes steady efforts to develop and strengthen the connectivity of India's northeast with the ASEAN region through physical infrastructure such as roads, airports, telecommunications and power as well as through trade, culture and people-to-people contacts.

Bilateral Trade and Investments

India's exports to ASEAN have grown from US$25 billion in 2015–2016 to US$32 billion in 2020–2021, and India imported goods worth US$40 billion in 2015–2016 which rose to US$47 billion in 2020–2021, according to the Indian Ministry of Commerce and Industry. ASEAN is India's fifth largest trading partner with trade expected to reach US$300 billion by 2025.

ASEAN-India trade witnessed a decline of 10.3 percent in 2020–2021 and 9.2 per cent in 2021–2022, owing to the COVID-19 pandemic. The decline in trade and India's increasing trade deficit in the last few years have led to a call for a review of the free trade agreements (FTA) with ASEAN. This review should be held with the objective of enhancing trade in both directions and aimed at the US$300 billion target instead of trying to achieve bilateral balance with the individual ASEAN member states.

Singapore, Indonesia and Malaysia are India's top ASEAN trade partners. Business cooperation between India and ASEAN in areas such as financial technology, start-ups and innovation, empowerment of youth and women and the development of micro, small and medium enterprises are important factors to consider while taking this multilateral connection to a higher growth trajectory. Engaging in new areas like energy, maritime safety and security, blue economy, digital connectivity and e-commerce will also effectively respond to the growing demand of new partnerships.

Indian businesses have a significant presence in ASEAN, including Tata, Aditya Birla, Bajaj Auto, ONGC Videsh, APTECH, HCL and Mahindra and Mahindra. Over 6,000 Indian companies have set up base in Singapore with an intent to address the wider ASEAN region. Business connectivity is growing in both directions with Singaporean, Indonesian and Malaysian companies expanding their presence in India.

India and the ASEAN member states should deepen trade and investments focusing on new technologies like artificial intelligence, infrastructure, healthcare, sustainable agriculture and alternative energy resources.

Physical/Infrastructure Connectivity

Three kinds of connectivity — physical, institutional and people-to-people — are crucial to strengthening economic relations between India and the Southeast Asian nations.

The seamless movement of goods and services across borders is highly dependent on effective transport links. The reality is that transport and infrastructure barriers exist between India and Southeast Asia — better quality of roads, filling gaps in railway links, adequate maritime and port facilities and customs cooperation can help to build trade in the region.

These have significant implications for any potential integration between India and Southeast Asia. India's northeast region is fundamental to efforts towards land connectivity with the ASEAN member states, given its strategic location with shared land borders with Myanmar. So far, the projects that have been undertaken by India with Myanmar include the Kaladan Multimodal Transit Transport Project and the India-Myanmar-Thailand Trilateral Highway. These have made progress, but all agree we could be moving faster.

India is working on setting up a special purpose vehicle to promote connectivity projects in ASEAN. In addition, there is immense potential to establish digital connectivity between ASEAN and India.

Institutional Connectivity

To deepen connectivity between India and ASEAN, it is essential to build effective institutional connectivity by harmonising trade, investment and financial policies. Physical connectivity (transportation and soft infrastructure requirements such as telecommunications) must be built in tandem with proper institutional arrangements to achieve improved cross-regional connectivity.

According to a 2015 report by the Asian Development Bank, there are ample opportunities for energy trading between India and Myanmar. Given the vast natural resources and hydropower reserves of Myanmar, it becomes a potential source of energy for India. However, due to lack of adequate physical and institutional infrastructure between India and Southeast Asia, energy trading remains underutilised.

Moreover, the presence of non-tariff barriers and restrictive institutional arrangements hinder the movement of goods and services. Trade facilitation measures to reduce the volume of documentation required and, thereby, the time of transit, are necessary to improve economic exchanges between India and the Southeast Asian countries. Close coordination at the institutional level can help achieve progress in these areas.

People-to-people Connectivity

India has a long history of people-to-people connectivity with Southeast Asia, particularly with Singapore, Malaysia and Indonesia, which are home to large populations of the Indian diaspora. Indian-origin citizens comprise nine and seven percent of Singapore's and Malaysia's populations respectively.

India and the ASEAN member states jointly organise regular exchange programmes for students, farming communities, diplomats and business and media personnel, among others. However, there are certain restrictions on the movement of professionals and labour between India and Southeast Asia.

Under the agreement on trade in services signed in 2015, India and ASEAN have agreed to liberalise trade in a few areas such as telecommunications and financial and insurance services while regulating the movement of natural persons. For the growth of the less-developed ASEAN member states (Laos, Cambodia and Myanmar), skilled labour and professionals are required. India can play an important role here.

Tourism generates large-scale foreign exchange earnings and many jobs. India hosts many students from the ASEAN member states. It has also positioned itself as an attractive destination for medical tourism. India can facilitate ASEAN to take advantage of this.

There is potential in promoting student exchange between India and ASEAN and collaboration between universities, mutual recognition of degrees and certificates, joint publication of research papers and conducting joint scientific research works through initiatives such as the Eminent Persons' Lectures Series. India has established English Language Training and Entrepreneurship Development Centres in the CLMV (Cambodia, Laos, Myanmar and Vietnam) countries.

Renewable and Conventional Energy

Linked as they are by both land and maritime borders, there are huge stakes in energy cooperation for India and ASEAN. Recognising their mutual needs for energy security, the two regions have been working on cooperation master plans which involve interconnecting power grids and gas pipelines, cross-border power projects and more liberal trade in energy commodities.

India has made good progress in solar and wind energy and, to some extent, hydro energy. Still, it is far from self-sufficient and depends heavily on external suppliers of oil and gas. It imports about 80 percent of its crude oil and 25 percent of its natural gas. It is the fourth largest energy consumer in the world and is still striving to fully exploit its abundant natural resources. It is placing special emphasis on power from wind, solar and biomass and renewables to make up 40 percent of its energy requirements.

India can harness untapped energy potential in the CLMV countries. For instance, Laos has a hydropower capacity of 26,000 megawatts (MW) but the installed capacity there is just 7,000 MW. It is now looking for foreign investments in its power sector. Cambodia and Myanmar are also inviting private investments in their energy sectors.

There are large opportunities for investments in solar power generation, biomass power generation and wind power generation on both sides. Coal-based power generation is also an area that foreign investors, especially India, can look into in ASEAN.

Agriculture, Crop Diversification and Food Security

India's expertise in agribusiness and horticulture will be of direct relevance to the agriculture-dependent and less developed ASEAN economies where agriculture contributes a major part of their gross domestic product (GDP). India has achieved extensive expertise in diverse fields of agro-science, including crop science, animal science, natural resource management, horticulture, fisheries, engineering, extension programme and the application of information and communications technology (ICT) in agriculture.

Agriculture accounts for 73 percent of Laos' GDP. It looks to India for assistance to improve its farm production and exports. Laos needs the know-how and strategy to develop its agriculture sector. Myanmar produces a lot of beans and pulses but consumes less than 10 percent of what it produces. India can be a lucrative market for the remaining 90 percent of production. The ASEAN member states are facing a bottleneck in the supply of quality seeds. India can help meet future food-related challenges with the use of farm and processing machinery to improve production.

India and ASEAN can collaborate in climate resistant, high-yield rice hybrids, reproductive technologies for buffaloes and small ruminates, capacity building in farm mechanisation, curbing post-harvest losses and managing food price volatility, among other areas. Both can benefit from an exchange of agricultural scientists, research fellows, students, farmers and women cooperative representatives to build the agri connect and share technology.

Information and Communication Technology

In terms of ICT, the economies of India and ASEAN are complementary. India's expertise as a software services provider, coupled with ASEAN's ICT manufacturing prowess, can lead to a win-win partnership.

In addition, ASEAN and India can share best practices in policy, regulation and technological development. India and ASEAN can work together in areas of capacity building, software development, e-governance, e-commerce, satellites and spectrum technology, radio frequency identification and ICT to mitigate the impacts of climate change.

Digital Economy

The ongoing COVID-19 pandemic has accelerated the digitisation of economies across the globe, and, as a result, it has brought an increase in digital payments. India's engagement with ASEAN on this front could allow for harmonious fund transfers across borders, incentivise innovations in payment systems and allow financial technology companies to expand their operations.

On the trade front, India can facilitate digital mechanisms by engaging with individual ASEAN member states through the Digital Economy Partnership Agreements, which aim to facilitate a steady and end-to-end digital trade and enable trusted data flow, thereby enhancing efficiency, reducing costs and increasing trust between businesses.

With ASEAN having the potential to become one of the top five digital economies in the world, its digital landscape presents a unique opportunity for businesses and investors. Given India's solid digital infrastructure and booming digital economy, engaging ASEAN through the digital means would prove advantageous.

Cross-border Investments

India and ASEAN need to take advantage of the opportunities created by the India-ASEAN FTA in goods, services and investments. The two regions can promote cross-border investments by linking investment promotion agencies, foreign investors and local entrepreneurs. Governments, industry bodies and relevant agencies can promote the dissemination of information on investment rules, regulations and policies related to investment in India and ASEAN.

With the adoption of these measures, India and ASEAN can foster a new era of seamless trade and investments, leading to shared prosperity and progress.

POLITICAL AND SECURITY RELATIONS

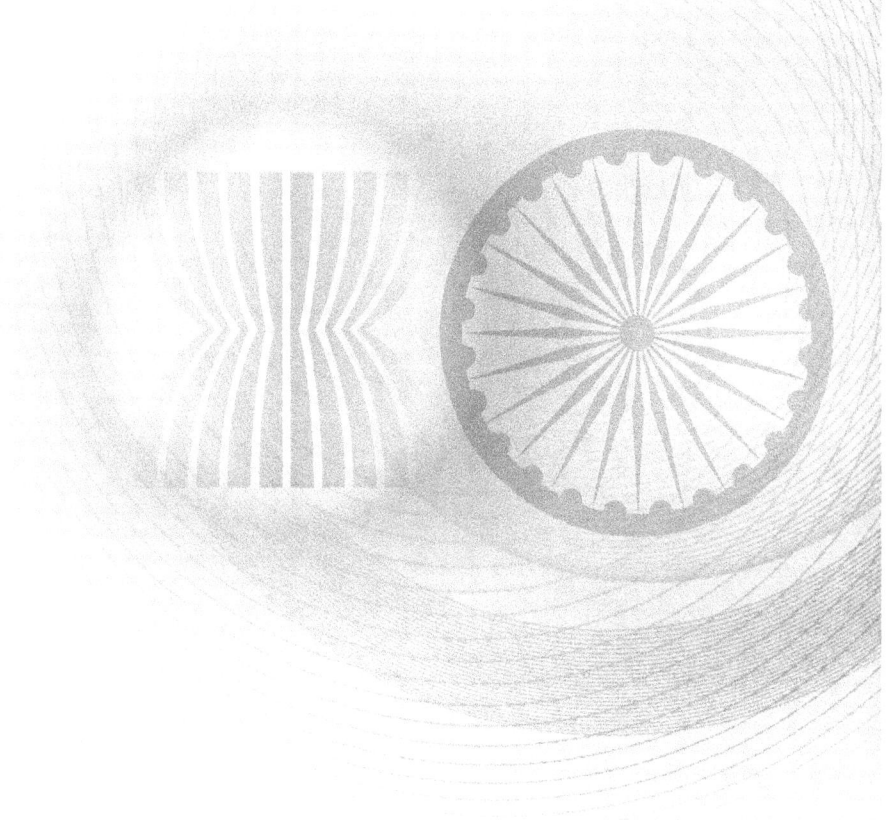

9

Relations between India and ASEAN: The 'ASEAN Way' and the Indo-Pacific Way

Sinderpal Singh

Introduction

This chapter has three main sections. The first section examines the early post-Cold War period and India's shift towards Southeast Asia via its 'Look East' policy. This is viewed as a period of growing strategic convergence between India and the Association of Southeast Asian Nations (ASEAN) as an organisation as well as with the individual Southeast Asian states. The second section considers the onset of the Indo-Pacific era, which signalled a growing divergence between India and ASEAN. The third section explores the various possible futures of the India-ASEAN relationship as India appears to be transiting into a new phase of its foreign policy.

The 'Look East' policy has been the subject of much academic and policy debate since its launch by India's Prime Minister Narashima Rao in 1991. Prime Minister Narendra Modi's government re-committed to the 'Look East' policy and upgraded it with the 'Act East' policy in 2014. Between 1991 and 2014, ASEAN responded to New Delhi's foreign policy shift by embedding India, in stages, into an ASEAN-led multilateral regional architecture in East Asia. India's entry as ASEAN's Dialogue Partner in 1995, joining the ASEAN Regional Forum in 1996, becoming a founding member of the East Asian Summit in 2005 and becoming part of the ASEAN Defence Ministers' Meeting-Plus in 2010 encapsulate this process of embedding India in an ASEAN-led East Asian regional order.

Since 2010, there have been a range of opinions about India-ASEAN relations. Within ASEAN, there has been widespread frustration, expressed both publicly and privately by member states, about India not fulfilling its promise as a key player in an ASEAN-led East Asian regional order. These frustrations were based on India's seemingly slow pace of economic liberalisation as well as a perceived reluctance or lack of capacity to play a more engaged role in the various multilateral institutions which ASEAN had facilitated India's entry into. Within India, however, there have been mixed reactions. On one level, there was an appreciation of the significant progress in economic ties between India and Southeast Asia since the 1990s. On the other hand, especially since 2014, there has been growing cynicism within India about ASEAN's ability to manage China's behaviour.

The advent of the Indo-Pacific, viewed within ASEAN as a geopolitical strategy to contain China, marked an adverse point in India-ASEAN relations. The official endorsement of this term by the United States (US), India, Japan, Australia and Indonesia compelled ASEAN, after some time, to articulate its ASEAN Outlook on the Indo-Pacific (AOIP). The AOIP attempted to re-assert an ASEAN-led regional security architecture in East Asia via existing ASEAN-led institutions. In contrast, India's articulation of the Indo-Pacific as a single strategic space is a means of firstly asserting India's position as a key player in the Indian and Pacific Oceans. Secondly, it is part of a wider strategy, together with the Quadrilateral Security Dialogue (also known as the Quad), of taking part in coalitions against China across the Indian and Pacific Oceans. The difference between the two visions points to the growing divergence between India and ASEAN on the shape of the desirable regional security order(s). This divergence is primarily shaped by India's shifting strategies in engaging the threat posed by China.

The 1962 India-China border war left a deep scar on Indian self-perceptions and entrenched a deep, structural distrust of Chinese intentions. It was not surprising that India pointed to China as a key reason for its acquisition of nuclear weapons in 1998. However, since 1998, India has attempted to manage the threat from China via a combination of improving its border defences while increasing economic engagement with China. This corresponded well with ASEAN's attempt to build a regional architecture that would possibly constrain Beijing within various multilateral structures whilst simultaneously hoping to socialise China into less aggressive behaviour within its neighbourhood. China's increasing presence in the Indian Ocean beginning in the 2010s, an area India traditionally deemed its strategic backyard, ushered in the beginnings of a shift in Indian foreign policy and a corresponding divergence from the 'ASEAN Way' of ordering regional geo-politics. Modi's attempts to reset relations by insulating economic relations with China from its security relationship faltered as India-China border skirmishes escalated and became more frequent. Increasingly, this led steadily to a shift in Indian policy on two fronts. Firstly, while India has traditionally been wary of being used as a pawn by the Americans in US-China relations, India has gradually shifted towards building a loose balancing coalition against China together with the US, Japan and Australia, embodied in the Quad. Secondly, it is increasingly reversing its earlier economic liberalisation trajectory and views economic ties with China as part of the larger threat posed by the latter. India's last-minute decision to not join the Regional Comprehensive Economic Partnership (RCEP) on the basis that joining it would be make India more vulnerable to China, marked a key moment in India-ASEAN relations. The upward trajectory in relations, beginning in the 1990s, seemed to be halting.

Looking ahead, this trend looks likely to continue as India increasingly demonstrates a lack of confidence in ASEAN-led institutions in moderating China's behaviour. India is increasingly looking towards the Quad process as a way of signalling a balancing strategy against China, and this goes beyond the military realm and extends into economic cooperation, joint infrastructural development, COVID-19 responses and other areas such as cyber security and artificial intelligence (AI). India's strong public statements in late 2020 on the Code of Conduct negotiations between ASEAN and China was another sign of the growing strategic divergence between India and the Southeast Asian region. A key aspect of Indian reservations stemmed from a growing perception that ASEAN was increasingly not able to stand up to China and would yield to Chinese demands to keep external powers like India out of the South China Sea. India's future strategy would most likely focus on adding Quad-Plus members in various activities like military exercises (France seems the key country in this respect), COVID-19 management discussions (Vietnam, South Korea and New Zealand) and other areas such as AI and cyber security. As these Quad-Plus processes mushroom, they will pose a significant challenge to an ASEAN-led order in East Asia and present even greater existential angst for ASEAN as an institution.

However, there are several positive trends in relation to India and individual Southeast Asian countries. ASEAN's disappointment at India's RCEP withdrawal notwithstanding, India's naval presence is still valued in sustaining a varied balance of power in the region. The recent India-Singapore-Thailand Trilateral exercise in the Andaman Sea is testimony to India's enduring role in the approaches to and in the Straits of Malacca. Other ASEAN member states such as Indonesia, Malaysia and Vietnam also continue to invest in stronger defence relations with India, cognisant of the weight India lends to a potentially more stable maritime balance of power within Southeast Asia.

Conclusion

The gap between the 'ASEAN Way' and the Indo-Pacific way is becoming increasingly clear. India appears to be transiting into a new phase of its foreign policy, progressively shedding its reservations about closer military ties with the US, resulting from its perceived inability to forge a viable great power compact with China since 2014. India's increased attention to the Quad and closer military relationships with the US, Japan and Australia have gradually led it to take part in balancing coalitions in response to China's actions, both on India's land borders and in the Indian Ocean.

In India's view, the ASEAN-led regional order looks increasingly unsuited to dealing with the threats presently posed by China. This seems to extend beyond the military domain and relates to economic multilateralism as well as other non-traditional spheres such as cyber security and infrastructure development.

In ASEAN's view, managing China's rise largely or exclusively via balancing strategies will likely lead to military confrontation between the great powers in East Asia, with adverse consequences for the Southeast Asian states. An approach lying somewhere between the 'ASEAN Way' and the Indo-Pacific way may be the future meeting point between India and some Southeast Asian states, signalling a new equilibrium in ties between the two sides.

10

India and ASEAN: Strong Base but Headwinds Ahead

T C A Raghavan

The year 2022 marks the 30th anniversary of India becoming a Sectoral Dialogue Partner of the Association of Southeast Asian Nations (ASEAN). The chronology of the past three decades shows linear progress in the development terms of an ever-closer political relationship between India and ASEAN and equally a widening and deepening interface across the fields of economic and cultural cooperation. In brief, if these past 30 years were contrasted with the preceding period, the latter would appear very much of a desert as compared to the strides made under India's successive 'Look East' and 'Act East' policies matched by strong ASEAN outreach, along with a consolidation of bilateral partnerships between India and the individual ASEAN member states.

Of course, the comparison is not entirely a valid one as the political and economic environment of the 1970s and 1980s cannot be compared with the post-Cold War situation of the 1990s, or that of the first two decades of this century. ASEAN's formation in 1967 with five member states took place at a time when India was deeply engrossed in its domestic churn and preoccupied with serious tensions and crisis with

China and Pakistan. The intensification of the Cold War from the 1970s saw new divisions emerging in Southeast Asia over Cambodia. It is no coincidence that it required dramatic developments in Europe, the Soviet Union and the end of the Cold War to restore balance to India's relations with Southeast Asia. The decade of the 1990s that saw India emerge as a Sectoral Dialogue Partner and the announcement of its 'Look East' policy thus also witnessed the expansion of ASEAN with Vietnam, Laos, Myanmar and Cambodia becoming full-fledged members.

By the mid- and late-1990s, the Cold War issues of the past had been comprehensively buried and the impact of this was very evident on the India-ASEAN interface. India thus became a full Dialogue Partner in 1996 and a Summit Partner in 2002. Thereafter, the political relationship grew in a near linear fashion taking on security aspects through the ASEAN Regional Forum and the ASEAN Defence Ministers Meeting-Plus processes. This has been further cemented since 2012 when the relationship was upgraded to a strategic partnership. In December 2012, an India-ASEAN Commemorative Summit in New Delhi was attended by all the ASEAN heads of state/government. Another commemorative summit in January 2018 to mark the 25th anniversary of the ASEAN-India dialogue partnership again saw a similar gathering in New Delhi. As stated earlier, 2022 is another milestone — the 30th anniversary of the India-ASEAN dialogue partnership.

The relationship, in brief, is today a dense network of inter-governmental processes and mechanisms cutting across different agencies and arms of the respective governments and an able testimony to the two millennium plus relationship between India and Southeast Asia. Alongside this, sub-regional arrangements such as the Ganga Mekong Cooperation and the Bay of Bengal Initiative for Multi-Sectoral Technical and Economic Cooperation (BIMSTEC) have added depth and vitality to regional cooperation as a whole.

While there is always the question to be debated of what has not been achieved or to what extent outcomes, expectations and capacities on both sides are in harmony, nevertheless, the point about linear progress in the cementing of this relationship will generally be accepted. In this context, how do we evaluate the political and security environments for India-ASEAN relations looking ahead?

The inauguration of India's 'Look East' approach from the 1990s had, of course, a strong economic rationale coinciding as it did with the opening up and reform of the Indian economy and the template that had been set by the East Asian 'Tiger' economies. However, the readjustment that took place in political and security priorities also had a wider context. The world immediately to India's west was conflict ridden and demonstrated minimal positive potential and enormous security threats and challenges. Looking East was, in a sense, a relief from the continental claustrophobia imposed on India's north and northwest by Pakistan, Afghanistan and numerous conflicts emerging from tensions between Iran and its maritime and continental neighbours.

The Bay of Bengal littoral offered, then as now, an obvious contrast with the Arabian Sea littoral. The former and beyond it, the wider Eastern Indian Ocean region merging with the Pacific, is a geography packed with geo-political rivalries as new and rising powers rub against older histories and conflicts. Yet, it is also a regional space intersected by numerous inter-governmental regimes, agreements and platforms. These temper and moderate rivalries to insulate the economic from the political and create an ecosystem with a positive narrative, notwithstanding all the existing tensions and potential conflicts. This in fact is the role of organisations and platforms such as BIMSTEC, ASEAN and the East Asia Summit process, among others. This gives a distinctive character to the Bay of Bengal and the wider Eastern Indian Ocean stretching to the Pacific.

To our west, there is a contrasting picture with the Arabian Sea littoral and its numerous political conflicts. The Iran-Saudi Arabia conflict in Yemen, India-Pakistan issues and the continued crisis in Somalia illustrate the point. The contrast, nevertheless, is not so much in the existence of conflict per se. The Rohingya issue in Myanmar, the tensions in the South China Sea and the still hovering shadows of numerous past conflicts in

Southeast Asia obviously stand out and will not disappear soon. The true contrast is the absence in the Arabian Sea littoral of regional platforms and inter-governmental agreements and associations that can moderate these conflicts or at least temper their intensity.

The relevance of this for India is self-evident. The countries of the Persian or the Arabian Gulf are vital as a source of employment and place of peaceful residence for millions of Indians, as a source of hydrocarbons and, increasingly, as a source of capital for much needed investment in India. The Arabian Sea is also, as it has always been, a conduit for ideas to India — benign in the past, radical more recently — and of security threats. The absence of an overall cooperative narrative multiplies the risks and threats as far as we are concerned. In this context India's eastward universe is less fragile.

As India further develops its external postures by engaging with the Indo-Pacific, a simultaneous disaggregation of this emergent maritime perspective and contrast between the East and West will be essential for India. These contrasting environments are, therefore, likely to remain an enduring feature of India's politics in the foreseeable future. Obviously, this means that a fundamental attraction for India to look and act East will be a constant. This obviously implies that the importance to India-ASEAN interface will not diminish, and ASEAN centrality will remain a key element in India's approach. However, the western theatre, for want of a better word, will also be ever present in India's concerns as a distraction, a worry but also one of great potential the harnessing of which has been suboptimal.

The second factor of importance is going to be the moving, in tandem, of the economic with the political. The global financial crisis, India's decision to stay out of the Regional Comprehensive Economic Partnership for the time being and what is loosely termed as the era of de-globalisation have played a role in dampening the economic momentum in the India-ASEAN interface even before the COVID-19 pandemic. The symptoms of this had been the flagging interest in India in free trade agreements (FTAs). There has, however, been a recent change in New Delhi's thinking on such agreements. India has signed FTAs with Australia and the United Arab Emirates. It is presently negotiating FTAs with Canada, the United Kingdom and the European Union.

Successive targets of trade in goods under the India-ASEAN FTA have not been met although this should not detract from the fact that trade growth has been impressive. There are numerous unresolved issues regarding more ambitious agreements on investments and services. The point in brief is that there are going to be roadblocks regarding any expectations that economic cooperation can continue to be the principal driver of the future political and security relationship. While the economic will obviously remain important but, unlike in the 1990s and in the first decade of this century, the coming decade is unlikely to see the political and the economic moving in tandem and supporting and consolidating each other. The way forward will, therefore, not be easy to chart. One possible course of action is for India and ASEAN to focus even more sharply on connectivity infrastructure through India's northeast. This will create new possibilities of widening economic relations, notwithstanding the structural impediments to their deepening.

The third and most obvious factor is China. India and China have interfaced in mainland and island Southeast Asia for over two millennia, but the situation now is different because of the power differentials that exist between the two and are likely to persist for the foreseeable future. There are differences of perception regarding China, both within ASEAN and between ASEAN and India. These are not unmanageable but require constant attention as these are not also easily reconcilable. Much, therefore, will depend on Chinese behaviour and approaches but it is unrealistic to expect that it will necessarily be uniform with respect to ASEAN or its constituent units and India. In this, India and ASEAN will constantly have to work towards a meeting of minds and convergence of approach as has been done, for instance, regarding the Indo-Pacific. Nevertheless, the China factor introduces an element of unpredictability which, for both India and the ASEAN member states, will pose numerous issues.

Finally, it is the question of the impact of the COVID-19 pandemic on political and security mindsets. Hopefully, the pandemic will pass soon but the question will remain of the lasting impact it will leave. If there is a lesson to be derived from the varied experiences of different countries since March 2020, it is that social infrastructure is as important a component of national and regional security as any other. How India and ASEAN integrate this perspective into their political approaches will be important to ensuring the relationship's future vitality and dynamism.

CONNECTIVITY

11

ASEAN-India Connectivity: Progress and Challenges

Myo Thant

Introduction

Physical connectivity between India and the member states of the Association of Southeast Asian Nations (ASEAN) has existed for eons and generated commercial, political and cultural exchanges. Connectivity has been strengthened by regional cooperation programmes and private sector-driven supply chains. This chapter examines the status and challenges of road and rail connectivity. This chapter also illustrates that in addition to political will and availability of financial resources, complementary institutions are critical to develop and maintain connectivity.

Background

Physical connectivity between the ASEAN region and India has existed for thousands of years. Complex patterns of land and maritime connectivity have resulted in rich cultural, commercial, technological and political exchanges. Physical connectivity between the two regions has been strengthened over the past three decades by public sector-led regional cooperation programmes and private sector-driven supply chains.

Immediately following the end of the Cold War, Southeast Asia witnessed a proliferation of regional cooperation programmes which sought to promote cross-border economic activity by removing structural obstacles such as missing roads, rather than through trade liberalisation. Prominent among these is the Greater Mekong Subregion (GMS) programme which was created by the Asian Development Bank (ADB) in 1992. The Indian subcontinent responded with the establishment of the Bay of Bengal Initiative for Multi-Sectoral Technical and Economic Cooperation (BIMSTEC) in 1998, which also includes Myanmar and Thailand. The Mekong-Ganga Cooperation (MGC) initiative involving India, Cambodia, Laos, Myanmar and Vietnam followed in 2000. A common denominator of these initiatives is the heavy emphasis on establishing efficient transport links to facilitate trade and investment flows between South and Southeast Asia.

Global and regional supply chains have been created by the emergence of networked production and inter- and intra-firm relations through which companies organise the entire range of business activities. Private sector supply chains knit together geographically dispersed regions. Underlying all the supply chains are reliable transport links which reduce trade transaction costs by establishing access, improve the quality and efficiency of transport services, minimise loss and damage to cargo and reduce inventory costs by ensuring timely delivery.

Land Connectivity: Land Bridge Challenges and Motivations

Physical connectivity between India and ASEAN requires the creation of a land bridge via Myanmar since there is no geographical alternative. The physical challenges of constructing such a land link are substantial. The distance from the northeast India-Myanmar border to the Myanmar-Thai border is about 1,500 kilometres. Land routes to both

India and Thailand exist but, until recently, have been rudimentary. Investment in cross-border road links was limited by the severe lack of financial resources and armed insurgency.

Myanmar's topography is a further hindrance to travel on an east-west axis. Three mountain ranges run in a north-south direction through the length of the country. In between the mountain ranges run three of the longest and widest rivers in Asia as well as innumerable streams which become raging rivers during the monsoon.

Establishing physical connectivity across countries is an exercise in engineering as well as political economy which requires understanding the differing motivations and expectations of the major stakeholders. Some of these motivations and expectations are as follow:

i. Myanmar is a passive participant in regional cooperation and more engaged with domestic concerns.
ii. The GMS programme tangentially and indirectly supports India-ASEAN connectivity. The pivotal event was the unveiling in 1998 of the economic corridor concept. The GMS ministers endorsed the concept and prioritised the 1,500-kilometre-long East-West Economic Corridor (EWEC) connecting Mawlamyine in Myanmar with Danang in Vietnam as a landbridge between the Indian and Pacific oceans. The three other road corridors originally proposed have been completed and facilitate networked production in mainland Southeast Asia, but the EWEC directly contributes to India-ASEAN connectivity as well.
iii. India is the most enthusiastic supporter of a land link to ASEAN, motivated by a desire to tap into new, large and growing ASEAN markets, plug into supply chains and develop border areas. The 1992 'Look East' policy was followed by the MGC and agreement between India, Myanmar and Thailand in late 2002 to establish a 1,360 kilometre-long Trilateral Highway connecting Moreh/Tamu on the Indian/Myanmar border with Myawaddy/Mae Sot on the Myanmar/Thailand border.

Land Connectivity: Road Transport

Road transport is a fast and reliable means of transport which can offer door-to-door services, thereby offsetting higher costs vis-à-vis maritime and rail transport, especially over short distances. Low entry costs for new users and wide flexibility of route choices are additional attributes.

The Asian Highway (AH) system, conceptualised by the United Nations in 1959, connected India and the present member states of ASEAN through two routes: AH1 Tamu-Mandalay-Meiktila-Myawaddy (1,650 kilometres) and AH2 Meiktila-Kyaingtong-Tachileik (788 kilometres). Progress was limited for 40 years until the GMS largely adopted the AH1 route for its own EWEC. The India-Myanmar-Thailand Trilateral Highway (2002), in turn, builds on the GMS projects as well as on Myanmar domestic projects. The implementation of the Trilateral Highway consists of three distinct components:

i. Myanmar massively invested in the transport sector between 1988 and 2012 despite lacking access to foreign aid. A new 600-kilometre-long highway along the central spine of the country has reduced travel time between Yangon and Mandalay to seven hours. Numerous bridges crossing the four major rivers, encountered on travel along an east-west axis, were completed by 2010.
ii. On the western side of the Trilateral Highway, a 150-kilometre-long road from Tamu to Kalemyo was financed and built by India in 2008. Over 60 bridges along this route are being renovated with Indian financing and, in 2016, the two governments further agreed to upgrade the 120-kilometre Kalemyo to Yagyi road for US$170 million.
iii. Construction of the EWEC, which constitutes the eastern portion of the Trilateral Highway, is financed by Thailand's bilateral assistance, the ADB's concessional loans and Japanese aid, which, by end 2019, amounted to a total of nearly US$1 billion. A completed EWEC will enable the 'Thailand Plus One' strategy under which Japanese

manufacturing plants in Thailand would migrate to neighbouring countries, according to economic, political and environmental variables.

Given the massive amount of secured financing, an all-weather land bridge connecting India with ASEAN, and capable of transshipping cargo from northeast India to Bangkok in four days or less, will be created by the end of this decade. Once in Thailand, transshipment to Hanoi or Singapore in less than three days and new supply chains will be possible. Heavy transport capacity and human skills are still needed as are common standards, regulations and efficient border crossing procedures. Nevertheless, the existence of a land bridge should provide a strong incentive for the countries to collaborate on removing the remaining challenges.

Land Connectivity: Rail Transport

Rail transport is a well-established but overlooked mode of transport in many ASEAN member states. It is particularly well suited to handle bulk cargo over long distances efficiently and in an environmentally positive manner. An India to ASEAN rail link would have a length of approximately 1,660 kilometres, of which about 600 kilometres is currently missing.

Substantive progress on a rail link occurred only after India proposed a Delhi-Hanoi rail link via Myanmar under the MGC initiative in late 2006. India simultaneously initiated a Jiribam-Tupul-Imphal 125-kilometre broad gauge link costing US$562 million to be completed by 2020. However, engineering challenges and centre-periphery political disagreements indicate that the link will only be completed by the middle of the decade. An additional 80 kilometres of track will still be needed to reach the Myanmar border.

Myanmar, which occupies the largest share of any rail link between India and ASEAN, has contributed towards connectivity by expanding track length from 3,180 kilometres prior to 1988 to 5,659 kilometres by

2010. The total route length is currently 6,110 kilometres, of which about 15 percent is double tracked. Despite significant expansion, the track is still missing on the Myanmar portions of an India-Myanmar-Thailand rail link. A 127-kilometre section between Tamu and Kalay and another 110-kilometre section on the Thanbyuzayat to the Three Pagoda Pass on the Thai border are missing. On the Thai side, a further 153 kilometres of track are missing.

An India-ASEAN rail land bridge would enable transshipment from New Delhi to Yangon in nine days, compared to 22 days by sea. The land bridge would feed into extensive domestic networks in Malaysia as well as India, Myanmar and Thailand, and rail transport could be competitive for distances of more than a thousand kilometres. The construction costs for such a link have been estimated at US$630 million in India, US$344 million in Myanmar and US$491 million in Thailand. Even allowing for decade-old estimates, the financial resources required are not exorbitant, given that the costs would be shared across three countries over several years.

The realisation of a rail-based land bridge may, however, depend less on the availability of investment and more on regional ability to agree on transit agreements, operating guidelines, signalling systems and other technical issues which prevent interoperability. State-owned rail companies may also require serious reforms to successfully meet the exacting needs of cross-border block trains and private-sector users.

Looking Ahead: Governance and Institutions

All major stakeholders involved in the Trilateral Highway should focus on its early completion and ensure that complementary institutions are developed in tandem. Research and past experiences indicate that three types of institutions are needed:

i. Transparent, efficient and predictable border crossing and customs clearance procedures;

ii. Transit agreements, including infrastructure charging for heavy goods vehicles; and
iii. A permanent body which provides rules that govern the use, maintenance and further development of the land bridge.

The need for a permanent body governing multi-country economic corridors has been long recognised. The institution should be strong enough to manage the expectations of the different countries, financiers and users. The institution must develop and apply a rigorous appraisal methodology to ensure an equitable distribution of benefits. Finally, the body must provide leadership by creating a long-term common template which different groups can work from.

Conclusion

A road-based land bridge, which acts as a catalyst in promoting trade and investment between India and ASEAN and establishes new supply chains, can be completed before the end of this decade. Regional connectivity is, however, time consuming, costly to achieve, requires trade-offs with domestic concerns and is difficult to maintain. Land-based connectivity requires Myanmar's active interest and its continuing access to concessional financing. Complementary institutions, which effectively govern and guide the development of physical institutions, are needed. A permanent body which efficiently manages the expectations of the different stakeholders and leads according to a common template, is highly desirable.

12

Thirty Years of ASEAN-India Connectivity

Prabir De

There has been steady progress in the relations between the Association of Southeast Asian Nations (ASEAN) and India since the 'Look East' policy was initiated in 1992. India became ASEAN's Sectoral Dialogue Partner in 1992. In 1995, this was upgraded to a full dialogue partnership. In 2002, India became ASEAN's summit-level partner. India's relations with ASEAN have also been the core foundation of India's 'Act East' policy, which was launched in 2014. In 2018, ASEAN and India commemorated 25 years of dialogue partnership and, 2022 marks 30 years of that partnership. During this period, ASEAN and India have not only strengthened trade and connectivity but also presented several best practices and important lessons. ASEAN and India require a strong and sustainable multimodal connectivity comprising road, rail, inland water transport, digital, maritime, air and logistics.

Roads and Highways

Road connectivity covers the Trilateral Highway and its extension to Cambodia, Laos and Vietnam, and the Kaladan Multimodal Transit

Transport (KMTT) project. The Trilateral Highway project requires the construction of a 1,360-kilometre highway connecting Moreh (Manipur) and Mae Sot (Thailand) through Myanmar. The Trilateral Highway is currently being constructed and is expected to be completed by 2023. The Economic Research Institute for ASEAN and East Asia has completed a study on the extension of the Trilateral Highway to Cambodia, Laos and Vietnam — except for one small section between Xieng Kok and Luang Namtha via Muang Sing in Laos, all sections of the suggested northern route are already designated as parts of the Asian Development Bank (ADB), United Nations Economic and Social Commission for Asia and the Pacific and Master Plan on ASEAN Connectivity 2025 transport corridor projects. All sections of the southern route of the eastward extension overlap with the East-West Economic Corridor, North-South Economic Corridor and the Southern Economic Corridor of the ADB. The Trilateral Highway would not work until the Trilateral Highway Motor Vehicle Agreement (T-MVA) comes into effect. Three participating countries have been negotiating the T-MVA, whose progress has been slow.

Another important cross-border connectivity project is the Mekong-India Economic Corridor (MIEC), which involves integrating four Mekong countries, namely, Myanmar, Thailand, Cambodia and Vietnam, with India. It aims to connect Ho Chi Minh City (Vietnam) with Dawei (Myanmar) via Bangkok (Thailand), Phnom Penh (Cambodia) and Chennai (India). A major part of the necessary investment is for the development of a port at Dawei and a Special Economic Zone. This corridor, when completed, is expected to augment trade between Southeast Asia and India by reducing the travel distance and removing the supply-side bottlenecks.

One of the objectives of the KMTT project is to provide attractive access to the Bay of Bengal to the landlocked northeast region of India. The components of this project include:

  i. Construction of an integrated Port and Inland Water Transport (IWT) terminal at Sittwe, including dredging;

ii. Development of a navigational channel along the Kaladan River from Sittwe to Paletwa (158 kilometres);
iii. Construction of an IWT-Highway transshipment terminal at Paletwa;
iv. Construction of six IWT barges (each of 300-tonne capacity) for the transportation of cargo between Sittwe and Paletwa; and
v. Building a double-lane highway (109 kilometres) from Paletwa to the India-Myanmar border (Zorinouri) in Mizoram.

India and Myanmar signed a framework agreement and two protocols (Protocol on Transit Transport and Protocol on Maintenance) in 2008. The construction of the integrated port and IWT jetty at Sittwe and the IWT terminal at Paletwa is completed. The 109-kilometre road from Zorinpuri on the India-Myanmar border to Paletwa in Myanmar is under construction. The KMTT project is yet to be operational.

Railways

Rail connectivity is critical to increasing bilateral trade and improving people-to-people contact. Rail connections will drastically shorten travel times for commodities and passengers. Rail India Technical and Economic Service Ltd completed a study for a rail link from Jiribam, Manipur, to Mandalay, Myanmar, in 2005. Within India, there is no rail link between Jiribam and Moreh, while, on the Myanmar side, there is no link between Tamu and Kalay. Therefore, connectivity between these points would enhance trade and passenger movements between the two countries. Following the construction of the Jiribam-Imphal-Moreh route, an India-Myanmar-Thailand-Malaysia-Singapore rail link and an India-Myanmar-Thailand-Hanoi train link may be possible. Recently, Indian Railways has given its sanction for the final location survey of the new Imphal-Moreh 111-kilometre railway line project. Initial survey work on a broad-gauge rail link between Imphal and Moreh has been completed by India's Northeast Frontier Railway.

Maritime

ASEAN and India are maritime neighbours and have a rich history of maritime trade. Over two-thirds of merchandise trade between ASEAN and India are carried through oceans. ASEAN-India cooperation in the maritime domain is one of the key areas of the ASEAN-India strategic partnership. India has endorsed the 'Blue Economy' as a new and central pillar of its economic activity. It encompasses both the coastal areas and the linked hinterland under the 'Security and Growth for All in the Region' policy. The ASEAN member states and India have been working closely in securing the trade routes, freedom of navigation in international waters, over flights, threat or use of force to intimidate, reducing piracy along the Straits of Malacca, cooperating in addressing traditional and non-traditional security challenges, including in areas of de-radicalisation, prevention of violent extremism, cyber-crime and natural disaster management. India is a member of the expanded ASEAN Maritime Forum. At the bilateral level, India and Myanmar have signed the standard operating procedure for the India-Myanmar Coordinated Patrol. India has signed a bilateral agreement with Indonesia and Thailand on maritime coordinated patrols. Coast guards of the ASEAN member states and India have taken part in search and rescue drill operations to strengthen their maritime security ties. Enhancing regional connectivity and trade through direct short-sea shipping and shipping facilitation agreements would strengthen maritime connectivity between ASEAN and India. At present, ASEAN and India have been negotiating the ASEAN-India Maritime Transport Cooperation Agreement. This agreement may provide greater access to maritime services, facilitate the flow of trade through sea and encourage private investments in the areas of maritime transportation and port development. ASEAN and India should take up issues such as the coastal shipping network (short sea shipping) and the development of maritime cargo routes, which hold immense potential.

Strengthening maritime connectivity will lead to economic integration through higher trade and investment, promotion of tourism, and building of seaports and shipping networks, cooperation in improving the efficiency of ports and joining the ASEAN Ro-Ro and Cruise Network.

Aviation

India and the ASEAN member states had many flights prior to the COVID-19 outbreak in early 2020. Bangkok, Kuala Lumpur and Singapore have been connected with major Tier-I and II cities in India by direct flights. Air connectivity between India and Myanmar is the only mode of transportation for religious and medical tourism. However, India is yet to be connected directly with Brunei, Cambodia, Indonesia and Laos by air. While the ASEAN-India open sky in cargo has been implemented, the same is yet to happen for passenger travel.

Digital

The progress in digital connectivity is moderate. Myanmar has set up cross-border fibre optic networks with many of its neighbouring countries, including India. The first cross-border fibre optic link between India and Myanmar was set up in February 2009, running from Moreh in Manipur to Mandalay in Myanmar and covering a distance of 500 kilometres. The 640-kilometre-long link passes through Tamu, Kampatwa, Kyi Gone, Shwebo, Monywa and Sagaing. The optic link is a high-speed broadband link for voice and data transmission. Besides, India has also offered over a US$1 billion special fund to the CLMV (Cambodia, Laos, Myanmar and Vietnam) countries to promote projects that support physical and digital connectivity and a Project Development Fund with a corpus of US$77 million to develop manufacturing hubs in CLMV countries, which can be used to strengthen digital connectivity between India and ASEAN. India has set up information technology (IT) centres in Myanmar — the India-Myanmar Centre for Enhancement of IT Skills and Centre of Information & Communication Technology Training in Yangon.

Nonetheless, there is ample scope to promote digital connectivity between India and the ASEAN member states, particularly in the areas of digital technology and digital economy.

Trade Facilitation

One of the key challenges to trade during these uncertain times is, therefore, to maintain the competitiveness in the global and regional markets by improving trade facilitation not only at home but also with the trade partners. Along with it, upgrading the ASEAN-India FTA and its effective utilisation may perhaps provide the required momentum to the bilateral trade flows while promoting sustainable and inclusive growth for both ASEAN and India. In addition, trade facilitation would be able to transform the cross-border clearance ecosystem through efficient, transparent, risk-based, coordinated, digital, seamless and technology-driven procedures that are supported by state-of-the-art land border crossings, roads and other logistics infrastructure and to reduce the overall cargo release time. Given that India and the ASEAN member states have ratified the World Trade Organization's Agreement on Trade Facilitation, they may resume the T-MVA negotiations at the earliest. To effectively implement the technical assistance, India's National Committee for Trade Facilitation (NCTF) may be engaged to design an appropriate strategy for technical assistance. This could help ASEAN and India effectively implement a paperless trading system.

Energy

While energy products are one of the major components of trade between ASEAN and India, commercial exchange of electricity is yet to happen between them. India already has grid interconnections with Nepal and Bhutan, but more energy market integration could take place if extended to ASEAN through Myanmar. Grids between ASEAN and India are yet to be connected in a larger way. Cross-border electricity exchange between ASEAN and India holds high promise. The energy cooperation between ASEAN and India appears to be more promising if we consider the countries commitments under the 2021 United Nations Climate Change Conference's agenda on climate change. The private sector should engage in both conventional and renewable energy in ASEAN's power projects. While moving towards a low-carbon growth path, trade in clean/green energy is essential. Therefore, India and ASEAN shall strengthen energy cooperation in clean energy products trade. India may develop a structure for a regional energy exchange, along with its operational procedures and regulatory and commercial requirements for cross-border trade with ASEAN. Besides, India and ASEAN should improve the investment environment for both electricity generation and transmission.

In the last 30 years, a review of regional connectivity projects between India and ASEAN suggests that the achievement on the connectivity front is mixed (see Table 12.1). India and ASEAN have witnessed good progress in air, trade facilitation and people-to-people connectivity, whereas digital, maritime and road connectivity have achieved moderate performance. Rail and energy connectivity have witnessed poor progress.

Table 12.1: ASEAN-India connectivity tally: 1992–2022

S/No	Sector	Performance
1	Road connectivity	Moderate
2	Rail connectivity	Poor
3	Maritime connectivity	Moderate
4	Air connectivity	Good
5	Digital connectivity	Moderate
6	Trade facilitation	Good
7	Energy connectivity	Poor
8	People-to-people connectivity	Good

Source: Author's own assessment.

The Way Forward

Economic corridors could provide the connection between gateways, economic nodes or hubs. This approach emphasises the integration of infrastructure improvement with economic opportunities such as trade and investment and includes efforts to address the social and other outcomes of increased connectivity.

The ASEAN-India Plan of Action (2021–2025) recommends transforming the Trilateral Highway into an economic corridor. The transformation of the transport corridors into economic corridors will have to pass through the logistics corridor in geographic space. Catalysts to move towards the economic corridors are trade facilitation, logistics services and border facilitation. The tasks are primarily three-fold: developing transport corridors; building corridor nodes; and linking corridor nodes and gateways. Creating an economic corridor on the Trilateral Highway would, however, require much more commitment from the ASEAN member states and India.

As a parting note, the seamless movement of goods and services along faster corridors will make ASEAN and India a truly united market.

CULTURAL TIES

13

Cultural Linkages between ASEAN and India: The Past to Post COVID-19

Sophana Srichampa

Introduction

India's geography shows a vast coastline of approximately 7,000 kilometres running along the Arabian Sea in the West and the Bay of Bengal in the East. Indian wisdom knew how to exploit the sea as mentioned in the *Rigveda*, the most ancient text of India, which refers to Indian merchants venturing to all corners of the known world in their quest for profit and gain. In the *Ramayana*, Yava Dvipa (India) and Suvarna Dvipa (Southeast Asia) are described as being connected in different ways especially through Java and Sumatra. In the 3rd century BC, during the Mauryan times, there was an administrative unit responsible for shipping and a commissioner of ports to supervise sea traffic. The Buddhist Jataka stories are also full of references to Indians taking sea voyages.

India and Southeast Asia have a long historical links, evidence of which can be found in Funan (2nd–3rd century AD), Sri Kshetra (4th–5th century AD), Pagan (5th–6th century AD), Khmer (8th–14th century AD),

Sri Vijayaand Sailendra (7th–11th century AD) and Majapahit (14th–15th century AD). Historically, Southeast Asia has been deeply influenced by Indian political ideas, religion, art and language, and local people in Southeast Asia willingly absorbed Pali-Sanskrit vocabulary into their languages. Moreover, architectural monuments, such as Angkor Wat, Borobudur and Prambanan temple, literary masterpieces like *Ramayana* and *Mahabharata* and the living Indian traditions found on the island of Bali, bear testimony to the courage and zeal of Indian princes, priests, poets, merchants and artisans and the ingratiating and assimilable qualities of Southeast Asians. The relationship between the Indians and the peoples of Southeast Asia was based not only on the economy but also on culture.

During the colonial period, many Indians migrated from India to Southeast Asia, mainly by force and due to various push factors. These migrants ultimately became citizens of the country in which they settled, and they represent significant elements of the human and cultural capital of these nations today.

This chapter presents some cultural linkages between ASEAN and India from the past to the post COVID-19 period.

Facets of India-ASEAN Cultural Linkages

Religious Linkages

Hinduism, Buddhism and Sikhism are religions that originated in India and have flourished in Southeast Asia. Many believers of these faiths in Southeast Asia undertake pilgrimages to the holy places of their religions in India. Moreover, religious linkages between these two regions are manifest in the existence of Indian priests who teach and perform rituals in many Southeast Asian countries. Classes and instruction related to the religious traditions of India are also popular in these countries by virtue of the interest and by satellite.

Pali and Sanskrit languages used in religious teachings are taught in some Southeast Asian countries. Higher education, including training scholarships in various fields through numerous schemes, are offered yearly to the Southeast Asian citizens by the Indian government, and many Buddhist monks and nuns take the opportunity to upgrade their knowledge of Buddhism by means of these scholarships. Furthermore, the Indian government promotes Sanskrit studies through the World Sanskrit Conference, which is held every three years, and is one of the biggest regular gatherings of Sanskrit scholars from around the globe. Vedic arithmetic taught in Sanskrit are learned by Southeast Asian students to equip them with the most effective techniques for rapid and precise calculation. This system can also be applied to the computer language in the digital era.

The Indian diasporic communities in Southeast Asia have succeeded in maintaining their unique identities through religious rituals and festivals during which the mainstream society is encouraged to participate and share in an atmosphere of learning and understanding. Some local followers of Indian gods and goddesses take part in annual festivals that are popular in India such as Ganesh Jaturathi in Mumbai. Furthermore, a country like Thailand, with its foundation in the concept of *devaraja* (god-king), holds tight to its Indian heritage in the form of Brahman ceremonies.

Ramayana Epic

The story of *Ramayana* was adapted from India and it flourished in Southeast Asia, though it is known by different names in different countries: *Reamker* in Cambodia, *Ramayana Jawa* in Indonesia, *Phra Lak Phra Ram* in Laos, *Hikayat Seri Rama* in Malaysia, *Yama Zatdaw Yamayana* in Myanmar, *Darangen-Singkil* in the Philippines and *Ramakien* in Thailand. The ancient epic remains part of the fabric of these cultures today, with each society creating its own version to reflect its specific values and beliefs and adapting the story accordingly. Furthermore, elements of the *Ramayana* in each country can be seen being performed in dance or experienced in literature, animation and the creative arts, and serve to inspire artists and startups to create products that appeal to the interests of the modern and younger consumers.

The *Ramayana* is considered an aspect of the vivid cultural diplomacy that reinforces the bond between India and Southeast Asia through regular exchange in the forms of conferences, seminars, books and performances.

Hindu and Buddhist Archeological Sites

There are several outstanding Hindu and Buddhist sites in Southeast Asia which are learning places as well as tourist spots.

These include Pagan in Myanmar to Nakhon Pathom, a central province in Thailand where Buddhism from India was first established. There are also several Hindu archeological sites in central, northeastern and southern Thailand; and Siem Reap in Cambodia is home to 10 Hindu temples, which are renowned archeological and tourist attractions. In central Vietnam, Hindu places of worship and museum can be found in Quang Nam, Da Nang and Nha Trang provinces. Selangor, Malaysia, has the famous Batu Caves, a popular Hindu shrine, and Yogyakarta in Java, Indonesia, prides itself not just for Prambanan, a Hindu compound, but also Borobudur, a Mahayana Buddhist temple- both world-rated tourist spots. Furthermore, the traditional Hindu lifestyle vigorously maintained as a unique feature of the Balinese culture and all these places serve to nourish the interest of Indians and international travelers alike.

In the post COVID-19 environment, both tangible and intangible heritages of India and ASEAN should be promoted, along with Hindu and Buddhist tourist routes in the ASEAN-India region.

Textiles

According to various sources of historical records, there has been a high demand for Indian textiles in Southeast Asia throughout history. Although many Southeast Asian countries carried out their own cotton productions, particularly in the wet zones of Sumatra, Peninsular Malaysia, West Java and Borneo, cotton could not be grown throughout the year. And despite weaving and spinning being household activities, commercial mass production of Indian cotton cloth made it cheaper than local products. Around the 5th century CE, after India and Southeast Asia had fully established sea connections, coloured cotton textiles started being imported into Southeast Asian ports in quantity.

In addition, the Indian textile techniques and designs influenced and mixed with certain Southeast Asian textile designs such as batik, which may have resulted from imitation with dyes used for South Indian painted cloth, probably before 1700 CE. Another Indian design, known as *ikati*, has been applied in some Southeast Asian textile production such as Thai *mudmee*, Cambodian *hol* and Indonesian *mengikat*.

Furthermore, the Mekong-Ganga Cooperation Asian Traditional Textiles Museum has been established in Siem Reap, Cambodia. Supported by the Indian government, the museum was inaugurated in April 2014 to exhibit textiles from the Mekong-Ganga regions as well as to provide interactive facilities. It also functions as an activity and learning centre, offering training and workshops on textiles and fashion design, and is a development space for traditional ethnic design. This museum has become one of the popular tourist spots of Siem Reap and symbolises the close linkages between India and Southeast Asia established by the textile industry.

To build on this, an annual ASEAN-India textiles exhibition should be initiated in the region, where knowledge can be shared among scholars and experts on innovation related to textiles and textiles products.

Films and Dramas

India is renowned to be one of the biggest world film production hubs for more than a hundred years. Its films and dramas are exported around the globe, including to the Southeast Asian countries. Nowadays, there are several international streaming platforms offering Indian and other

Asian films. This is another easy way to learn from each other. Prior to the COVID-19 outbreak, a number of Indian films used specific locations in Southeast Asia as settings which attracted Indian tourists to these countries, and others benefitted from special promotions in India in documentaries and travel and lifestyle programmes centred on Southeast Asia.

An India-ASEAN film festival should be organised annually in all ASEAN member states and India. Furthermore, knowledge and experience sharing through conferences or seminars involving producers, scholars, relevant government offices and audiences should be initiated through online meetings which would also be a convenient platform for international exchanges.

Conclusion

These cultural linkages between ASEAN and India are only part of the 'soft power' which sustains and enhances our historical and contemporary linkages. They are valued and vital in the everyday lives of the peoples of India and Southeast Asia, and they continue to survive and function in both regions. Furthermore, adaptations and innovations will undoubtedly contribute more to these established links, regardless of the challenges posed in the post COVID-19 era.

14

ASEAN-India Rhapsody of Cultural Exchanges

Rajeev Ranjan Chaturvedy

Introduction

The member states of the Association of Southeast Asian Nations (ASEAN) and India have been friends and neighbours since time immemorial. Shared cultural markers and footprints bear testimony to a rich tapestry of exchange of cultural ethos. Our habits, customs, folklores, textiles, cuisine, art and architecture enlighten us about our shared cultural legacy. Further, our religions, philosophies, trade and commerce connect us. We continue to cherish the living streams of cultural ties that flow through the hearts of the people of ASEAN and India. The cultural embrace between the ordinary people of ASEAN and India has immense potential to transform this partnership.

Amid the churning of the world, ASEAN and India are celebrating their three decades of companionship. However, a miasma of suspicion and anxiety negates the spirit of collegiality, particularly due to a limited understanding of each other and, sometimes, due to broken communication. ASEAN and India need to relive the intimate contacts of the past by nurturing the epistemology of pluralism and creating a wide profusion of distinctive yet ever-shifting cultures in one of the most dynamic regions in the world.

An aesthetically enriched cultural integration calls for an innovative cultural framework to cultivate the true spirit of friendship. When emerging challenges create an environment of despondency and cynicism, profound heterogeneity and asymmetrical prosperity of ASEAN and India make it imperative for both to optimise the existing institutional mechanisms and inject more robustness to enrich the cultural aspects of their relations. Underlining past splendour is not enough to convert present challenges into opportunities. It requires the active participation of all stakeholders.

Interwoven Legacies of the Past

A peninsula of numerous cultures, religions and cults, the Southeast Asia region has been a meeting ground for cultures and civilisations; the region has nurtured its own myths, legends, arts and an amazingly broad spectrum of styles that portray most Southeast Asian states. While there is evidence of intimate cultural and civilisational contacts between Southeast Asia and India, a lack of understanding of some unbroken cultural links and traditions, perhaps due to autochthonous norms and values, has resulted in a visible gap in understanding and sensitivities.

Numerous historical currents have fashioned ASEAN-India cultural connections over centuries. The diversity of cultures and traditions is multifarious in the ASEAN member states. The cross-pollination of Indian culture, ideas and religion across the region played a considerable role in the politico-cultural landscape of ASEAN. India's cultural and civilisational imprints influenced the emergence of statehood and inter-state system in Southeast Asia. Even today, the influence of ancient India can be seen in places and personal names, in commonly used words and in the arts and crafts. Studies show that during the first 600 years or so, Indian cultural symbols, including writing and statuary, were adopted in whole with little to no modifications. However, the 7th century onwards saw the creative adaptation of Indic culture by the Southeast Asians, resulting in interesting local variations. Thus, the countries in this region adapted and modified a whole range of foreign ideas and rules to suit their interests and local context. This process of imaginative adaptation preserved and, in some cases, amplified local beliefs and practices while producing a significant but evolutionary historical change in domestic politics and inter-state relations. The Indian cultural influence, therefore, was an adaptation and not an acceptance; for example, the localisation of Indian influences can be seen in the depiction of mythological traditions and various adaptations of religious and cultural performances such as the exhibits of the legendary bird, *Garuda*, or depiction of *Samudra Manthan* (churning of the Ocean) in various Southeast Asian countries.

Moreover, the Southeast Asians gave as much as they learnt from Indian cultures and civilisations. The influence of Indian civilisation on the ASEAN region is highly evident. Also, much literature is available on India's influence in this region. Southeast Asia's impact on cultural and historical events in India has not drawn adequate attention. However, the evidence suggests that the cultural influence flowed both ways. Southeast Asia has also contributed to enriching India's culture and traditions. This cross-pollination of ideas and the spiritual interaction between them has left an indelible mark on the regional art, architecture, culture, language and people-to-people exchange stimulated by a spirit of creativity, corporation and collaboration.

Southeast Asians established cultural contacts and came to study at Nalanda University. Some research suggests that several Southeast Asian innovations such as rice cultivation, bronze production, ideographs, outrigger canoes and iron technology, among others, were transmitted by traders and sailors to coastal India. In a fascinating episode of history, a 12-year-old boy was brought from Champa (modern-day Vietnam) from a distant family branch of the Pallava to the capital

Kanchipuram and crowned as King Nandivarman Pallavamalla, who ruled with great distinction and built the grand Vaikuntha Perumal temple. Similarly, *idli*, one of the favourite foods in Southern India, traces its origin to Southeast Asia.

Blooming of Culture and Creativity

Better connectivity and connection through social media have led to greater people-to-people connectivity and collaboration between India and the ASEAN region.

The cuisines of the Southeast Asian region, once found only in metro cities, are making rounds in small Indian towns. India is witnessing a culinary revolution in which Thai and Vietnamese cuisines make their presence felt in most parts of India. In Indian wedding feast, *khow suey* and *laksa* are eaten with gusto.

With its scenic natural beauty, historical monuments and rich biodiversity, India is attracting the attention of tourists from the ASEAN region. All this has led to a better appreciation of each other's cultures.

Creating a Tapestry for the Future

Despite a rich cultural heritage legacy, ASEAN and India's cultural connectedness and communications are limited. We live in an interconnected world in the age of diffused culture based on a modern outlook that relies on science and rationality to address emerging challenges. While we celebrate our past and continue to follow several rich cultural traditions, we also witness modifications, adaptations and infusion of new elements in our artistic journey.

The contemporary dynamics of the region and the fast-changing global society bring new ideas and pose different challenges. Therefore, ASEAN and India need to deliberate upon issues on which they could share their expertise and experiences and learn from each other.

This section identifies five key issues that require attention for greater collaboration between ASEAN and India.

The first and most important is the safety of cultural heritage. The sale of antiquities is a lucrative source of income, and illegal trade in art and historical artefacts funds terrorist activities. Terrorist groups use the black market to sell art and historical artefacts obtained illegally from conflict zones and then use those funds to support their activities around the world. Therefore, the protection of cultural heritage is related to national security and requires greater coordination and cooperation to end such transnational crimes. In today's world of swift communications, policymakers should work proactively to highlight the positive things in their countries and engage more constructively to address pressing global problems.

The cultural aspect of external interface is a powerful tool in the governments' diplomatic schemes. A pragmatic cultural policy could drive a convergence of interests towards cooperation in finding common solutions. The fusion of our cultural past could be enriched further through robust collaboration between ASEAN and India.

The second issue is that of intercultural communications. Culture is dynamic, and it changes with time and circumstances. Cultural groups face continual challenges from such powerful forces as environmental upheavals, pandemics, wars, migration, the influx of immigrants and the growth of new technologies. As a result, culture changes and evolves. More importantly, the knowledge remains limited due to a lack of intercultural communications. Intercultural communications are vital to develop a better understanding of each other's practices and sensitivities, likes and dislikes. This could be helpful in boosting mutual interaction. Digital technology can be an important medium for effective communications. Public digital infrastructure offers immense opportunities to directly reach out to ordinary people. ASEAN and India can transform the intercultural communication space by using digital technology. This can also empower the people to strengthen their capability to become trusted collaborators.

The third issue is the management of cultural resources. Culture and cultural resources represent a vital asset in the efforts to develop tourism across the ASEAN member states. Moreover, tourism is highly dependent on cultural icons, and proper management strategies will ensure that cultural heritage is preserved and contributes significantly to the material well-being and stability of their societies. ASEAN and India should enhance their technological and professional cooperation in cultural resource management.

The fourth issue is dealing with the culture industry. Both ASEAN and India have experienced an explosion of popular cultural products such as movies, pop music, animation, comic, television programmes and fashion magazines, among others, that have expanded and deepened their reach domestically and internationally and across regional and even national borders. Multi-directional flows of popular culture have intensified to reach consumers in different national and linguistic areas and have substantially decentralised the region's popular culture market.

As a result, consumers are exposed to various popular cultures to a great extent and are characterised by a diversity of consumption habits and lifestyles. Indeed, there is a realisation among governments that cultural industries are an excellent source for enhancing the countries' soft power and have the potential of cultivating lucrative export enterprises. How the culture industries of ASEAN and India collaborate will depend much on the governments' policies and support. Indeed, it requires greater coordination and a structured approach.

Finally, though ASEAN and India have initiated programmes on cultural and civilisational linkages, it is equally important to document civilisational ties and shared cultural symbols and disseminate them widely through various mediums and platforms to enhance general awareness on both sides.

Although culture is increasingly becoming an essential aspect of engagement, there are no culture ministry dialogues among the existing annual institutional mechanisms between ASEAN and India. ASEAN and India need to work on collective, consultative and inclusive approaches for greater coordination and a structured approach to deepen cultural ties further. The culture ministry dialogue can play a significant role in this regard.

Conclusion

India and ASEAN have much in common in the cultural realm. From religion, archeology, customs and folklore to literature, cuisines, the arts and dramas, the two sides have a legacy that they should be proud of. However, it is important for India and ASEAN to constructively address common challenges to ensure that their cultural ties continue to flourish.

PEOPLE-TO-PEOPLE TIES

15

ASEAN-India: Strengthening People-to-people Ties

Tan Ming Hui and Nazia Hussain

The year 2022 marks the 30th anniversary of the dialogue relations between the Association of Southeast Asian Nations (ASEAN) and India and has been designated the 'ASEAN-India Friendship Year'. On top of a long history of cross-civilisational linkages and people-to-people exchanges, ASEAN-India modern-day relations have seen positive and steady improvements since the end of the Cold War.

Under Prime Minister Narasimha Rao's leadership and his 'Look East' vision, relations with ASEAN took off in 1992 with the signing of a Sectoral Partnership, which later matured into a Strategic Partnership in 2012. India's major foreign policy initiatives — its 'Act East' and 'Neighbourhood First' policies — are testimony to New Delhi's priorities vis-à-vis Southeast Asia. These initiatives, however, progressed more slowly than expected in terms of functional collaborations, and they can be bolstered by renewed attention to people-to-people relations.

The role of people-to-people ties in forging strong bilateral relations should not be underestimated. Personal connections and informal networks encourage citizens from both sides to develop a deeper and informed understanding of each other beyond stereotypes and what we see on the news. Furthermore, the success of foreign policy objectives, such as connectivity projects, trade deals and defence cooperation agreements, often rely on whether there is enough understanding of local nuances and unique conditions. In the absence of strong official or formal diplomacy between countries, having informal linkages and bonds at the grassroots level becomes even more important in maintaining bilateral goodwill.

Ties that Bind

Historical linkages lay the foundation for modern-day people-to-people ties between ASEAN and India. Spanning back thousands of years, the impact of India's civilisational influence on the region's cultures, traditions, values and languages is notable. According to Milton Osborne in his book, *Southeast Asia: An Introductory History*, there had been a gradual expansion of Indian cultural contacts with Southeast Asia since the 2nd and 3rd centuries CE, with varying degrees of cultural influences depending on the geographical locations and the different centuries. The two regions saw a great flow of people, ideas and goods — ancient traders and priest-scholars brought Indian culture in various forms with them. Languages and literature, religions, art and architecture and administrative and legal frameworks were among the most important legacies of Indian influences. Some of these travellers also settled in the region and filled significant roles in the emerging Southeast Asian kingdoms.

Osborne also suggests that the indigenous population of Southeast Asia borrowed and adapted parts of Indian culture as they fitted with the existing cultural patterns and religious beliefs of the locals. We can observe the impact of these early linkages in historical sites such as the Angkor Wat in Cambodia, Pagan in Myanmar and Borobudur and Prambanan in Indonesia. The *Ramayana*, the ancient Indian epic, is also a shared cultural legacy treasured and retold by generations of Southeast Asians.

According to India's Ministry of External Affairs, 20 percent of the Indian diaspora have also established roots and found homes in many ASEAN member states, particularly in Singapore, Malaysia and Indonesia, playing a formative role in strengthening bilateral ties. Singaporean Indians form approximately 7.4 percent of its total population, while Malaysian Indians form approximately 6.4 percent of its total population.

Examining the Multifaceted Ties

Tourism across the ASEAN-India Neighbourhood

Tourism is a good metric of people-to-people flows between ASEAN and India. Despite their geographical closeness and cultural linkages, the potential of tourism has not been fully tapped. While travel between both regions was supported by improved air connectivity over the years, the COVID-19 pandemic caused disruptions to this trajectory. Pre-pandemic tourist arrivals from India in Southeast Asia were approximately 5.3 million in 2019, with numbers more than doubling from 2.4 million in 2010. Statistics published by India's Ministry of Tourism indicate that tourists from the region arriving in India also increased from 439,043 in 2010 to 930,540 in 2019. With the increase of vaccination rates, international travel is likely to gradually recover to pre-pandemic levels.

This presents an opportunity for ASEAN and India to forge closer collaboration to rejuvenate the industry safely, bring about a more resilient sector and enhance people-to-people relations in the long run. Both sides can reap mutual benefits from increased coordination on joint tourism campaigns, sharing best practices and building better infrastructure connectivity. Given their historical and cultural ties, there remains great potential for the expansion of educational, heritage and religious tourism. For example, sacred sites like Bodh Gaya, Rajgir and Nalanda are essential destinations for the Buddhist tourism circuit, attracting pilgrims and learners from across Southeast Asia.

Collaboration through Education and Think Tanks

ASEAN and India engage in various educational exchange programmes and capacity-building workshops for students, members of the media and farmers to foster people-to-people exchange. The Indian initiative to fund 1,000 integrated PhD fellowships for ASEAN students who wish to attend one of the 23 highly competitive Indian Institutes of Technology (IITs) is particularly salient as it is the largest capacity development initiative in India's engagement of ASEAN, with a budget of approximately US$45 million. Given the disruptions brought on by COVID-19, ASEAN students have commenced classes at the IITs, albeit virtually for the time being. Moreover, India is also working to launch a network of ASEAN and Indian universities to facilitate the exchange of faculty and students. The universities seek to undertake joint research projects, including the revival of Nalanda University for students from across Asia, one of the oldest centres of learning in the world, particularly renowned as a seat for Buddhist studies between the 5th and 12th centuries.

Apart from university exchanges, ASEAN and India have also initiated exchanges to inform discussions at the policy level through think-tank collaborations. The ASEAN-India Network of Think Tanks Roundtable, established at the 7th ASEAN-India Summit in Thailand in 2009, affords a platform for academics, think tanks, policymakers, media and business representatives to provide policy inputs to governments on the future direction of cooperation. The forum serves to provide long-term perspectives to further strengthen ASEAN-India cooperation and dialogue. At the recently concluded 7th ASEAN-India Roundtable organised under the theme, 'Post-Covid-19 Recovery: Regional Cooperation Agenda for ASEAN-India Partnership', the participants deliberated on the common challenges faced by the people on the ground, such as healthcare and sustainability, as the region embarks on a post COVID-19 recovery.

Consolidating efforts to strengthen the people-to-people and institutional linkages, the Asian Confluence, India, the ASEAN Studies

Centre of ISEAS-Yusof Ishak Institute and the ASEAN-India Centre at the Research and Information System for Developing Countries, New Delhi, launched their first joint programme in 2021 entitled 'ASEAN-India Development Partnership Programme', a training and capacity-building programme for scholars and practitioners of the ASEAN member states and India. This week-long training programme comprised lectures by eminent scholars on overarching themes pertinent to ASEAN-India relations.

Efforts in the Sub-regions

Geographical proximity and ensuing cultural similarities between the people of India's northeast and the Mekong countries provide an impetus to enhancing people-to-people linkages in the sub-regions. Myanmar shares a land border with four northeast Indian states, stretching over 1,600 kilometres, and forming a land bridge connecting the two neighbours. In fact, the people in northeast India share more similarities with those in the Mekong countries, in terms of culture, traditions, languages, religious practice and food habits, than with their counterparts in the Indian mainland. This includes over 200 ethnic and tribal groups in India's northeast which share ethnic ties with Southeast Asia.

Existing cultural ties will benefit from improved physical connectivity. The Bay of Bengal Initiative for Multi-Sectoral Technical and Economic Cooperation (BIMSTEC) sub-regional mechanism, involving India, Myanmar and Thailand, among other members, has several projects in the pipeline, all of which are set to provide a much needed push for enhanced people-to-people connectivity. Nevertheless, multiple missed deadlines of key projects, such as the India-Myanmar-Thailand Trilateral Highway and the Kaladan Multi-modal Transit Transport Project, have largely kept physical connectivity between India and the sub-regions limited with slow progress. The 5th BIMSTEC Summit in March 2022 saw the adoption of the Master Plan for Transport Connectivity. This could offer a framework to accelerate the key projects and bring people in the sub-regions closer.

Seeking Closer Ties Ahead

Since August 2021, Singapore has begun its three-year term as country coordinator for ASEAN-India Dialogue Relations and is poised to play a critical role in forging deeper engagement with India. Singapore's Prime Minister Lee Hsien Loong emphasised the importance of people-to-people relations and highlighted the priority areas of cooperation, including digital transformation.

Digital Future

India is known for its thriving technological sector, boasting the world's third largest start-up ecosystem, while ASEAN is at the cusp of its own digital revolution. People-oriented partnerships could include the promotion of industrial networking and enhancing training and capacity-building programmes for skilled labour, information technology professionals and business leaders. This could help bridge ASEAN's digital gap, facilitate the transfer of technology and know-how, human resource development, poverty alleviation as well as support joint research and development projects.

Next Generation

With a combined youth population of over 700 million, ASEAN and India could accelerate and expand their joint efforts and investments in future-oriented education and training, such as in online education. The pandemic has greatly normalised the need to build reliable virtual learning systems across the world. Importantly, both sides can boost efforts of youth-focused initiatives such as dialogues and hackathons. Besides promoting stronger ties, trust and understanding, having regular youth exchanges also helps to encourage the younger generation to work collaboratively and find innovative solutions for its common future challenges, such as climate change, healthcare, transnational threats and inequality.

Overall, deep historical linkages, cultural similarities and geographical proximity are a strong foundation to propel the ASEAN-India partnership forward. Moreover, the people of ASEAN and India face common challenges that require coordinated efforts and constant dialogue to identify common solutions. Strengthening interactions on the ground among the ordinary people creates a strong basis for mutual trust and confidence building, and, critically, it can promote public support for positive bilateral relations in the long term.

16

People-centred: Advancing India-ASEAN Ties through People-to-people Contacts

Shankari Sundararaman

Introduction

In diplomacy, states are moving beyond processes that are confined to the official arena and enlarging the scope and interaction of communities to advance closer ties between countries. This aspect of diplomatic leverage, known as public diplomacy, allows for a wider exchange through which interstate relations can be strengthened. The advantage of public diplomacy extends beyond the immediate official processes and its efficacy can help to maintain relations even when the official processes are strained or stressed.

This is where the role of people-to-people contact becomes significant. The strength and flexibility of the informal nature of people-to-people interaction often remain viable even where the formal processes are unable to make much headway. People-to-people ties provide greater leverage through a multi-pronged approach rather than relying on official processes. While it offers a more personal and engaging interaction, people-to-people ties cannot be limited to information exchange but require more robust interaction.

ASEAN's Move towards Community Building

During the 9th Association of Southeast Asian Nations (ASEAN) Summit in Bali in 2003, ASEAN initiated the genesis of its approach towards community building, a process through which ASEAN sought to establish three critical pillars of the wider ASEAN community it envisaged. Known as the Bali Concord II, which was the agreement that became the basis for establishing the ASEAN community, it endorsed the Vientiane Action Plan in the 10th ASEAN Summit in 2004 through two broad frameworks for ASEAN integration: the Initiative for ASEAN Integration and the Roadmap for Integration of ASEAN.

The move towards community building within ASEAN had three critical elements: the ASEAN politico-security community; ASEAN economic community and ASEAN socio-cultural community — all of which contributed to the formalisation of an overarching ASEAN community that the grouping sought to establish. This approach to community building aspired to follow the processes set up by the European Union (EU) even while it was limited in some sense, as the ASEAN principles and those of the EU are distinct. Within the context of the ASEAN socio-cultural community, the move towards a more people-centred ASEAN was advocated. According to the ASEAN Secretariat's *ASEAN Socio-Cultural Community Blueprint* (2009), it sought to enhance the "quality of life through cooperative activities that were people-oriented". The core objective of this approach looked at promotion and advancement of cultural diversity as a right of all people within the region, while simultaneously addressing the development of all member states. In this context, it is important to view the core areas where India and ASEAN can synergise their relations while promoting the ASEAN socio-cultural community's objectives.

India-ASEAN Relations: The Overarching Context

While the overarching relationship with ASEAN has been improving steadily, India's engagement with the wider regional processes have seen ups and downs. Particularly relevant in this regard is India's withdrawal from the Regional Comprehensive Economic Partnership (RCEP). India's decision to pull out of the RCEP was not a welcome decision from the ASEAN perspective since it considers both economic and security ties with India to be complementary to each other. The impact of the RCEP withdrawal has made it more critical to re-evaluate the focus on India-ASEAN relations, where both cultural and public diplomacy can play a critical role in re-engaging the two regions to further their engagement across a multi-pronged approach.

People-to-people Ties: A Weak Link

One of the weakest links in ASEAN-India relations is their people-to-people ties. As India's 'Look East' policy evolved over the first few decades, the focus was primarily economic, even while security cooperation was evident in the first decade itself. In 2014, the 'Look East' policy was renamed the 'Act East' policy with three critical areas of focus — commerce, connectivity and culture, referred to as the three 'Cs'. However, even as India's RCEP withdrawal led to a downslide in regional ties, both connectivity and culture were not focused on. There has been a clear delivery deficit in terms of the connectivity projects — the Kaladan Multimodal Transport Corridor and the India-Myanmar-Thailand Trilateral Highway have been delayed repeatedly leading to little progress on connectivity projects. Furthermore, several other projects boosting India-ASEAN connectivity remain only in the nascent stages and are far from being implemented, with little tangible results. For ASEAN, India's exit from the RCEP is considered a lack of commitment to furthering economic integration, while for India, the question of protecting key sectors of its domestic economy is a critical part of both political and economic rationale.

The fourth 'C' in the 'Act East' policy is capacity building. It is within this context that the furthering of India-ASEAN people-to-people ties must be evaluated. The role of India's soft power and the country's ability to foster ties based on cultural diplomacy becomes a critical area to be addressed. India's soft power in the context of Southeast Asia is clearly visible in the cultural linkages that are a vibrant part of Southeast Asian society. This includes two key components.

The first is India's civilisational heritage that spread across the region through the historical interconnectedness that India shared with the region. The elements of that shared cultural impact are spread across three religions — Hinduism, Buddhism and Islam — that have impacted the region through contact with India. This has led to the robust exchange of cultural ties with the region over a period of 2,000 years of contact, reminiscent in the architectural wonders that abound in the region.

Cultural diplomacy has been seen as a key plank on which India's ties with its near neighbourhood can be effectively enhanced; this has been reiterated by the focus on five core aspects which are considered the key elements of India's soft power diplomacy. Ambassador Bhaswati Mukherjee, in a lecture on 'Diplomacy, UNESCO and Soft Power' (2016), identified five core elements as reflected by India's Prime Minister Narendra Modi — first, *samman* or dignity, which encapsulates interstate relations as respect for one another; second, *samvaad* recognises that dialogue and negotiation are key to building relations; third, *samriddhi* which is co-prosperity for all; fourth, *suruksha* that implies both regional and global security; and fifth, *sanskriti evam sabhyata* which reiterates the importance of civilisational and cultural links. While these five objectives promote the space for opening up the areas of cultural diplomacy and soft power, a key component of this is people-to-people contact. This form of interaction provides two advantages, according to Gregory Payne in his 2009 article 'Reflections on Public Diplomacy: People-to-People Communication' — first, it broadens the onus of public diplomacy from reliance on government agencies and brings in non-government players in enhancing ties along a wider spectrum; and second, by building ties at the grassroots level, it promotes sharing of ideas and experiences, while building synergies that accept mutual differences.

Optimising Existing Mechanisms

With regard to people-to-people ties, there are few areas in which India-ASEAN relations have taken modest steps in recent times. The Indian government initiated the Indian Council of Social Science Research fellowships and the Indian Technical and Economic Cooperation Programme to promote assistance to students and other areas of capacity building. However, these tend to remain somewhat underutilised. In the context of assisting the Mekong countries of ASEAN, India has offered the Quick Impact Projects which cover a wide range of critical areas. A more robust focus on areas of education has been considered crucial as this acts as a form of cultural bridge that can fill the existing gaps in the ties.

India has been instrumental in enhancing capacity-building projects; for example, it offers 1,000 integrated doctoral programmes for students from ASEAN member states to study at the prestigious Indian Institutes of Technology in India. This is an area which can develop and sustain a core network of scholars. This was started by the Ministry of Human Resource Development in 2019 and aims at promoting people-to-people ties within the region. Dipanjan Roy Chaudhury wrote in *The Economic Times* on 11 November 2020 that the budget outlay for this initiative is one of the largest in the context of India's ties with ASEAN at the capacity-building level.

Another focus on education relates to starting exchange programmes between the universities of India and ASEAN member states through which the promotion of academic interaction and exchange is expected to grow in the coming years. One of the recent efforts that has seen some leverage in addressing the lacuna in people-to-people ties has been the ASEAN-India Students Exchange Programme. This has led to a network of youth connecting the two regions together and can evolve as a dynamic option to explore the furtherance of people-to-people contact. This is an option that allows for community building through fostering a dialogue among the youth and it has the potential to reshape generations of interaction between the two regions.

The second key area where India and ASEAN can evolve better mechanisms to enhance people-to-people ties is through the development of the tourism sector between the two regions. While Southeast Asia remains an important tourist attraction for Indian travellers, the reverse is not the case. In terms of broadening the scope for tourism, two key areas need be addressed — first, the measures for connecting all the ASEAN member states with India through direct flights falls short of expectations outlined in the Comprehensive Economic Partnership Agreement (2003) which highlighted the provisions for an open skies agreement to promote tourism. Writing for the *Hindustan Times* on 24 January 2018, Ambassador Shyam Saran identified this as an issue in promoting deeper contact between the regions. The potential to create twin cities or sister cities between important historical and architectural sights between India and ASEAN would be a welcome step. In a 2014 article, 'Modi in Myanmar: From 'Look East' to 'Act East'', I suggested linking Bodhgaya, Lumbini and Yangon together in the form of a Buddhist circuit, connecting India, Nepal and Myanmar. Jogjakarta, Siem Reap and Thanjavur could become another tourist hub as the architectural similarity between these sights is a magnificent indicator of the cultural ties between the two regions.

The ASEAN socio-cultural community aims to achieve this kind of integration promotion and understanding of cultural diversity and community building through cultural exchange. This is an area that needs to evolve significantly between India and ASEAN. The most important of the India-ASEAN ties have been reflected in the restoration process of ancient monuments in which the Archeological Survey of India was involved. This has been an important area of collaboration in reviving and supporting the tourism sector in many ASEAN member states.

Conclusion

The potential for further expanding people-to-people contact in the context of India-ASEAN ties remains critical. Several opportunities, particularly in the areas of English language training and capacity building along areas of technological sectors, particularly information technology, remain areas that can be explored further. Student exchange programmes need to be coordinated and developed further, particularly through regular meetings and interactions that expand across the entire region. Another area which can be promoted is language training where both Indian and Southeast Asia languages can be used as a leverage to foster closer people-to-people contact. This is an area that remains under explored.

Economic relations need a clear revamp in the aftermath of India's RCEP exit and the delay in the India-ASEAN services sector free trade agreement. There is also growing emphasis on areas of cooperation at the security level through expanded naval diplomacy that is orchestrated by the official state-level interactions. However, beyond the process of official interaction, robust ties can be leveraged by deeper integration through people-to-people ties.

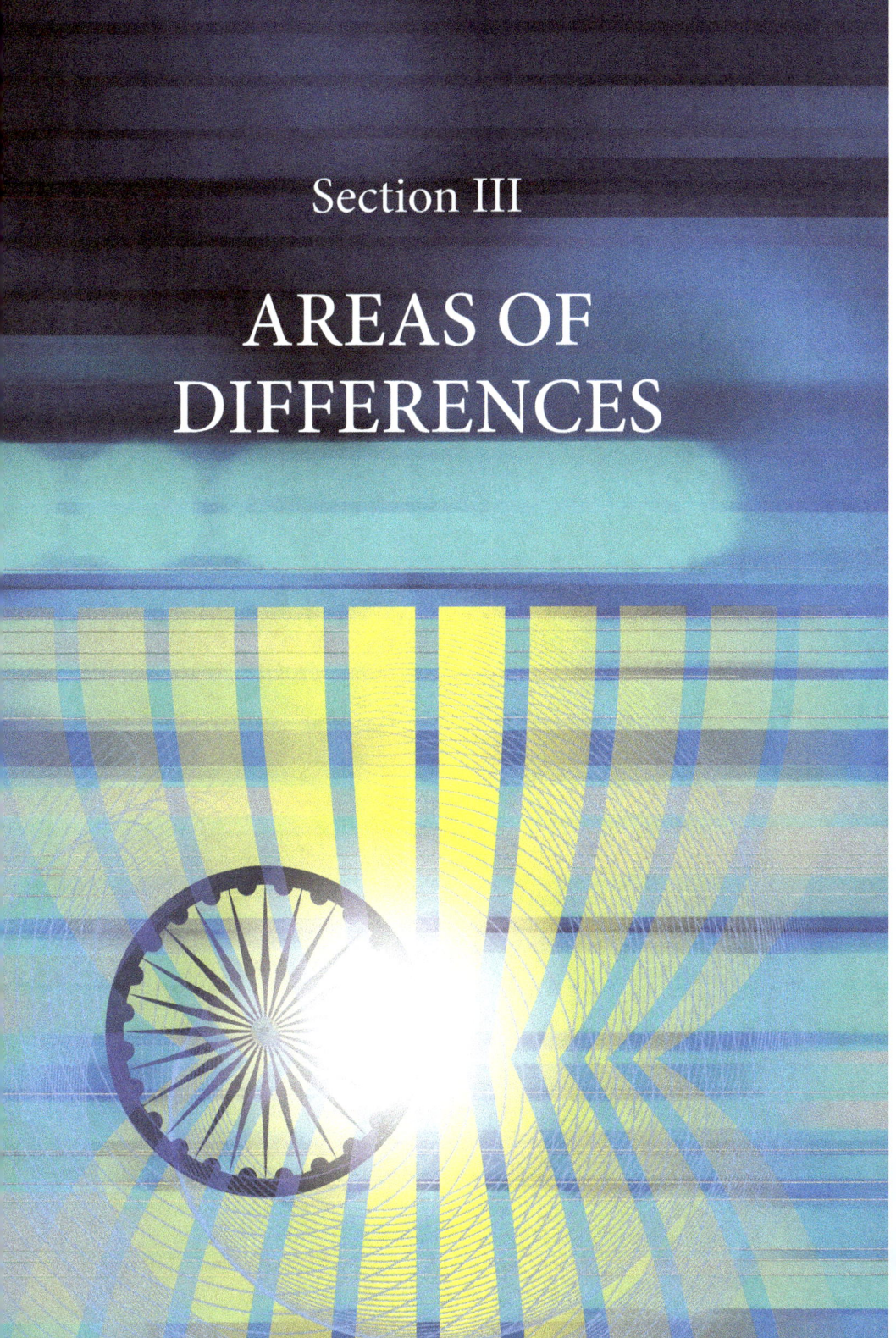

Section III
AREAS OF DIFFERENCES

THE REGIONAL COMPREHENSIVE ECONOMIC PARTNERSHIP

17

The Regional Comprehensive Economic Partnership: The Journey

Sulaimah Mahmood

I have often been asked asked why it took almost a decade to conclude the Regional Comprehensive Economic Partnership (RCEP) agreement. I knew that taking up the role as Singapore's chief negotiator would not be a walk in the park. The initial 16 RCEP participating countries (RPCs) included a wide range of levels of development, ambition levels and political considerations.

The RCEP was signed on 15 November 2020 and entered into force on 1 January 2022 after Australia, New Zealand, Brunei, Cambodia, Laos, Singapore, Thailand, Vietnam, China and Japan ratified the agreement. The journey, however, was not a straightforward one. Against the grim backdrop of the COVID-19 pandemic. I recall the sense of anticipation — perhaps even anxiety — as well as the lingering doubts that the signing might not happen due to evolving circumstances. The collective joy and pride of the RCEP negotiators and officials during the signing will always be a deeply treasured moment of my career.

2006: The Beginning

It may not be commonly known but the first steps towards the RCEP began as early as 2006.

The Association of Southeast Asian Nations (ASEAN) played a critical role in setting the foundation, taking cues from the commentaries on developing the regional trade architecture, calls for closer economic integration and, more importantly, business needs. With the increasing number of free trade agreements (FTAs) in the region, it was increasingly difficult and complex for businesses to navigate the interwoven and overlapping trade rules.

As a result, we began to consider how to consolidate ASEAN's existing five FTAs involving six FTA partners, to untangle the 'spaghetti bowl' effect to form a common regional partnership in Asia with ASEAN at the centre. It was also an opportunity to "significantly build upon" the standards set out in the existing ASEAN FTAs. This eventually formed part of the Guiding Principles adopted prior to the launch of the RCEP negotiations.

2012: Launch of the RCEP

ASEAN did not start with the ambition of consolidating all five FTAs into a single agreement. We had the option of either embarking on an East Asia Free Trade Agreement comprising ASEAN, China, Japan and South Korea (ASEAN+3) or the Comprehensive Economic Partnership in East Asia, which also included Australia, India and New Zealand (ASEAN+6). After much deliberation, in August 2009, ASEAN and the ASEAN FTA partners agreed to look into merging these two processes into a single process to consolidate all concluded ASEAN Plus One FTAs into a wider regional FTA.

This gave birth to the RCEP which was formally launched at the 21st ASEAN Summit in November 2012. The first round of negotiations at the level of the RCEP Trade Negotiating Committee was held in Brunei in May 2013. I recalled it being a productive first five-day meeting, which finalised a detailed work plan for next three years, foolishly thinking that we would conclude the RCEP by end 2015.

2019: The RCEP near Conclusion but Surprising Withdrawal by India

At the eleventh hour, where the 16 RCEP leaders were ready to announce that we "have concluded text-based negotiations for all 20-chapter texts, and essentially all their market access issues", India withdrew from the RCEP on 4 November 2019.

In the words of India's Prime Minister Narendra Modi, "The present form of [the] RCEP…does not address satisfactorily India's outstanding issues and concerns. In such situation, it's not possible for India to join the RCEP."

I literally froze from shock and disappointment as we believed that India was satisfied with having settled its interests and the 20 chapters could be closed. It was unfortunate that India chose to leave the RCEP. India's departure came as a surprise and was deeply disappointing for all RPCs, especially after so much time and effort were exerted to align the RPCs' concerns and India's position.

India faced great domestic pressures to reconsider its participation in the RCEP due to concerns that the influx of imported goods could hurt local industries and that India's bilateral FTAs were contributing to India's trade deficit. Throughout the negotiation process, the RPCs made significant efforts to address and accommodate one another's concerns, making difficult compromises and tough decisions. Despite our best efforts, India unilaterally announced its decision to withdraw from the RCEP.

The withdrawal of India from the RCEP was met with mixed reactions even in India. Some of those who were directly involved in the negotiations expressed some disappointment not only because of the time and effort they had dedicated to the RCEP negotiations but, more importantly, also the opportunities that Indian businesses, especially those that are part of the regional supply chain, may miss. India's most influential business chamber, the Confederation of Indian Industry, was also a vocal proponent of India being part of the RCEP.

Despite our collective disappointment, we acknowledge India's difficulties and concerns in joining the RCEP; its decision not to join the RCEP so near the conclusion must have been difficult. We respect India's decision. Nevertheless, as a founding member, India holds a 'special status' and the doors are still open for India to join the RCEP any time it so wishes.

Long-term Interest for India to Join the RCEP

The RCEP was an opportunity to bring the region together with a modern, comprehensive, high quality and mutually beneficial agreement, which will lead to opportunities for our businesses and our people. With ASEAN at its core, the RCEP brought our FTA partners together, becoming the first FTA between China, Japan and South Korea. The RCEP could have been India's first FTA with China and would have enabled India to strengthen its linkages with other ASEAN FTA partners. Joining the RCEP may cause short-term pains for India's domestic industries. However, the prioritisation of long-term reforms would serve India well, integrating it into the global value chains, supporting its ambitions to be a US$5 trillion economy by 2025 and doubling its exports to US$1 trillion by 2025. Bold economic actions to open up and connect with the world could be the right direction for India.

I believe that India's participation would also benefit the RPCs, creating a win-win situation. With India, the RCEP would cover 45 percent of the world's population and further promote regional integration and strengthen supply chains in the region.

2020: Signing of the RCEP

The RCEP was signed when the region was in the midst of the COVID-19 global pandemic. The signing was a strong testament of the region's determination and commitment to deepen economic integration amidst difficult times. In the final stages, the meetings were conducted entirely virtually — this was unprecedented and unfamiliar for most of us as FTA negotiators, who are well-tuned to negotiations in a physical setting.

Looking back, I am proud of the tremendous tenacity displayed by all the negotiators in forging ahead through the difficult situations to deliver the final agreement and I am thankful for the excellent assistance provided by the ASEAN Secretariat throughout the entire journey. Truth be told, it was ASEAN's centrality and leadership by Indonesia as the ASEAN country coordinator for the RCEP that enabled us to overcome differences to finally reach consensus. In particular, the stewardship, dedication and hard work of the Chairman of RCEP Trade Negotiating Committee Chairman, Pak Iman Pambagyo, throughout these eight years brought the RCEP across the finish line.

Benefits of the RCEP

The RCEP is a big step forward for the region. It improves upon ASEAN Plus One agreements to allow for more comprehensive trade facilitative measures, enhanced services commitments, enhanced investment rules and expanded scope and commitments in new areas. It is a centralised framework that has improved upon existing agreements and facilitates regional integration efforts via a common rulebook for the 15 RPCs. According to 'The RCEP's Impact on Trade and Growth in the Asia Pacific', *Macroeconomic Review*, published by the Monetary Authority of Singapore (MAS) in 2021, the RCEP could add between 0.4 percent and 0.6 percent to the gross domestic product of the RPCs. The MAS reports also stated that the common and alternative product-specific rules of origin under the RCEP are also expected to boost various production patterns and lower costs for businesses; this is because companies can more optimally source for raw materials and intermediate inputs from other RPCs, while enjoying lower tariff rates. In the long term, the RCEP will increase our region's competitiveness through the strengthening of our intra-regional supply chains. We also worked diligently and boldly to ensure that the RCEP is comprehensive in its coverage — its 20 chapters include many new areas not typically included in ASEAN Plus One FTAs, such as e-commerce, competition policy, intellectual property rights and government procurement.

In addition, the RCEP recognises the importance of enabling and benefitting smaller businesses with a dedicated chapter on small- and medium-enterprises (SMEs). One of the areas of sustained effort in the RCEP that is useful for SMEs is e-commerce and digital trade. It represents the fastest and easiest way for SMEs to connect to suppliers, consumers and firms across borders. I recalled that when the RCEP negotiations were launched in 2013, ASEAN held reservations about including an e-commerce chapter in the agreement, feeling unprepared to discuss the issue as e-commerce was a novel area for FTAs in general and unfamiliar to ASEAN. We gradually grew in confidence after several rounds of informal Experts Group meetings and eventually agreed to start a formal Working Group on E-commerce. Finally, this led to discussions on broader e-commerce provisions, including market access provisions, which was a significant step beyond ASEAN's initial position of only accepting cooperation and promotion-related provisions.

Conclusion

The signing of the RCEP does not mark the end of the journey. For now, 13 of the 15 member states of the RCEP have ratified the agreement. Indonesia and the Philippines are working to expedite their domestic ratification of the RCEP in order to realise its wealth of benefits to our businesses and people.

I am confident that the RCEP will provide a boost to the trade ties between the RPCs and create long-lasting benefits for the region. Having been a part of the RCEP since its nascence, I am glad to have contributed to its formation and development. In my capacity as Singapore's chief negotiator, I would like to thank the Singapore team for their support, dedication and contributions throughout negotiations, especially Singapore's former Trade and Industry Minister Lim Hng Kiang and Minister Chan Chun Sing for their leadership and guidance. I am grateful to have been a part in this journey and will always treasure this experience.

18

Withdrawal from the Regional Comprehensive Economic Partnership — Where Does It Take India?

Sudhir T Devare

India's last-minute decision at the November 2019 Bangkok meeting of the East Asia Summit not to be a signatory to the Regional Comprehensive Economic Partnership (RCEP) agreement came as a major surprise to the business and strategic communities in India. Although New Delhi's reservations to certain provisions of the draft agreement (under negotiation since 2013) were known, there was hope among a number of Southeast and East Asian countries that a settlement would finally be reached and that India, the third largest economy in Asia, would remain within the regional economic grouping which accounts for nearly 40 percent of the global economy.

With the parties to the agreement insisting on the elimination of nearly 90 percent of tariff lines within the member states, the focus was placed on market access and the issue of rules of origin. India had demanded a three-tiered structure with respect to tariffs reduction — for the Association of Southeast Asian Nations (ASEAN), free trade agreement (FTA) partners like Japan, South Korea and Australia, and non-FTA countries like China and New Zealand. India, already having a huge trade imbalance with most East and Southeast Asian countries, and especially with China (US$56.9 billion in 2019) asked for an automatic trigger safeguard mechanism which would ensure countermeasures to raise tariffs on products when their imports crossed a certain threshold. This was, however, not acceptable to a majority of the members. India did not feel confident enough to allow unhindered market access, especially when its products, such as generics in which India had export capacities, were not receiving due access to the East Asian markets, bilaterally or under existing FTAs. The issue of the rules of origin was also a bone of contention between India and the export-oriented East Asian states. While India expected 25 percent or more value addition in the final country from where the export of a particular item would take place, some of the East Asian countries held the view that a cumulation of the value could occur in any of the countries. For these countries, this was one of the most desired provisions which India could not accept as it ran counter to the basic principle of the rules of origin. India had also sought some phasing in terms of agreeing to the common rules of origin.

India's experience with FTAs or comprehensive economic cooperation agreements (CECA) with countries in the region is mixed. Although these agreements entered over the past two decades have helped India to move closer to the objective of economic integration with ASEAN and East Asia, the results, especially with respect to India's exports of goods, have been disappointing. Barring a few items, such as automobiles and components, and pharmaceuticals, India's exports have basically been primary products or raw materials. In services, the opaque regulatory barriers such as the non-availability of visas in time or excessive restrictions on the operation of banks, or the language factor in many RCEP countries have come in the way of Indian information technology (IT) companies to expand their operations. In the CECA with Japan, South Korea, Singapore, Malaysia and ASEAN, the trade balance has been substantially unfavourable to India. With non-FTA countries like China and New Zealand, there are large trade gaps. India has had a trade deficit with 11 out of 15 RCEP states. India's apprehension that the aggregate imbalance with all RCEP members would be unsustainable and weighed heavily in India's decision to pull out of this important negotiation. Perhaps a more flexible and back-loaded tariff reduction schedule, particularly with countries like China, with which India already had a large deficit, may have helped.

India also expected that ASEAN, with its centrality in the process of decision-making, would lean on the East Asian states, particularly China, with respect to key elements of the agreement, namely, the rules of origin and market access, to enable India to have some flexibility. However, in absence of this, India had to essentially deal bilaterally with China.

The decision for India to leave the RCEP is no doubt very difficult and comes at an inopportune time when the country is under severe economic stress on account of the COVID-19 pandemic. However, it reflects India's independent view of the economic and political landscape of the region today identified as the Indo-Pacific. India's 'Act East' policy, which is premised on a strong strategic and economic relationship with the countries of the region (which constitute the membership of the RCEP), may find the economic dimension greatly affected. As it is, India is virtually absent when it comes to participation in regional economic groupings in Asia. It is not a member of the Asia-Pacific Economic Cooperation or another major regional grouping, namely, the Comprehensive Progressive Trans-Pacific Partnership, led by Japan. This no doubt impacts on its association with supply chains in the dynamic region of East and Southeast Asia. With the centre of geo-economic gravity shifting from the Euro-Atlantic to the Indo-Pacific, the advantage of being an active part of the global value chains could be lost for India.

Clearly, India's compulsions, as outlined above, were so overwhelming that it felt necessary to resort to a decision which can have far-reaching implications. The loss is as much for India as could be for ASEAN and others in the RCEP. India needed some initial flexibility to enable it to catch up. Likewise, some accommodation in areas of India's strength, such as services, could have brought greater balance and equity that also figured in the initial RCEP mandate. The 'Guiding Principles and Objectives for Negotiating the RCEP', adopted by the economic ministers in August 2012, lay down some principles like broader and deeper engagement with significant improvements over the existing FTAs while recognising the individual and diverse circumstances of the countries.

It is important to see why the existing FTAs have not generally come to the expectation of the volume of trade and investment. India's existing FTAs are currently being reviewed. The India-Singapore CECA, the first that India signed with a developed economy in 2005, was found to be a dynamic instrument for the expansion of trade, investment and services between the two countries. The CECA enabled India to substantially increase the presence of its commercial and economic institutions in the international business space of Singapore which found it to be mutually beneficial. It may, however, be necessary to evaluate how effectively it is contributing to that end today. In the absence of the RCEP, there is a greater need for the optimal implementation of the agreements with Singapore, Japan, South Korea, Malaysia and Thailand. If need be, these agreements may be suitably modified.

India is also simultaneously exploring the option of expediting the finalisation of such comprehensive agreements with the European Union (EU), the United Kingdom (UK), the United States (US) and the African Union. With each of these, there may be different outstanding issues. However, India's market size and growing technological capacity can act as attractions. Its active and supportive role in the Indo-Pacific could also be an important geo-political consideration for the above powers to conclude the agreements with India at an early date.

India's export performance has been a matter of concern for some time since its exports have remained around US$300 billion in the last decade. India's absence from the RCEP may further hamper its exports to the destinations within the membership since the latter are very likely to give preference to their fellow member states, There would be some exception, namely, in products that India enjoys competitiveness such as automobiles, pharmaceuticals, and certain IT services.

What is true of exports can also be true with respect to investments. Investing countries from within the RCEP may prefer intra-RCEP investments. India, which has received a low level of greenfield foreign direct investment (FDI) in manufacturing over the past two decades, needs high technology investments from the East Asian countries. In the current COVID-19 situation in India, where there has been massive unemployment, the infusion of FDI in job-creating enterprises will be much welcomed. The developed economies in the RCEP are able to invest in infrastructure, electronics, construction and renewable energy, among others. The opportunity to receive their investments in India may be lost because of India's absence from the RCEP.

Another issue related to investment is the current trend towards the diversification of investment away from China. Since the surfacing of US-China trade rivalry, several foreign enterprises have relocated from China. Japan has offered economic assistance to the tune of US$2.2 billion to enterprises — Japanese and from other countries — for such diversification. The list of countries for possible relocation includes several RCEP countries as well as Bangladesh and India. Vietnam has already attracted sizeable investments. Whether India's withdrawal from the RCEP would impact India's attractiveness with respect to such investments remains to be seen.

India's decision not to be part of the RCEP may serve as a protective step in the short term, given the imbalanced nature of several of the agreement's provisions. However, will India's absence from such a regional agreement help the country in the long term? On objective evaluation, it appears that both India and the RCEP countries may stand to lose in many ways. India may also be giving up a large economic and strategic space to China even as the Chinese large-scale exports and economic outreach in India may not substantially reduce soon.

As stated earlier, among the options available to India to strengthen its external commercial and economic position, the conclusion of CECAs with the US, the UK, the EU and Australia could be advantageous. The EU and India have lately shown keen interest in resuming negotiations on a comprehensive trade pact. The UK and India also recently launched an Enhanced Trade Partnership that envisages facilitating market access in specific sectors. Both the UK and India appear open to moving towards a strategic relationship in which trade and economy would be key components. With Australia too, the prospects of an FTA may be good, in view of a relatively better access for India's IT service sector. The agreement with the UK and Australia could serve as a useful template for future discussions on India's FTAs with developed states and the RCEP countries.

Economic integration with ASEAN has been India's objective for the past three decades under its 'Look East' and 'Act East' policies. In order to achieve it, India may have to continue to engage intensively with ASEAN and the East Asian countries. With deeper economic reforms and emphasis on *Atmanirbhar Bharat* (Self-reliant India), India should hopefully be able to reduce its huge import dependence on China and the other RCEP countries. India already has the experience of complex negotiations within the RCEP and could suggest flexibility till a later date — a few years from now — for its participation. Needless to say, such reciprocity may also be necessary on the part of the RCEP countries since a broad-ranging agreement like the RCEP can only be achieved through mutual accommodation and benefit.

ATTITUDE TOWARDS CHINA

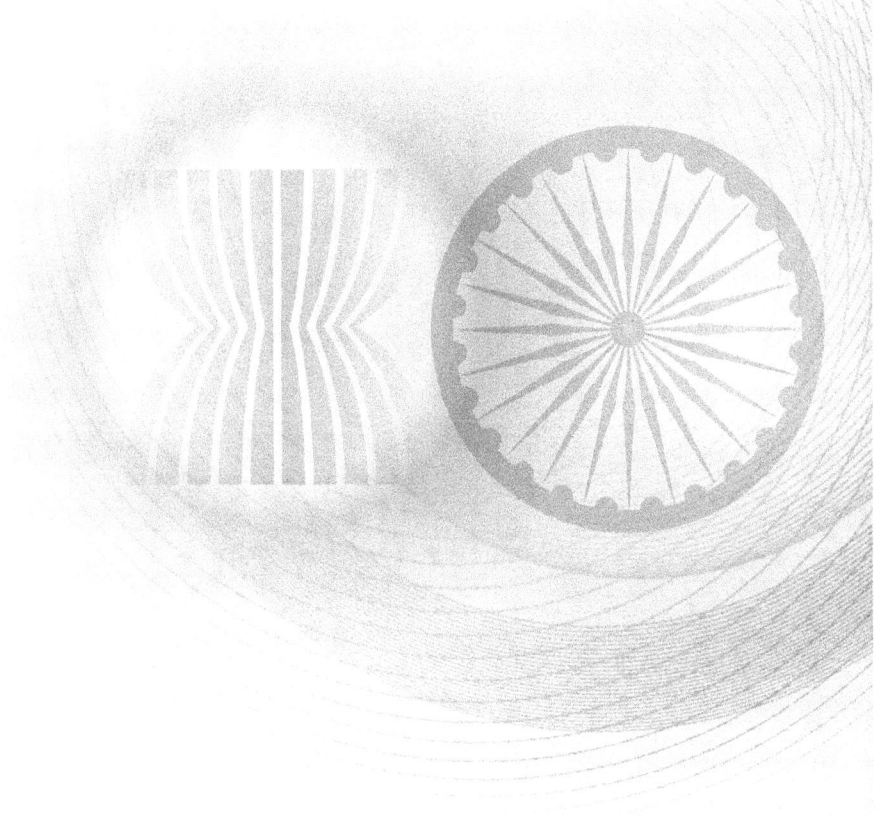

19

ASEAN and India's Relations with China: Perceptions and Priorities

Kavi Chongkittavorn and Moe Thuzar

Since 1991, when the Association of Southeast Asian Nations (ASEAN) and China first established Sectoral Dialogue relations, their ties can be said to have advanced with the right moves that enabled China to obtain full Dialogue Partner status in 1996 and, later, in 2003, Strategic Dialogue Partner. China was the first among ASEAN's Dialogue Partners to obtain Strategic Partner status. Also, in 2003, China acceded to the Treaty of Amity and Cooperation (TAC) in Southeast Asia, the first major/regional power to do so. Beijing also indicated an interest to sign up to the 1995 Southeast Asia Nuclear Weapons Free Zone, differing from other nuclear powers' seeming lack of interest (or commitment).

Beijing's 'enthusiasm' for such key ASEAN security frameworks has the main aim of obtaining and remaining in place one of ASEAN's top-ranked dialogue partners. China was a founding member of the ASEAN Regional Forum (ARF), established in 1994, and of the East Asia Summit (EAS) in 2005. India, the other regional power or 'big neighbour' to Southeast Asia, is perceived to be somewhat lagging behind China. India was admitted to the ARF only in 1996, two years after the ARF's establishment. Even though India signed the TAC in the same year as China and succeeded in joining the EAS at its inception, ASEAN-India dialogue relations do not have the same coverage as ASEAN-China interaction in key sectors of ASEAN cooperation. There are approximately 50 different committees under the ASEAN-China aegis, covering the whole gamut of ASEAN's key sectors of cooperation.

The most cited 'success stories' for ASEAN-China relations have mainly been in economic and people-to-people exchanges. For instance, trade volume between the two sides leapt from just under US$8 billion in 1990 to US$684.6 billion in 2019. Before the COVID-19 pandemic, there were nearly 4,500 flights between cities in China and the 10-member ASEAN community. More than 200,000 students from China and the ASEAN member states were recipients of education exchange/scholarship programmes. China has also kept track of sister cities between ASEAN and China; China's Ambassador to the Philippines Huang Xilian stated in 2021 that there were now 200 such pairs.

After 30 years of interactions, China and ASEAN are now 'comprehensive strategic partners'. The move to elevate the relationship a step further was first mooted by China in 2020 but the ASEAN member states spent more than one and a half years deliberating this proposal at various levels. This is an indication of the prevailing attitude and mood of each ASEAN member state towards China at that point in time.

Indeed, the 'State of Southeast Asia 2022' survey, conducted by the ISEAS-Yusof Ishak Institute's ASEAN Studies Centre, found that the region is worried about China's growing economic influence (64.4 percent) as well as its regional political and strategic influence (76.4 percent). The 'perceived geo-political reality' is reflected in 76.7 percent of the respondents continuing to see China as the most economically influential country in the region, and 54.4 percent viewing China as the most politically and strategically influential. Since the first survey in 2019, China has been ranked first on both counts. These perceptions reveal a continued unease about China's role and reach in the region, evidenced in 41.7 percent of the respondents viewing China as a "revisionist power" that "intends to turn Southeast Asia into its sphere of influence". Most Southeast Asian respondents to the survey (58.1 percent) have little or no confidence in China "[doing] the right thing to contribute to global peace, security, prosperity, and governance". Over 57 percent of the region chose to align with the United States (US) over China.

Among the top three reasons given for factors that could potentially worsen any positive impressions of China, the respondents cited China's economic and political assertions in the Southeast Asian countries, its "strong-arm tactics in the South China Sea and Mekong" and its "use of economic tools and tourism to punish [my country's] foreign policy choices" as the main concerns.

The survey findings give an indication that the past 30 years of cordial relations do not necessarily provide firm assurance for the future, and perceptions and priorities do matter in ASEAN's dialogue relations. As the 'State of Southeast Asia 2022' survey findings highlight, three 'pain' points inform ASEAN's relations with China: (a) China's behaviour in the South China Sea; (b) China's conduct in the Mekong River; and (c) China's practice of using its economic power punitively to pursue (and entrench) its strategic and economic interests in the Southeast Asian/ASEAN member states.

The South China Sea may well be one of the main barometers of ASEAN-China relations, as expectations are high on both sides on shaping the Code of Conduct (COC) in the South China Sea to suit respective interests. The pandemic disrupted negotiations on the first consolidated draft of the COC for well over a year. Work resumed in June 2021, with virtual meetings to negotiate the less sensitive parts, but progress has been slow.

China's State Councillor and Foreign Minister Wang Yi stressed in a keynote speech on 28 July 2021 at a teleconference with ASEAN-based think tanks that China is willing to step up dialogue and consultations with the concerned parties on the South China Sea. He also urged

ASEAN to speed up the negotiations on the COC "…in order to reach a substantive and effective COC that conforms with international law, including UNCLOS [United Nations Convention on the Law of the Sea]". Wang Yi's language seemed to be more accommodating than earlier occasions, manifesting Beijing's desire to conclude the COC within an earlier timeframe. Even so, at the in-person meeting of ASEAN and Chinese foreign ministers in Chongqing in June 2021, ASEAN could not reach a consensus on the language Beijing used to describe the ongoing negotiations. While ASEAN member states welcomed Beijing's willingness to reach a substantive and effective COC, they could not agree on the word "conform" due to the different interpretations pertaining to its legal implications. This nitty-gritty discord has undermined the so-called big picture of cooperation between ASEAN and China and will delay the COC's conclusion even by end-2022. The reasons include differences between ASEAN and China on several contentious issues, including Beijing's attitude towards the growing presence of the US, the United Kingdom, Japan and Australia in the Indo-Pacific region under security arrangements separate from the ASEAN track.

The crisis that erupted in Myanmar following the country's military's takeover of state power on 1 February 2021 has also had some impact on ASEAN's relations with China and India. Both are ASEAN's Dialogue Partners, and both share borders with Myanmar. The security implications of the Myanmar crisis present an increasing potential for cross-border spillover, as the military's use of lethal force has continued despite the ASEAN Five-Point Consensus call for the cessation of violence, creating a cycle of violence in Myanmar. As Myanmar's neighbours, both China and India will be affected by the humanitarian and security aspects of displacements following the intensified armed conflict in Myanmar after the February 2021 coup.

As ASEAN's Dialogue Partners, China and India have voiced support for ASEAN's Five-Point Consensus and to follow ASEAN's practice of constructive engagement. Bilateral interests and concerns, however, will affect the pursuance (and upholding) of the Five-Point

Consensus priorities. China and India's separate bilateral engagements with the State Administration Council regime in Myanmar may thus have unintended consequences for the centrality of ASEAN's political decisions.

Though Beijing followed ASEAN's October 2021 decision to invite only a 'non-political representative' to the special ASEAN-China Summit commemorating 30 years of dialogue relations, it initially sought an exception to this decision. The 'China factor' in India's foreign policy towards the Southeast Asian countries as well as India's domestic concerns related to security issues along its border with Myanmar have also influenced New Delhi's overall policy towards the current Myanmar crisis and in engaging with the State Administration Council regime. Like China, India has also taken a more cautious approach to the coup. As the negative consequences of the Myanmar coup wear on, however, both China and India may need to consider how engaging with the state in Myanmar may serve their respective economic and security interests in the region.

In the foreseeable future, the heightened emphasis on strategic competition by both the US and China in Southeast Asia will also present ASEAN with a dilemma on several fronts. Though ASEAN will refrain from taking a definitive side, due to the consequences that may be visited upon the group's economic and security well-being, each of the ASEAN member states may be compelled to reveal its preferences at the bilateral level. The Myanmar crisis has also shown that maintaining a strategic balance between the US and China may be affected by how ASEAN's Dialogue Partners, particularly those neighbouring Myanmar, will consider the US' influence on matters pertaining to human rights and global governance.

As a bloc, ASEAN must find ways to manage both great powers and help them find common ground, thereby enabling multidimensional cooperation in the future. New areas such as climate change, cyber security, sustainable development and the digital economy could form a new platform on which the US, China and ASEAN could compete and cooperate without resorting to what is frequently described as a doomsday confrontation.

Though ASEAN-China ties — and how India responds to those dynamics either bilaterally or collectively with the ASEAN member states — may be difficult to accurately predict, one thing is certain, strengthening mutual trust and respect is the main tenet that ASEAN upholds in its internal and external interactions. The emphasis on peaceful co-existence and a mutually beneficial partnership has been a feature of ASEAN-China relations in the last three decades, while ASEAN-India relations have been primarily occupied with finding areas of mutual interest to push forward pragmatic cooperation. In the post COVID-19 pandemic world, the strategic environment and unintended consequences that follow from the security implications of developments in the Southeast Asian countries/ASEAN member states and new shifts in alignments with powers in the region and beyond would provide a fertile ground for varying degrees and combinations of close cooperation or fierce competition with and between ASEAN's Dialogue Partners in the region.

20

How India and China View Each Other

Shivshankar Menon

India and China have long regarded each other in complex and not always complimentary ways. Apart from the problem of mirror imaging, there are multiple asymmetries in the way that Indians and Chinese see each other. The images that Indian and Chinese elites created of the other have often diverged considerably from reality. It is fair to say that India and China have considerable experience of misunderstanding each other and display a continuing ability to build on that past.

Some reasons for this unusual situation between two neighbours can be found in history, in the differing paths that India and China chose when they became republics and in contemporary India-China relations.

History

In reaction to the British colonial assumption of superiority and denigration of things Indian, the Indian national movement found it useful to stress the greatness of Indian civilisation in history and to emphasise that India was not alone; another great Asian civilisation, China, had suffered a similar fate. This narrative drew on an inspiring history of exchanges of ideas, technologies, goods and monks in the first millennium, and a rapid expansion of trade links in the second. Figures like Xuan Zang dramatised in the fabulous Chinese novel, *Journey to the West*, ensuring the story's popularity. A narrative of centuries of friendly exchanges fed a pan-Asian sense of worth, heightened by the fact that the exchanges had been peaceful.

The peace could equally be attributed to the fact that for most of history, Indian and Chinese polities did not figure in the other's political or security calculus, each living in its own multiverse. The narrative also ignored the fact that for most of early history, India-China exchanges were mediated through third parties, whether on land through the Silk Road running across Central Asian cities and states, or by sea across the maritime kingdoms and city-states of Southeast Asia. This is not to deny awareness of each other. It is just to say that such contact was remote, sporadic and intermediated.

With the coming of Western imperialism, India and China began to be directly linked politically. However, their experience of colonialism was different. Each drew different lessons from it. To ordinary Chinese, the Indians were visible enforcers of colonial dominance. The British Indian Army troops fought in every British military engagement in the Chinese empire after the Opium War of 1840. Under unequal treaties, Indian policemen enforced British law in the international concessions and settlements of the treaty ports along the China coast. They became a common trope in early 20th century Chinese literature. For the reformer, Kang Youwei, fleeing China and visiting India after the failed Hundred Days of Reform, India was a negative example of an enslaved people who served their colonial master — a fate that China must avoid at all costs.

Rising Indian nationalism did not reciprocate emerging Chinese nationalism's negative view of India. Indian leaders like the great poet Rabindranath Tagore and Prime Minister Jawaharlal Nehru saw China as a collaborator in their pan-Asian project. The idea that Asians would build a common future in opposition to colonialism and restore their historic greatness was an attractive one in India. China was assigned a starring role in this construct. Unfortunately for its advocates, it could not survive Japan's role in dismembering the Qing empire, taking Korea and Taiwan, and invading Manchuria and then mainland China itself, all in the name of pan-Asianism. Even so, the mixed and somewhat hostile reception provoked by Tagore's 1924 visit to China could not quench his conviction of the value of the cultural and other connections between India and China. It led him to found Cheena Bhavan (a centre of Sino-Indian cultural studies) at the Vishwabharati University he founded in Shantiniketan. There is no parallel to this belief or institution on the Chinese side.

For Nehru, who saw the potential of India and China working together to remake Asian politics free of great power dominance after World War II, China was an important partner. He was aware of the strength of Chinese nationalism, as is clear from the letters he wrote after visiting China briefly in 1939 — when he had to rush back to India as World War II was declared — but he thought it a force that could be channelled to do good. However, the seeds of differences between China and India were apparent as early as spring 1947 at the Asian Relations Conference in Delhi. Tibet was invited as a separate country and was mentioned as such in Nehru's speech.

If there was a moment when Indian and Chinese attitudes to each other were close and buttressed by mutual need, it was during World War II. India was a rear area for China in its war against Japanese aggression. As many as 20 Chinese divisions trained in India. However, again, mutual incomprehension arose. During his February 1942 visit to India, Chinese leader Chiang Kai Shek attempted to persuade Indian nationalist leaders Mahatma Gandhi and Nehru to work with the British to support China's war of resistance against Japan. To the British, Chiang argued that a promise of self-rule leading to independence for India after the war was the least Britain could do. This naturally fell on deaf British ears, especially those of the Prime Minister of the United Kingdom, Winston Churchill. The British would not let Chiang visit

Sevagram to see Gandhi, so they met at Shantiniketan. Chiang was unimpressed by Gandhi's advice to use non-violent means. Gandhi too was not impressed with the meeting. He wrote to Sardar Vallabhbhai Patel, "I would not say that I learnt anything, and there was nothing that we could teach him."

Little in history prepared India and China to cope with each other when they emerged as modern nation states in the mid-20th century. Besides, history left both countries with very different understandings of the boundary, which for the most part, had been traditional and customary between India and Tibet, sanctified by treaty, custom and usage.

Two Republics

When the Republic of India and the People's Republic of China were formed in mid-20th century, both chose divergent paths. China chose a more radical internal social and economic restructuring amounting to a socialist revolution and built a Leninist state. India chose to reform, building on what was, seeking a mixed economy, along with social stability in a democratic polity. Externally, India chose to go it alone and non-aligned; China chose alliance, first with one superpower and then with the other.

India-China gaps in comprehension grew after failed attempts to bridge it in the mid-1950s. A primary cause was the state and nation-building exercise and rising nationalism that China and, to a lesser extent, India manifested in the transition to becoming modern Westphalian states, a transition that Tibet never made. The Chinese occupation of Tibet in 1950, creating a Chinese presence on India's borders for the first time in history, and the subsequent boundary dispute are corollaries of this historical process. So is Chinese hyper-sensitivity on Tibet. Then Chinese president, Mao Zedong, ascribed China's failure to assimilate Tibet to Indian and United States (US) hostility rather than to the nature of that forcible integration. The

Tibetan refugee influx into India and the Dalai Lama's exile did much to further worsen Indian views of China and remain a significant factor in the Indian attitude to China.

The Chinese decision to describe the entire boundary with India as disputed in 1959, going against the practice and experience of centuries past, strengthened negative perceptions of China in India. In the buildup to the 1962 conflict, the Indian leadership failed to anticipate China's use of force. On the Chinese side, Mao told the Politburo that in 30 years, the Indians would forget about the war and that the two sides would be friends again, underestimating the effect of the 1962 attack and its continuing effect on both elite and public opinion in India to this day. This is one reason why China did not achieve its objective stated in the official People's Liberation Army (PLA) history of the war as "quickly achieving peaceful, stable borders in the west". Indeed, one sees a fundamental asymmetry of world-views and attitudes to the use of force between Indian and Chinese leaders in the 1950s and 1960s.

After 1962, India and China found themselves on opposing sides on most Asian issues, whether it was the Soviet invasion of Afghanistan, Kampuchea, Pakistan's nuclear weapons quest and so on. China chose, since the 1980s, to integrate its economy into Asian and global value and production chains while India remained aloof and has opted out of the Regional Comprehensive Economic Partnership. Indian distrust of China hardened over time.

India-China Today

The present crisis in India-China relations, caused by China's military build-up and attempts to change the Line of Actual Control since the spring of 2020 leading to the first deaths by military action on the border in 45 years, has worsened attitudes on both sides. Today, over 100,000 troops of both armies confront each other at forbidding heights for a second brutal winter. The entire India-China border is live.

China's actions have given new strength to the narrative of betrayal established in Indian minds by China's attack in 1962. By August 2020, 84 percent of Indians believed that Chinese President Xi Jinping had betrayed Indian Prime Minister Narendra Modi — they had met 18 times in six years — and 91 percent said that they would not buy Chinese products. The latter threat has not been acted upon. India-China trade in 2021 has broken records. Polls showed that over 70 percent of Indians believed that the simultaneous COVID-19 pandemic was a "Chinese-hatched conspiracy". Official Indian spokesmen still publicly express a lack of understanding of why China chose to do what it did on the border since 2020. In India, the levels of trust in China, never high, have dropped drastically because of China's actions on the border.

In China, the border crisis saw an initial eight months of relative restraint in official statements despite strong quasi-official propaganda in the *Global Times* and others. Since then, however, we see concerted efforts to play up the heroic role of the PLA in the events on the border and to denigrate India in official and social media. This could signal a Chinese assessment that the crisis is not likely to be resolved soon. Unlike previous face-offs and crises, this one has been presented by China as a sovereignty issue, making a negotiated solution less likely. Two governments relying on legitimacy of their nationalist credentials have not found it possible so far to engage meaningfully, or to return to the status quo before spring 2020, or to establish a new equilibrium in the relationship.

Separate Dreams

There is another asymmetry in Indian and Chinese attitudes towards each other. Most Indians look at China through a bilateral lens. Chinese officials and scholars look at India through the lens of China-US relations. Indian commentary tends to judge China by its actions on bilateral issues — the border, the trade deficit, situation in Tibet, Beijing's support to Pakistan and by China's presence in India's periphery, namely, the subcontinent and the Indian Ocean region. Chinese elites and media, on the other hand, focus on India as part of China's larger geo-political environment and problem. Today, that problem is with the US.

There are thus multiple levels of mutual incomprehension built into the way Indians and Chinese see each other and, over time, this has been baked into the relationship. That would not matter if both states had agreed a roadmap to deal with their differences. Its absence, however, amplifies the potential effects of mutual misunderstanding, with worrisome results if incomprehension is acted upon, as China probably did in 2020.

THE ASIA-PACIFIC VERSUS THE INDO-PACIFIC

21

India and ASEAN's Visions of the Indo-Pacific: Same Dream, Different Beds

Hoang Thi Ha

At the 2018 Shangri-La Dialogue in Singapore, India's Prime Minister Narendra Modi charmed Southeast Asian audiences with his vision of an "open, stable, secure and prosperous Indo-Pacific", and with his praise of the Association of Southeast Asian Nations (ASEAN) as a force that "has laid the foundation of the Indo-Pacific" and "can integrate the broader region". Modi and Indian diplomats, time and again, reiterated the importance of ASEAN as "the heart of India's 'Act East' policy and the gateway for India to the Pacific". Likewise, ASEAN sees Southeast Asia lying "in the centre" of the Asia-Pacific and Indian Oceans and serving as "a very important conduit and portal" to these dynamic regions. The grouping also envisages ASEAN centrality as "the underlying principle to promote cooperation in the Indo-Pacific region".

Among many articulations of the Indo-Pacific by the United States (US) and its like-minded partners, the Indian vision is considered the most aligned with the ASEAN Outlook on the Indo-Pacific (AOIP).

India's vision of an Indo-Pacific of "pluralism, co-existence, openness and dialogue" echoes ASEAN's emphasis on "an Indo-Pacific region of dialogue and cooperation instead of rivalry". Modi's positive rendition of the Indo-Pacific — one that is not directed against any country — was also meant to assuage ASEAN's underlying concern that the Indo-Pacific strategy is aimed to confront and contain China. Notably, in terms of institutional vehicles to realise a cooperative, inclusive and prosperous Indo-Pacific, both Modi's Shangri-La Dialogue speech and the ASEAN Outlook highlighted the importance of the East Asia Summit (EAS) and the Regional Comprehensive Strategic Partnership (RCEP) trade deal in embracing the Indo-Pacific geography.

Yet, just a year later, at the EAS in 2019, Modi shocked his ASEAN counterparts by announcing India's withdrawal from the RCEP, saying that "[n]either the Talisman of Gandhiji nor my own conscience permits me to join [the] RCEP". Driven by its prevailing domestic political agenda and long-held protectionism, India's estrangement from the RCEP was a major setback for both New Delhi's 'Act East' policy and ASEAN's strategic interest to deepen economic integration with India. With India staying outside of both the Asia-Pacific Economic Cooperation and the RCEP, the centrality of China in the regional supply chains continues to entrench. To paraphrase Singapore's former Prime Minister Goh Chok Tong, the China wing of the ASEAN jumbo jet continues to soar while the India wing has hardly taken off.

For the Southeast Asian countries, the analogy of the ASEAN jumbo jet fuelled by the two Asian powers on its northern and western flanks makes both economic and strategic sense. Long before the advent of the Indo-Pacific construct and the emergence of India as a centre of power to be reckoned with in today's multi-polar regional order, ASEAN had displayed its strategic foresight by proactively embracing India in the regional architecture as an ASEAN Dialogue Partner and a member of the ASEAN Regional Forum in 1996, and as a founding member of the EAS in 2005 and the ASEAN Defence Ministers Meeting-Plus in 2010. Especially, the inclusion of India, alongside Australia and New Zealand, made the EAS a broad-based institution that embraced the Indo-Pacific geography right from the beginning. It was a judicious decision that effectively re-negotiated the nature of East Asian regionalism at a time when the more exclusive East Asian identity remained prevalent.

ASEAN's track record in keeping India engaged and invested in the region — be it called Asia-Pacific then or Indo-Pacific now — demonstrates its 'omni-enmeshment' strategy that seeks to engage all major powers near and far to create "a complex balance of power", according to scholar Evelyn Goh. For the Southeast Asian countries, this omni-enmeshment helps to diversify their policy choices with a range of external powers, dilute the influence of a single hegemon in the regional architecture, and resist the pull towards bipolarisation in regional politics due to the US-China strategic rivalry. At the same time, this omni-enmeshment duly recognises New Delhi's role in the region's balance of power and provides the necessary institutions for New Delhi to shape the regional order and governance beyond the Indian sub-continent. ASEAN-led mechanisms have always been welcoming avenues for India to 'Look East' in the 1990s and to 'Act East' today. India and ASEAN's visions of the Indo-Pacific are also aligned in terms of upholding the regional rules-based order through adherence to international law and renunciation of force in settlement of disputes.

Yet, the operational reality of India's Indo-Pacific strategy thus far has focused far more on deepening security and economic cooperation with the other Indo-Pacific powers than with ASEAN and Southeast Asia. In his articulation of India's Indo-Pacific vision, Modi spoke highly of "India's faith in multilateralism and regionalism" but New Delhi's approach to multilateralism is no longer confined to broad-based, inclusive multilateral structures. In recent years, India has become increasingly invested in minilateral and plurilateral coalition building with the other major powers, given their growing strategic convergence in responding to the China challenge. In April 2021, India's Ambassador to China, Vikram Misri, emphasised the importance to afford space to plurilateral initiatives rather than prejudge them.

Likewise, India's Permanent Representative at the United Nations, Syed Akbaruddin, noted that "the 'plurilaterals' and the emerging 'minilaterals' each have their place in terms of international agenda setting" and that "as a growing power, India needs to avail of such avenues". Indian Foreign Minister S Jaishankar framed these multiple engagements as part of hedging in a multi-polar world, that is, "having many balls up in the air at the same time and displaying the confidence and dexterity to drop none".

India's more forward-leaning approach towards major power-centric minilaterals in the Indo-Pacific has been a critical enabler for the revival of the Quadrilateral Security Dialogue (also called the Quad) in 2017 and its consolidation ever since. Especially, after the border clash with China in mid-2020, India's China policy has hardened, and New Delhi has pivoted further towards balancing against China through closer military-defence cooperation with the other Indo-Pacific powers. Apart from the Quad, India has actively embraced other trilateral security platforms such as India-Australia-Japan, India-US-Japan, India-Australia-Indonesia and India-France-Australia. In 2020, India signed Mutual Logistics Sharing Agreements with Australia and Japan, and the Basic Exchange Cooperation Agreement with the US. Joint military exercises in different configurations — bilaterally, trilaterally and multilaterally — between India and the other Indo-Pacific partners have become a regular feature of the Indo-Pacific waters. Although a balance of power has always been a defining feature of the regional order, the entrenchment of hard balancing by these Indo-Pacific powers would likely entail their less reliance on ASEAN's normative persuasion and their reduced investment in ASEAN-led institutions in substantive ways.

With the expansion and deepening of its security relations with the other Quad members, India was ranked 7th in terms of "defence networks" in the Lowy Institute's 'Asia Power Index 2021'. However, its ranking in "economic relationships" dropped to 8th position, which was attributed in no small part to India's absence from mega trade deals in the region — from the RCEP to the Comprehensive and Progressive Agreement for Trans-Pacific Partnership. As a result, India has increasingly stood on the margins of the ever-deepening trade integration and production networks that are central to Southeast Asia's economic growth.

Of note, India's economic cooperation with the other Quad members has grown at a faster pace than with ASEAN in recent years. According to the United Nations International Trade Statistics Database, India-ASEAN trade grew by 12.88 percent between 2018 and 2021 while India's trade with Japan, Australia and the US grew by 18.59 percent, 23.61 percent and 33.80 percent respectively in the same period (see Table 21.1). In 2021, the US returned to its position as India's largest trading partner while ASEAN continued to be China's largest trading partner since 2020. With trade and geo-politics increasingly intertwined in the Indo-Pacific, these trendlines suggest that China is making headways in binding its economic future with that of Southeast Asia whereas India's tryst with a common destiny with the region remains a far-off aspiration.

Given these hard realities, ASEAN and India's efforts to synergise and coordinate their outlooks on the Indo-Pacific should focus on practical areas of cooperation that are of common interest and concern. The seven central pillars of India's Indo-Pacific Oceans' Initiative, namely, (i) maritime security; (ii) maritime ecology; (iii) maritime resources; (iv) capacity building and resource sharing; (v) disaster risk

Table 21.1: India's trade with ASEAN, Australia, Japan and the US (2018–2021)

Trade Partner	Trade Volume, 2018 (US$ billion)	Trade Volume, 2021 (US$ billion)	Growth Rate, 2018–2021 (%)
ASEAN	93.48	105.61	12.88
US	84.38	112.90	33.80
Japan	17.28	20.49	18.59
Australia	17.81	20.02	23.61

Source: United Nations International Trade Statistics Database (UN COMTRADE).

reduction and management; (vi) science, technology and academic cooperation; and (vii) trade connectivity and maritime transport, are very much aligned with the five priority areas of the AOIP, that is, maritime cooperation, connectivity, sustainable development and economic and other possible areas of cooperation. India should also join efforts with the other Indo-Pacific powers — especially Japan and South Korea — in enabling infrastructure connectivity between northeast India and mainland Southeast Asia. High on this connectivity agenda should be the India-Myanmar-Thailand Trilateral Highway and its potential eastward extension to Laos, Cambodia and Vietnam.

New Delhi should also leverage the reservoir of goodwill among the Southeast Asians towards India. Compared to China, whose influence is viewed with both admiration and fear by many Southeast Asians, India is welcomed as a benign power with no historical baggage, no territorial disputes and no hegemonic intention in the region. According to the *State of Southeast Asia 2022* report by ISEAS-Yusof Ishak Institute in Singapore, there is little fear among Southeast Asians that India's economic and military power could be used to threaten the interests and sovereignty of their countries. However, they maintain a prevalent scepticism about India's political will and capacity to exercise its regional leadership role. India's trust ratings among the Southeast Asians are the lowest among the four Quad countries and significantly lower than those of China (Table 21.2).

On its part, ASEAN and its member states need to overcome their strategic reticence regarding the Indo-Pacific construct and actively leverage the AOIP to push forward their security, economic and functional cooperation with India. They should seek to amplify the Southeast Asia content and focus in various initiatives and facilities put forth by India and other Indo-Pacific partners, for example, in COVID-19 vaccine support, supply chain resilience, green technologies and quality infrastructure. They should look at the Indo-Pacific through the lens of unfolding possibilities rather than as a limited set of choices.

Table 21.2: India's trust ratings compared to Australia, China, Japan and the US

Survey Questions	India	Australia	Japan	US	China
Most influential economic power in the region	0.1%	0.5%	2.6%	9.8%	76.7%
Most influential political-strategic power in the region	0.2%	0.8%	1.4%	29.7%	54.4%
Leadership in maintaining the rules-based order and upholding international law	0.1%	1.9%	7.7%	36.6%	13.6%
Leadership in championing the global free trade agenda	0.1%	1.4%	9.0%	30.1%	24.6%
Confidence in the country to "do the right thing" to provide global public goods	16.6%	N.A.	54.2%	52.8%	26.8%

Source: State of Southeast Asia 2022 Report, ISEAS-Yusof Ishak Institute.

The Indo-Pacific discourse in recent years has proven to be dynamic and adaptable, with an evolving agenda that can cater to a wide range of common interests and concerns for both the Southeast Asian states and India. However, there exists a considerable risk of strategic and economic divergence and lack of coordination in the execution of ASEAN and India's Indo-Pacific visions. Both sides should take a long, hard look at the current situation, renew their political commitments and revitalise existing mechanisms to ensure that they do not act past each other in pursuing their common goal of forging a peaceful, prosperous and inclusive Indo-Pacific region.

22

The Asia-Pacific or the Indo-Pacific: Changing Geo-political Priorities

C Raja Mohan

Introduction

The introduction of a new geography, the Indo-Pacific, has created much unease in the Association of Southeast Asian Nations (ASEAN) that has grown most comfortable with the notion of the Asia-Pacific. The context in which the new geography has been framed is part of the problem. Among many quarters of the world, the Indo-Pacific has become inseparable from the unfolding conflict between the United States (US) and China. It is no surprise that China has vehemently opposed the Indo-Pacific concept. Russia has been equally vocal in opposing the Indo-Pacific construct. Reinforcing the Chinese and Russian opposition to the Indo-Pacific has been the revival of the Quadrilateral Security Dialogue (also called the Quad) that brings together India, the US and two treaty allies of Washington — Japan and Australia.

The Quad, formed in 2007, quickly became moribund but was revived in 2017 and elevated to the summit level in 2021. Questions have arisen about the Quad's potential to undermine the centrality of ASEAN that has been leading the efforts to develop a cooperative regional order. ASEAN's concerns and India's embrace of the Indo-Pacific and the enthusiastic participation in the Quad underline the dangers of deepening misperceptions between the two. Preventing the emergence of a strategic divergence over the Quad and the Indo-Pacific and ensuring sustained regional cooperation are important tasks for the leadership of ASEAN and India.

Fluid Geographies

While the political concerns about the Indo-Pacific are real, it is important to note that Asia has continuously invented and reinvented regional geography over the last many decades. For example, the Asia-Pacific is itself a relatively new term that became popular in the 1990s as the US and the Latin American economies began to integrate with those of East and Southeast Asia. However, the terms East and Southeast Asia are also not too old either. The term Southeast Asia was not used until halfway through World War II when the allies set up the Southeast Asia command under Lord Louis Mountbatten in Kandy in Ceylon (now Sri Lanka) to reverse the Japanese aggression in the region. Imperial Japan had invented the term 'Greater East Asia Co-prosperity Sphere' in the 1930s.

Contemporary "Asian identity" is also itself a political construct that dates back to the early 20th century when pan-Asianism began to emerge as a political force in the East. However, it was never easy for the Asianists to define where exactly Asia began and where it ended. For many of the Western chancelleries, the terms Near East, Middle East, the Indian subcontinent, East Indies and Far East were some of the more common ways of describing these regions well into the second half of the 20th century. That would tell us that regions are politically, economically and ideologically constituted rather than through fixed geographic markers. As the economic and political realities in a space change, regions are constructed and deconstructed.

Although the idea of the Indo-Pacific was first articulated by Japan's Prime Minister Shinzo Abe in 2007 in an address to the Indian

Parliament, it took a while for it to gain acceptance. Sitting astride the Indian and Pacific Oceans, Indonesia adopted the Indo-Pacific as a concept in 2013 but it was quite different from the Japanese or the later American ideas. It was more rooted in principles of inclusion and multilateralism. The same ideas were eventually incorporated in the ASEAN Outlook on Indo-Pacific in 2019. The idea gained real traction only after Washington adopted it in 2017. Throughout his visit to Asia at the end of 2017, US President Donald Trump consistently used the term Indo-Pacific rather than the Asia-Pacific. Trump's national security aides had apparently concluded that drawing India into the Pacific was necessary to construct a balanced Asia that had been destabilised by China's rise.

Washington's growing concerns on China's rise and its consequences for Asia convinced the Trump administration that the old framework of US bilateral alliances in East Asia and the ASEAN-centred multilateralism rooted in Southeast Asia were no longer sufficient to secure the regional order. Bringing India into the Asian equation had become vital; hence, the Indo-Pacific and the construction of the Quad. However, the big question was whether India would welcome the ideas of the Indo-Pacific and the Quad.

India's Strategic Autonomy

If the Washington surprised Asia with its new initiatives, the traditionally non-aligned India did much the same by embracing the US' initiatives. That did not come about quite easily. There was much hesitation and internal argumentation on the Indo-Pacific, after Abe's speech in the Indian Parliament. The question of India's non-alignment and strategic autonomy were at the heart of this Indian debate, which had actually preceded the Indo-Pacific becoming the focus of the discourse. As India's relations — political, economic and military — with the US began to improve through the 21st century, the question of New Delhi's alignment with Washington in Asia inevitably arose. The very suggestion of such ideas was anathema to the foreign and security policy establishment in New Delhi, which saw non-alignment and strategic autonomy as central to India's world-view.

Linked to this was also the deeply held Asianist sensibility of the Indian foreign policy elite that saw partnership with China as a critical element in building a post-World War II global order. It is a tradition that goes to pan-Asianist sentiments in the early 20th century and India's support to the Chinese national movement's resistance against Japanese occupation in the inter-war period. India's romance with China did not end with the brief border conflict between the two nations in 1962. India turned to the Soviet Union rather than the West to balance China. The Sino-US partnership since the 1970s further deepened India's political distance from the West. The collapse of the Soviet Union, the emergence of the unipolar moment and the normalisation of India-China relations led New Delhi to a modified version of non-alignment — coalition with Russia and China (and later with Brazil and South Africa) to promote a multipolar world. Although India's engagement with the US steadily improved in the 21st century, New Delhi was reluctant to consider explicit balancing strategies against China. Three important factors changed this and nudged India closer to the US.

One was the relentless effort in Washington, across successive administrations — George Bush, Barack Obama, Trump and Joe Biden — to overcome India's suspicion of the US. This involved setting aside the Western activism on the Kashmir dispute between India and Pakistan, resolving the differences over the non-proliferation question, liberalising the transfer of advanced weapons and dual-use technologies and offering strong cooperation on counter-terrorism to India. The US' pull was interesting but not enough to break India's commitment to non-alignment. It needed a Chinese push. China's growing assertiveness on the boundary dispute with India provided it.

The second was a series of military crises along the long and contested border in 2013, 2014, 2017 and 2020 underlined the Chinese determination to change territorial status quo by military means. There was no way New Delhi could duck this issue of balancing the Chinese military power.

Third, beyond the boundary, China's great power ambition began to undermine India's regional primacy in South Asia and the Indian Ocean. China also actively blocked India's attempt to join the Nuclear Suppliers Group and opposed India's quest for a permanent seat in the United Nations Security Council. All these factors steadily shifted the debate in New Delhi.

India's formal acceptance of the Indo-Pacific was finally articulated by Prime Minister Narendra Modi at the 2018 Shangri-La Dialogue in Singapore. Like Indonesia, Modi was trying to develop India's own approach to the Indo-Pacific. In his 2018 speech, the Indian Prime Minister affirmed that New Delhi's conception of the Indo-Pacific "stands for a free, open, inclusive region, which embraces us all in a common pursuit of progress and prosperity. It includes all nations in this geography as also others beyond who have a stake in it." He also declared that Southeast Asia was at the heart of the Indo-Pacific and that "ASEAN has been and will be central to its future. That is the vision that will always guide India, as we seek to cooperate for an architecture for peace and security in this region."

These principles remain at the core of the Indian approach to the Indo-Pacific and have been repeatedly reaffirmed by New Delhi. Equally important is that India has not abandoned its independent foreign policy in adopting the Indo-Pacific and joining the Quad. Under Modi who, riding a political wave of nationalism, has no desire to be a camp-follower of the US. Modi's advisers are convinced that as the only non-treaty member of the Quad, India can shape the pace and direction of the Quad.

New Delhi's reluctance to turn the Quad into a military alliance has already seen the US shift the focus of the forum to non-military areas like connectivity, climate change and combating the COVID-19 pandemic. New Delhi has neither abandoned its special relationship with Moscow nor has it given up its diplomatic engagement with Beijing. India's membership of the Quad has not stopped India's participation in the China-led forums such as the BRICS that link the two countries to Brazil, Russia, and South Africa and the Shanghai Cooperation Organisation.

India and ASEAN

That Asia is a very different geo-political juncture is not in doubt. The creation of new strategic conceptions like the Indo-Pacific are unlikely to reverse four decades of economic interdependence and political cooperation across the Asia-Pacific. It would be reasonable to assume that the Quad and the AUKUS military alliance between US, the United Kingdom and Australia are here to stay but must coexist with the older and stronger institutions like ASEAN and the Asia-Pacific Economic Cooperation forum. It is, therefore, more important that ASEAN and India intensify their political consultations and expand their own security cooperation. Only deeper trust between the two sides will prevent the current misperceptions turning into differences and divergence.

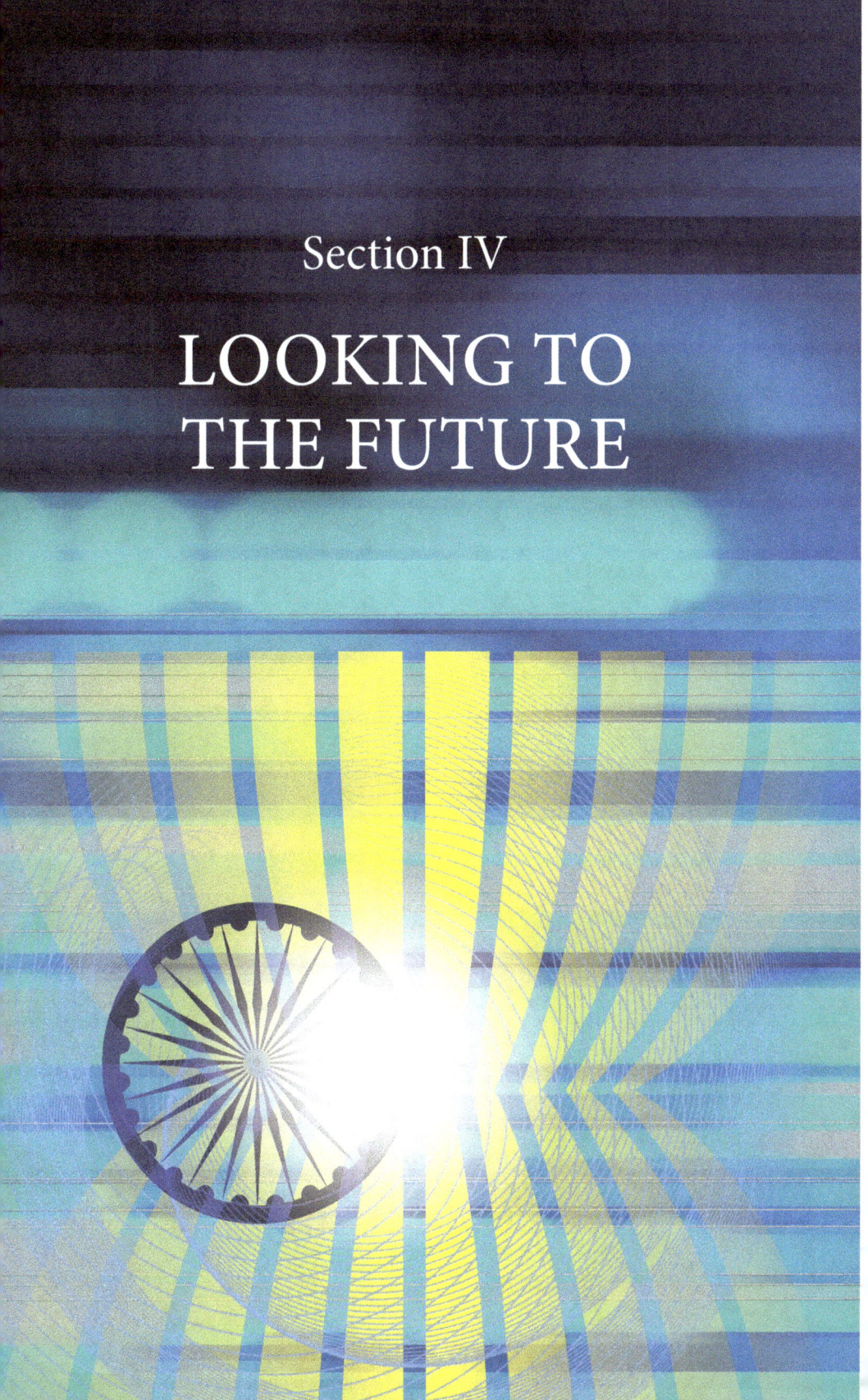

Section IV

LOOKING TO THE FUTURE

SMART CITIES

23

From a Smart to a Learning City: The Singapore Model for ASEAN and India

Limin Hee and Aaron Maniam

Introduction

In 2014, Singapore unveiled its Smart Nation vision, which aims to harness technology to boost the country's economic productivity while improving life for its citizens. Since then, sensors, modelling tools and a slew of innovative technologies have been steadily integrated into the city's urban planning systems. These have given Singapore a new layer of 'digital intelligence', deepening the city's 'smart-ness' in how it tackles increasingly complex urban challenges.

At its core, Singapore's approach is to use technology as an enabler for the larger goal of urban development. The city state has been consistently recognised as one of the world's leading smart cities. In 2019 and 2020, Singapore topped the Global Smart City Index published by the Institute for Management Development, in partnership with Singapore University of Technology & Design.

While these accolades recognise Singapore's progress, there is no room for complacency. Attaining and sustaining 'smart-ness' as a city requires humility and a process of constant reinvention and refinement. Singapore cannot afford to stay comfortable in the status quo but must be a 'learning' city that embraces a culture of dynamic experimentation. This chapter describes the ways in which Singapore is doing so, as it pursues its smart city vision. In doing so, it is hoped that there would be possibilities and opportunities for India and the Association of Southeast Asian Nations (ASEAN) member states to work together in the development of smart city projects and initiatives on both sides.

Whole-of-society Approach

Cities face increasingly complex, existential challenges: from resource scarcity to climate change and from economic disruptions to public health risks. Coupled with governance challenges, such as building and maintaining the citizens' trust, this makes the effective management of cities ever more difficult. These urban challenges are deeply intertwined, and Singapore has learned that finding solutions requires an integrated, whole-of-society effort.

In Singapore, all stakeholders in society — government, business and the community — have specific roles to play. The government lays a strong foundation of infrastructure and leads by example in spearheading the systematic use of smart technologies. These technologies are typically first trialled and monitored in pilots, then improved over time as more is learned about their use. For instance, Housing and Development Board (HDB) planners use computer simulations to analyse wind flow, solar irradiance and shaded areas within towns to determine how new flats can best be designed and located to conserve energy and optimise comfort for residents. The HDB is also designing flats that will enable the residents to easily adopt a range of smart home solutions, such as the Utility Management System, which enables the residents to track their energy and water usage in real-time for both personal cost optimisation and more sustainable practices at the aggregate level.

The government drives the widespread adoption of smart technologies throughout the economy and society by creating 'living laboratories' for companies to create, test and develop innovative urban solutions in real-life settings before they are scaled up for use. This way, the private sector can experiment and develop innovations within a supportive digital environment. For example, the Land Transport Authority has partnered with Nanyang Technological University and Swedish firm Volvo to trial the viability of autonomous electric buses as a future form of transport. The western region of Singapore has been specially designated to test the use of autonomous vehicles to provide inter-town services and longer-haul journeys. This 'test-and-learn' approach provides a safe but rigorous space for innovation, allowing Singapore to assess the effectiveness of any new technology before implementing it more widely.

Lastly, the citizens are not only the eventual beneficiaries of these smart technologies but also active participants providing feedback and suggestions for improvement. One prime example of this is the OneService mobile application, developed by the Municipal Services Office, which has enabled residents to easily give feedback on municipal issues that they spot in their neighbourhoods. The application automatically routes feedback to the respective agencies in charge, thereby eliminating inefficient red tape, while its geo-tagging and photo-taking functions allow agencies to ascertain the exact location and nature of the issue so that they can respond expeditiously.

High Technology, High Trust, High Touch Smart City

Technology alone is not the key to becoming a smart city. Ultimately, a city is made up of people, and a smart city can only be enabled and sustained by the citizens' trust in it, its technologies and the technology providers. This is an important point for all of us in ASEAN and India.

In Singapore, the Smart Nation Sensor Platform is a nationwide sensor platform that collects and shares real-time data, enabling public agencies to provide more pre-emptive and responsive services to citizens. This data can be used for good in various ways, including tracking virus outbreaks, monitoring local environmental pollution and analysing transport routes to reduce road and rail congestion.

To build trust with the citizens, the Singapore government has made the collection of sensor data more transparent through sharing information with the community. Singapore has also acknowledged the importance of articulating the use of this data and ensures that the community benefits from it.

Singapore emphasises the importance of data protection and security because strong cybersecurity infrastructure is critical to gaining the citizens' trust towards the use of smart technologies. The National Cyber Security Masterplan reinforces Singapore's cybersecurity by enhancing the security and resilience of critical infocommunication infrastructure, promoting the adoption of appropriate infocomm security measures among individuals and businesses, and growing a local pool of infocommunication security experts. The Infocomm Media and Development Authority (IMDA) and the Personal Data Protection Commission have also introduced the Trusted Data Sharing Framework to put in place stronger safeguards for regulatory compliance. These enhanced data security measures aim to reassure consumers that their data will not be abused, hopefully making them more willing to share their data with businesses. These businesses would, in turn, use this data to innovate and customise their services, benefitting the consumers in return.

Singapore is learning that apart from having high levels of trust, a smart city must also be digitally inclusive and 'high-touch', not just 'high-tech' — with two-way interactions between smart technologies and the people. In other words, the citizens should neither be passive subjects for sensor data collection nor passive beneficiaries of smart city management.

To enable this, cities must ensure that its citizens are digitally literate. Digital literacy and readiness are important pillars of

Singapore's smart nation vision to ensure that no one is left behind in the country's digitalisation efforts. The IMDA set up the SG Digital Office in May 2020 to accelerate Singapore's adoption of digital tools and raise the digital literacy of less digitally savvy individuals and businesses. Within its first few months, the SG Digital Office had recruited 1,000 digital ambassadors to help microenterprise owners, such as those at hawker centres or coffee shops, as well as seniors, to 'go digital' under the 'Hawkers Go Digital' and 'Seniors Go Digital' programmes respectively.

International Collaboration and Knowledge Sharing

Just as the best minds from different fields flourish when they can exchange knowledge and views with other luminaries — learning from each other — cities can become more liveable by learning from each other and constantly challenging themselves.

Singapore has always learnt from others, and will continue to do so, while also supporting the learning of others. By openly discussing and sharing our respective knowledge and experiences, each city learns and grows more intelligent. Such inter-city collaborations and learning are vital as cities in ASEAN, India and worldwide develop their respective smart cities.

The biennial World Cities Summit, which Singapore has organised and hosted since 2008, is a prime example of the kind of city-to-city mutual learning and sharing that Singapore believes in and supports. Together with its accompanying series of environment-related events, the Summit has traditionally drawn thousands of participants from government and the business and research sectors from around the world.

ASEAN has also committed to learning from and helping each nation's cities to develop smart urban solutions through the ASEAN Smart Cities Network (ASCN). Inaugurated in 2018, the ASCN is a collaborative platform for ASEAN's cities to share good practices, exchange solutions, and discuss common problems, ranging from waste management to traffic control, and from energy to basic infrastructure. The network has 26 cities from the 10 ASEAN member states, including Johor Bahru, Phuket, Yangon, Phnom Penh, Vientiane and Singapore. The regional initiative has also partnered with about 100 companies, multilateral institutions and other external partners to kick-start commercially viable smart city projects.

Conclusion: Smart Cities must be Learning Cities

While the term 'smart city' has come to dominate discussion on the use of technology in urban development, cities must not get carried away with its adoption through merely investing in technology but must frame policy towards enabling inclusivity and social innovation. While the aim is to create cities that are 'smart', what matters in practice is that the technology and the city should also be able to take a flexible approach in a state of constantly becoming a 'learning city'.

Rather than define the smart city as an end state, the smart city is itself an enabler as much as it is a desired outcome. An examination of several smart city indices shows that only a handful of those doing well, that is, cities which have invested in smart infrastructure and have an innovation eco-system, have the same top rankings in liveability indices. Singapore's past and recent experience has shown that it is crucial to develop, preserve and deepen the capacity to be agile and learn. This is an experience that is relevant to the rest of ASEAN and India.

Most recently, the COVID-19 pandemic has been a litmus test for not only cities' 'smartness' but also their capacity for quick and agile learning. Singapore has had to swiftly develop and introduce technologies to aid in contact tracing, monitoring of crowd levels and enforcing of safe distancing, while companies had to adapt to remote working.

Even as Singapore's contact tracing application, TraceTogether, was developed and rolled out, the government recognised the need for a physical TraceTogether token for groups such as the elderly or low-income who may not have smartphones. The Urban Redevelopment Authority and National Parks Board urgently created digital platforms 'Space Out' and 'Safe Distance@Parks' respectively, which use geospatial data to give the public information on crowd levels in malls and parks. Meanwhile, the Government Technology Agency produced simple but powerfully effective platforms in local lingo — 'Flu Go Where' and 'Mask Go Where' so that people with flu symptoms would easily know their nearest clinic and on the collection of free masks. And when vaccines were available, the agency even created 'Vaccine Go Where' to direct people to the online vaccination registration portal.

In the private sector, travel companies and tour guides reinvented their business models, curating virtual instead of physical tours for locals and would-be international tourists. And Singapore's MICE (Meetings, Incentives, Conferences and Exhibitions) sector was one of the first to bounce back by introducing infection control measures that boosted the confidence of business travellers. Developing Connect@Changi with hotel rooms and innovative new safe-distanced meeting rooms with air-tight glass panels separating the participants was a world first and has also allowed international business travel and physical business meetings to resume.

The need for a culture of learning and adaptation is becoming even more critical as the problems of climate change, changing demographics, social and technological disruption and pandemics point to a world that is becoming increasingly complex. By being 'Learning Cities', Singapore and other cities in ASEAN, India and beyond will be able to find ways to survive and bounce back, despite the unpredictability presented by the global pandemic. Ultimately, this process of learning and adapting, with the help of technology, where relevant and possible, will be what makes a city truly smart.

24

Indian Smart Cities: The Challenges Ahead

Pushpa Pathak and Marie-Hélène Zérah

Introduction

The origins of the 'smart city' have been widely discussed and so has the circulation of the idea of 'smart' itself. There is a consensual view that a smart city is to create a better living environment through ease of living for people and better governance. It also points towards significant reliance on information and communications technology (ICT) and digital solutions to do so. There are regional variations as well. In Europe, the focus of smart cities has been to improve the environmental conditions through largely providing appropriate transport and street design solutions to facilitate a smooth flow of traffic.

In Asia, and more so in India, augmenting urban infrastructure and enhancing cooperation have been more prominent. In the wake of the 2008 financial crisis, IBM and other ICT companies saw the urban as a new market to enable data driven governance. This led to the idea of the 'smart city' worldwide and later to the Smart City Mission (SCM), launched in India in 2015. However, the process of implementing the SCM in India has not been linear and tracing its trajectory demonstrates two main directions. The first, more focused on infrastructure projects, continues to drive city action plans and was dominant between 2015 and 2018. The second relates to the role of data-driven governance, which has been pushed more seriously since 2018.

Therefore, the pertinent issues to be raised in the Indian smart city context are twofold: How do we realise the goal of better ease of living? Does it come from better governance, service delivery and more information? And how are digital solutions introduced and what do they mean for the future of urban India and city governance?

Urban Governance and Infrastructure Development

The SCM was designed for a period of five years and has been extended till June 2023 to complete the projects delayed due to the COVID-19 pandemic. The purpose of the SCM is to drive economic growth and improve the quality of life of people. The programme is currently being implemented in 100 smart cities selected based on a competitive application process. The total central allocation for the mission is approximately US$31 billion, with 80 percent of the fund earmarked for area-based development and the remaining 20 percent for pan-city interventions. Local area development aims to transform the existing areas (retrofit and redevelop), including slums, into better planned ones, thereby improving liveability of the whole city as well as new areas (greenfield) development around the cities to accommodate the expanding urban population. The pan-city initiatives include smart technology solutions covering larger parts of the city that lead to smart outcomes in the key urban sectors such as water supply, sanitation, electricity, mobility, housing, energy and environment.

The SCM puts in place new institutional structures for its implementation, which are: (i) special purpose vehicles (SPVs) for the overall programme design and management at the city level; (ii) Project Management Consultants (PMCs) for various programme components; and (iii) Smart Cities Advisory Forums (SCAFs) to advise and enable collaboration among various stakeholders. Such private modes of urban governance are also becoming increasingly common in the management of specialised urban spaces such as the Special Economic Zones, special investment regions, infrastructure corridors, industrial corridors and industrial townships. The PMCs have also assumed a greater role in urban policy decision-making, planning and programme designing as well as other urban management functions at the central, state and local governance levels. The emergence of such parallel urban local governance structure raises several questions.

The SPVs, registered under the Companies Act 1956 (last amended in 2015), and set up under the state government, function as independent entities with some of their own revenue generation potential, mainly from the commercialisation of their land assets. The most important concern pertaining to the SPVs relates to the fact that these entities function outside the decision-making domain of the democratically elected urban local governments. Another issue is the relationship between the state and the urban local governments in the context of the centralisation-decentralisation debate. While, in principle, the need for greater decentralisation to the urban local governments is widely recognised and endorsed by the 74th Constitutional Amendment Act 1992, the SPVs, set up under state governments, reinforce the state control over urban local governments. In addition, there are a whole range of associated issues that relate to the role of the SPVs in areas such as the frequency and effectiveness of interdepartmental and territorial coordination, financing and legal mechanisms for project evaluation and the inclusion of the lower-income areas for infrastructure development in project design, funding and implementation.

The issues pertaining to the PMCs include the kinds of roles assigned to the consultants, diversity of consultants, exchanges of learning and circulation of models — often the same consulting firms selected for several cities reproducing the same models without much local context knowledge and understanding, and new roles being given, as compared to previous forms of consultocracy. The questions relating to the SCAF are the kinds of participative platforms created, inclusion of private actors, representation of academics and experts with specialised knowledge, consultation with civil society and the induction of other forms of expertise.

The SPVs are expected to deliver urban infrastructure development and service delivery at speed as there are still huge gaps in urban basic services such as water supply, waste management, education, health and transport while the future demand is likely to increase with the urban population growth and spatial expansion. The performance of the SPVs also varies from city to city with a few examples of good inter-agency coordination; likewise the success of infrastructure projects varies in terms of their design and timely completion. Capacity enhancement or injecting extra capacity in the form of the SPVs and PMCs may work in the short run but may undermine urban governance capacity building in the long run. There is clearly a need to rebalance the need for the urban local governments' capacity building and rapidly expanding urban infrastructure. There is also the issue of scaling up infrastructure development from the area-based interventions to city-wide provision and how this can be done. Evidence from the field also suggests that the preferred solution of many cities has been to review the share of funding initially proposed in favour of pan-city projects.

Shift towards Data-driven Smart Urbanism

Since 2018, the thinking within the Indian Ministry of Housing and Urban Affairs (MoHUA) shifted towards linking the implementation of the SCM with more systematic data collection through platforms, the digitalisation of a range of sectors and processes such as smart metering or smart roads, for instance, and the data integration at the city level using the Integrated Command and Control Centres (ICCCs). Though these interventions had been planned since the onset of the SCM, they have been given a strong impetus by the central government in a shift towards data-driven smart urbanism, as defined by Rob Kitchin in 2018 in a book titled *Data and the City*, "wherein the generation of data is continuous, exhaustive to a system, fine-grained, relational and flexible across a range of domains". This transformation is occurring at multiple scales, two are being discussed here — the central government initiatives and the city level implementation on the ground.

At the central level, the current focus is on creating instruments and templates to enhance integrated data sets production and data handling capacity at the city level, and to create data assessment frameworks. A dedicated Mission Management Unit, located within the MoUHA, headed by a consultant from Deloitte and a cell at the National Institute of Urban Affairs, is responsible to track the cities' progress. This 'digital turn' is organised around a set of initiatives. Among them, the DataSmart Cities Strategy accelerates the incorporation of digitalisation solutions at the city level. As a support, cities must appoint a City Data Officer whose role is to incentivise the reliance on data analytics platforms created with the SMC's funding. The setting up of a National Urban Learning Platform, an Indian Urban Data Exchange and an Urban Observatory are further steps towards aggregating big data sets and create conditions for dissemination and use of data through exchange also through collaborations with academic institutions, for instance, or through the commercialisation of data. The progress at the city level is tracked through a Data Maturity Assessment Framework created at the MoUHA and, as of today, the focus has been towards helping cities build their data infrastructure.

Two points need to be highlighted. Though these are impressive steps, the construction of a data institutional architecture is not fully stabilised. It would need to be assessed prior to its planned expansion to all Indian cities through the National Urban Digital Mission launched in February 2021. This points to the importance of taking stock and dialogue with cities to scale up. Further, the reliance of the central government on consultancy firms is a worrying trend. These firms are seen as having higher skills and expertise and they are instrumental in creating the data policies, monitoring mechanisms and emerging platforms. However, they might not understand the complex challenges facing Indian cities and knowledge asymmetries between the public and private stakeholder could be detrimental in the long run, as highlighted in the previous section.

Looking more closely at the city level, all the cities have appointed their Chief Data Officer and many Urban Local Bodies have devised their data policy, created open data portals and started to integrate big data sets into their ICCCs. There are several positive outcomes that have been shared and disseminated. This is the case in Surat where there is the creation of an integrated smart grievance redressal system through phone, website and a unique phone number. Many cities have not only developed technology solutions for traffic, mobility, solid waste management but also surveillance, underlining both the range of sectors covered and raising concerns around control, data property and ownership. The COVID-19 crisis has accelerated the adoption of digital solutions, as seen in Gwalior, through the combination of a data-centric technology to track COVID-19 cases, monitoring movement, understanding infection hotspots and managing hospital beds.

Conclusion

While looking to the future of urban India, the notion of 'smart cities' is increasingly important for public decision-makers. This is particularly so with the concrete reality of a 100 Smart Cities programme that is currently being rolled out. By tracing the short history of the Indian SMC, we have highlighted two of its main domains of intervention — infrastructure-led projects and emerging data-driven governance. Though these two domains have their own challenges, in conclusion, it is important to highlight two key similar structural and long-term issues which, if not resolved upfront, will hamper the will to improve the lives of urban citizens.

The first is that the funding of infrastructure — physical or digital — needs to be accompanied by public sector strengthening. In the context of weak and fragmented governance, and a fragile history of innovation in urban management, the capacity of Urban Local

Bodies to absorb both the challenge of expanding, maintaining and overhauling infrastructure and to shift towards digital technologies remains limited. The importance of enhancing capacity-building and knowledge production within municipal cadres remains as urgent as ever when big data becomes instrumental for urban governance. The increasing role played by private consultants in the deployment of the smart city programme could be seen as a worrying trend.

The second concerns the unresolved question of inclusion and better living conditions for all. The creation of new infrastructure needs to focus on basic needs rather than focusing on wealthy areas as has been the case in some cities. It also requires strong coordination with other existing urban programmes. In addition, there is an urgency to accompany the potential of digital technologies with a solid framework to protect data privacy and the usage of data. For instance, the rapid deployment of closed-circuit television cameras in most cities needs reflection. Many examples worldwide have shown how surveillance systems tend to be used to control social activities or to stigmatise certain groups by reinforcing prejudices.

DIGITAL ECONOMY AND E-COMMERCE

25

Race towards a Digital Future: The Case for Greater ASEAN-India Cooperation

Jayant Menon

Introduction

Although economic relations between the Association of Southeast Asian Nations (ASEAN) and India have a long history that dates back several centuries, more recent engagement started to strengthen only following the 'Look East' policy of Prime Minister Narasimha Rao in the early 1990s. Following this policy, various bilateral, sub-regional and regional initiatives were pursued. The ASEAN-India Trade in Goods Agreement was signed in 2009 and entered into force a year later, while the negotiations for a free trade agreement (FTA) in services and investment were concluded in 2012.

The next step in consolidating the relationship within the broader regional context was to take place through the Regional Comprehensive Economic Partnership (RCEP) but India opted out of this agreement before it was signed in late 2020. Nevertheless, there has been rapid growth in trade and investment, with bilateral ASEAN-India trade surpassing US$90 billion before the COVID-19 pandemic hit in 2020.

Future growth in trade and investment between India and ASEAN will be intricately linked to developments relating to the digital economy and e-commerce, especially in terms of how they develop domestically as well as policies that encourage the exchange between the two. India aspires to have a digital economy worth US$1 trillion in the next five years while its e-commerce sector could reach US$350 billion by 2030. ASEAN's digital economy policies and reforms are being pursued through bilateral and regional agreements, including the RCEP, while the ASEAN Agreement on E-commerce entered into force in December 2021. While both India and ASEAN are emphasising the development of these sectors domestically, specific arrangements and policies facilitating an exchange between them could be strengthened.

In this chapter, the likely impacts of the COVID-19 induced acceleration towards the digital economy are considered, starting with its distributional consequences. Although much has been written about how the Fourth Industrial Revolution (4IR) may worsen existing inequalities between and within countries, we consider ways in which it may offset some of these effects. There will be significant disruption to labour markets, especially in the lower skill categories, as digitalisation and the 4IR progress. The ways in which to address these adjustment costs at the bilateral and regional levels that could benefit both India and ASEAN are also considered in this chapter.

Distributional Impacts: The Good and the Bad

One of the supposed positive aspects of the pandemic is the acceleration towards embracing 4IR. Although there is optimism that many aspects of the 4IR such as artificial intelligence, robotics, blockchain and 3D printing may have sped up, it is the transition towards a digital economy that has captured our attention. Lockdowns and other social distancing measures have accelerated the creation and adoption of new technologies that enable work-from-home and remote learning. The rapid growth in e-commerce has accompanied these digital transformations. Looking forward, firms are already starting to restructure their operations to better adapt to a new normal that will involve less human interaction and be restricted by other risk mitigation regulations.

The adoption rate of these technologies favours the more developed countries, which threatens to widen the digital divide in Asia.

Digital infrastructure in the developing countries is limited and access to what is available can vary by income class. The urban poor may not have the financial means to fully participate, and technology may not reach rural or isolated regions. The threat to their jobs is more concerning as automation and robotics take hold initially in low- and mid-skilled jobs.

This increases the risk of unemployment in the low- to mid-skilled job categories. Low wage growth rates in these sectors, relative to rates in higher-skilled sectors, will exacerbate wage and income inequality. Inequality between the countries in Asia is likely to increase and a rise in income and wealth disparities within them appears unavoidable.

Though attention has focused on how the 4IR may exacerbate inequality, various countervailing effects are often overlooked, perhaps because they will take time to materialise. The 4IR may produce offsetting effects that enhance economic inclusion by increasing connectivity, improving agricultural incomes and supporting micro, small and medium enterprises (MSMEs).

The 4IR technologies will enable citizens to connect and trade with each other through increasingly affordable mobile phones. In Indonesia, Myanmar, the Philippines and Vietnam, less than a third of the population have a bank account. The share of the unbanked is even higher in India. Innovations such as the *Aadhaar* — a digital identification system — is driving financial inclusion and bringing banking services to more than a billion people in India who had previously been excluded. These financial services enabled by technology allow households to save in secure instruments to enlarge their asset base and escape cycles of poverty and inequality.

Mobile phones enable the poor to access new sources of information, including high-frequency news and market prices that can affect their incomes. A famous study undertaken in South India by Robert Jensen in 2007 titled 'The Digital Provide: Information (Technology), Market Performance, and Welfare in the South Indian Fisheries Sector', which was published in the *Quarterly Journal of Economics*, showed how smartphone adoption by fishermen and wholesalers reduced price dispersion and eliminated waste, increasing consumer and producer welfare.

Smartphones also enable new forms of education, such as online courses and virtual classrooms, and new healthcare services, such as telemedicine linked to diagnostic pills. Platforms like Kenya's *Ushahidi* are democratising access to new technology and innovation while aiding improvements in governance and accountability. Access remains unequal but is improving with the advent of such platforms.

Mobile phones give farmers better access to prices, weather information and knowledge about soil, seeds and fertiliser. They may also enable a 'sharing economy' to develop, whereby farmers who cannot afford to buy expensive mechanical equipment can rent it by the hour from other farmers via online sharing sites, like Trringo in India, developed by equipment maker Mahindra & Mahindra.

More than 90 percent of the enterprises in the formal sector within both ASEAN and India are MSMEs. They have become almost synonymous with the informal sector. These enterprises in the formal and the informal sectors account for the overwhelming majority of employment in ASEAN and India. However, the MSMEs are often constrained by a lack of access to business and financial services.

Blockchain technology could potentially increase the security of cross-border financial transactions and logistics even in the poorer parts of Southeast Asia and India where these services are underdeveloped. The rise of online marketplaces also provides platforms for the MSMEs in India to access markets in ASEAN and vice versa.

These factors demonstrate that the 4IR can aid economic inclusion. Countries must still tackle rising unemployment among low- to mid-skilled workers and widening wage disparities due to the skills premium to address inequality.

Policy Response: Addressing the Need for Greater Trade and Factor Mobility

Despite the ability of the 4IR to increase inclusion in various ways, the overriding impact in the short to medium term is to increase inequality and unemployment, especially among the low-skilled. Although the long-run effect of the 4IR on employment could be positive, labour churning will dominate the adjustment phase with possible increases in unemployment of low-skilled workers. Enabling greater cross-border mobility of such workers would curtail unemployment in labour-abundant countries and help sustain growth in labour-importing ones. India is a labour abundant, labour exporting country while there is a mixture of both in ASEAN. Even in labour-abundant countries like Indonesia and the Philippines, importing skilled labour can bring in valuable competencies while capital can come with diffused technology, both of which can drive productivity of the local economy.

Despite being a populous and labour abundant developing country, India has the skill content in its exports that more closely resembles that of a developed country. This reflects positive and negative factors: a strong skills base in key digital and 4IR technologies, and a still restrictive policy environment, especially in relation to trade, capital and labour flows.

Divergent demographic trends will add to the need for greater factor mobility. While India and the newest member states of ASEAN, especially Cambodia, Laos and Myanmar, have relatively young populations, the rest of ASEAN and East Asia is ageing rapidly. Countries in the region with young populations also tend to be capital importers, while ageing economies tend to be capital exporters. Policies that enable greater factor mobility can help reduce differences in capital-labour ratios and assist in increasing productivity to promote more inclusive growth.

The economies of the ASEAN member states have signed several mutual recognition agreements (MRAs) to increase the mobility of skilled labour. However, implementation has been stymied by domestic rules and regulations on employment and licensing requirements. Furthermore, these MRAs will have to be more responsive to the rapidly changing skills needs because of the pandemic and the 4IR.

Removing barriers to labour more so than capital mobility through regional arrangements may be politically difficult, given the sensitivities involved. Therefore, bilateral agreements may be more feasible than regional ones. For instance, the India-Singapore Comprehensive Economic Cooperation Agreement is one such bilateral deal that has enabled short- and long-term employment visas, ranging from two months to three years, to nationals of both countries. Similar agreements involving the other ASEAN member states would be of mutual benefit.

Such policy changes must first overcome anti-globalisation forces that have been strengthened by the pandemic. However, these forces can assume deceptive forms, such as 'reshoring' under the guise of supporting supply chain resilience.

Such moves would curtail rather than promote factor mobility. In this environment, regional initiatives that aim to liberalise trade can help, such as the ASEAN Economic Community, ASEAN-India agreements and the RCEP. Even if these agreements cannot promote factor mobility, they can help equalise factor prices by increasing commodity trade. Increased trade can produce similar results in reducing adjustment costs.

Conclusion

Although ASEAN-India economic relations date back several centuries, it was not until the 1990s that these ties were formalised through FTAs, which spurred robust growth in trade and investment. Future growth will be linked to digital trade and e-commerce; this potential will be realised if policies are implemented at the national, bilateral and cross-regional levels. The ASEAN-India cooperation agreements need to be upgraded to address this fast-evolving area of international commerce.

The pandemic's push towards a digital economy may worsen inequality but it will also increase inclusion in some areas which will serve as a partial offset. There will be significant disruption in the short to medium term, however, particularly to labour markets.

This would be best addressed by policies that increase the mobility of capital, labour, data and technology across borders — these flows are currently quite limited between ASEAN and India. The need to increase such flows will be compounded by divergent demographic trends between the two, with a bulging labour force in India and a shrinking one in most of ASEAN.

FTAs could play a role but sensitivities, especially relating to labour mobility, may stand in the way of broad, regional agreements, leaving bilateral deals to fill in the gap. Regional cooperation arrangements are effective tools in promoting trade. This can go some way towards substituting for factor flows by equalising their prices — wages and rentals.

The rise in anti-globalisation sentiment that has increased with the pandemic may limit trade and factor mobility at a time when it is needed the most. This needs to be overcome in India and ASEAN, and together, if possible, if the enormous potential in digital trade and e-commerce is to be realised.

26

India and ASEAN: Enhancing Collaboration in the Digital Economy and E-commerce

Arpita Mukherjee

Introduction

During the past decade, India and the member states of the Association of Southeast Asian Nations (ASEAN) have seen rapid growth in the digitalisation and adoption of Fourth Industrial Revolution (4IR) technologies, which have been accentuated by the recent COVID-19 pandemic. The need for social distancing has fast-tracked the requirement of automation of manufacturing, work-from-home, growth of e-commerce and online delivery of services, such as education and healthcare. The governments in India and the ASEAN member states have accelerated the adoption of technology for e-governance and to provide pandemic-related support directly to vulnerable groups such as women, farmers and small- and medium-enterprises (SMEs).

India's digital economy is projected to be US$1 trillion by 2025, constituting around 18–23 percent of the gross domestic product (GDP). The digital economy of ASEAN is around seven percent of its GDP and with digital integration across its member states, it is projected to be

US$1 trillion by 2025. Thus, both economies are expected to reach the same size by 2025. India's e-commerce market was valued at US$38.5 billion by volume in 2017, and is estimated to reach US$165.5 billion by 2025, while the ASEAN market is estimated to reach US$90 billion by volume by 2025. Although the growth of e-commerce varies across the ASEAN member states, most of them are experiencing a high double-digit growth like India. Cities such as Bengaluru, Singapore, Bangkok, Kuala Lumpur, Jakarta and Manila have emerged as start-up hubs in the region. There are several examples of collaboration, cross-border investments and partnerships.

ASEAN-India Bilateral Partnership in the Digital Economy and E-commerce

The collaboration between ASEAN and India in the digital economy and e-commerce is primarily at two levels: government-to-government (G2G) and business-to-business (B2B).

G2G Collaboration

At the G2G level, the two economies have identified certain areas for collaboration in information and communications technology (ICT) under the 'Plan of Action to Implement the ASEAN-India Partnership for Peace, Progress and Shared Prosperity (2021–2025)' and are deliberating on the steps to implement it. This plan includes:

 i. capacity building and knowledge sharing in e-commerce and 4IR technologies, such as artificial intelligence (AI), Internet of Things and the use of ICT in disaster management and smart cities, among others;
 ii. strengthen cooperation, capacity building and policy coordination on cybersecurity, including personal data protection and the implementation of the ASEAN Cybersecurity Cooperation Strategy;

iii. promote sustainable and inclusive economic growth and prosperity through increasing digital trade, entrepreneurship, preparing micro, small and medium enterprises (MSMEs) for digital transformation;
iv. developing a digital-ready workforce equipped for the 4IR; and
v. support digital skills development for women and youth.

The two economies have already started collaboration in digital connectivity. For example, in July 2017, India announced a concessional line of credit of US$1 billion to develop connectivity infrastructure, both physical and digital, as part of its commitments for integration with ASEAN. It involved the installation of a regional high-capacity fibre-optic network, supplemented by national rural broadband networks and digital villages in remote areas of ASEAN, among others. In January 2018, India announced a pilot project on rural connectivity in the CLMV (Cambodia, Laos, Myanmar and Vietnam) countries at the ASEAN-India Commemorative Summit.

India and the ASEAN member states have signed several memoranda of understanding (MOUs)/partnership agreements. For example, in 2018, India signed an MOU with Singapore to constitute a Joint Working Group on Financial Technology for regulatory cooperation and sharing of best practices and with Vietnam to enhance cooperation in the field of information and broadcasting. It includes the implementation of a tracking and data reception station and data processing facility in Vietnam under the ASEAN-India Space Cooperation. The India-Singapore Entrepreneurship Bridge, launched in 2018, is a digital platform that enables start-ups, investors and aspiring entrepreneurs to connect with one another with a focus on knowledge exchange, networking and capacity building. CERT-In, Ministry of Electronics and Information Technology, India, and VNCERT, Ministry of Information and Communications, Vietnam, signed an MOU on cybersecurity during the ASEAN-India Special Foreign Ministers Meeting on 15 and 16 June 2022. In February 2022, an MOU was signed in science, technology and innovation between the Department of Science and Technology, India, and the Ministry of Trade and Industry, Singapore, to facilitate technology exchanges.

B2B Collaborations

Several Indian technology businesses have invested in the ASEAN member states and vice versa. For example, Tata Communications has joint ventures in Malaysia and Singapore in digital solutions and cloud infrastructure services. Singapore-based Temasek Holdings has invested around US$400 million in technology-based Indian start-ups such as Ola Cabs, Policy Bazaar, Zomato and Pine Labs.

Some Concerns

While India and ASEAN have strong complementarities and synergies in the digital economy and e-commerce, there are some challenges.

First, the digital regulations are evolving in both economies. ASEAN is yet to be an integrated market and there are differences in views across the members on data governance, data protection, data localisation and storage, use of data and content in social media and digital taxation. The ASEAN member states also differ in their willingness to participate in plurilateral discussions, for example, India and Indonesia have expressed concerns about participating in the World Trade Organization's plurilateral e-commerce negotiations, while Singapore has taken an active role in the discussions. While some countries such as Singapore have comprehensive digital plans, targets and policies, others, including India, have more generic policies or regulatory gaps in areas such as consumer data privacy, cybersecurity, cross-border data flows and transactions. In some areas, India's trade policy is more aligned to some ASEAN member states, for example, India and Indonesia have similar concerns on "sharing of data with a trust". The two countries are keen to support the growth of their domestic digital economies and are concerned about competition from global technology giants. Many ASEAN member states have introduced start-up visa to facilitate the entry and stay of foreign start-ups, but India is yet to introduce one.

Second, there are infrastructure and connectivity issues in India and some ASEAN member states. There are wide differences in broadband penetration, quality and speed, telephone/mobile connectivity and access at reasonable prices.

Third, while the governments are trying to adopt technology, the pace of adoption may be slow, and technology may not be used efficiently in areas like a robust risk management system to ensure food safety and standard and fast-track clearances of perishables. All government processes are not online, or even if online, responses and query resolution processes may not be well-developed, resulting in lower ease of doing business.

Fourth, in some ASEAN member states (for example, the Philippines and Vietnam) and India, the adoption of online financial services has been low. In Myanmar, there are policy restrictions on using domestic credit/debit cards to make international purchases. There are restrictions on accepting dollar payments and international online payment providers, and these vary across countries. Digital financial inclusion, onboarding SMEs in digital platforms and use of digital technology by SMEs and other vulnerable groups like women are low in many countries, including India. Further, issues regarding security and reliability of digital payment modes have been a concern for businesses and consumers in India and ASEAN.

Fifth, India-ASEAN bilateral engagement in digital space has so far been limited to MOUs, regulatory information sharing and intent to cooperate. India opted out of the Regional Comprehensive Economic Partnership (RCEP) and commitments on both sides in the India-ASEAN bilateral trade agreement and India's agreement with the ASEAN member states are lower than the autonomous regime. India also discontinued its bilateral investment treaties with many countries.

Recommendations and the Way Forward

India and the ASEAN member states are going through a difficult time due to the COVID-19 pandemic-related lockdown and disruptions of supply chains. The pandemic has also created opportunities to leverage digital technology for exports and to revive growth. For example, digital connectivity and e-commerce channels can be used to link SMEs to the global markets at a low cost. Through e-commerce, SMEs can reach their consumers across the globe while consumers can access and compare a wide range of products and services, purchase from any location and at any time as per their convenience and get the product delivered to the place of their choice. The e-commerce business is growing in both economies, but cross-border trade and partnership is low, which can be further enhanced. In this context, to move the Plan of Action forward, the following steps can be taken by India and ASEAN:

i. Address regulatory gaps and enhance regulatory cooperation: While the digital regulations are evolving and each country should have the right to regulate, regulations should be non-discriminatory, technology neutral and should not be a non-tariff barrier to trade. There can be a framework for the harmonisation of policies across India and ASEAN through discussions/consultations. There is need for more detailed discussions on digital connectivity and e-commerce during the review of the trade agreements and through other forums. The Plan of Action referred to regulatory corporation and knowledge sharing. Regular meetings between regulators and nodal government departments can be held to understand each other's policies and concerns and find a way to address them. India and ASEAN can explore the possibilities of sharing data with a trust to facilitate cross-border trade. Regulatory commitments and cross-border recognition of standards and regulations can facilitate trade and provide businesses with a secure regulatory environment. While both sides have defined the areas of collaboration, there is a need for targets, road maps and regular monitoring of the initiatives and their outcomes.

ii. Remove barriers for SME exporters and start-ups: It is important to conduct a comprehensive study to identify the barriers faced by SME exporters in India and ASEAN in onboarding into e-commerce platforms. The two economies can then prioritise and address the barriers. They can work together to develop an integrated e-commerce platform which can provide information and go-to-market strategy for SMEs. Start-up visas can support cross-border mobility of SME entrepreneurs. India and ASEAN can start discussions on start-up visas since high-skilled labour mobility is a core demand for India in trade discussions. The two sides should strengthen the initiatives on joint start-up hubs and they should explore options for more cross-border financing of start-ups.

iii. Address infrastructure gaps: Cross-border investments in infrastructure will help to address infrastructure gaps and enhance technology penetration. The governments need to collaborate to facilitate private investments in this area and remove barriers to cross-border investments.

iv. Engagement and collaborations in international and regional forums: Countries should participate actively in discussions on the digital economy and e-commerce in international and regional forums and, at the same time, try to leverage their strengths in such forums. For example, India can leverage its competitive advantage in highly skilled manpower. There is a need for deeper understanding of each country's strengths, concerns and requirements. Forums such as India-ASEAN summits and the Indo-Pacific can be good platforms for collaboration and to take up joint initiatives needed to leverage digitalisation and e-commerce. In such forums, countries can present their needs, discuss their concerns and learn from each other's best practices. Joint initiatives can be launched in areas such as digital skill development for women and youth. India and ASEAN can collaborate on 4IR technologies in twin cities like Chennai, India, and Kuala Lumpur, Malaysia. Joint working groups can be set up in areas like AI for social benefit.

v. Collaborate in cross-border digital payment and digital financial inclusion: India and ASEAN can develop an efficient and secure cross-border digital payment system through applying best practices within the region. Innovative technology start-ups and multinational firms can be roped in. The restrictions on online payment methods may be addressed.

Conclusion

While India and many ASEAN member states are today importers of digital products and services, they are fast developing their capabilities which will enable them to export in future. Jointly, they can target third country markets leveraging their mutual strengths. Technology and digital innovations will be the key drivers of growth in the post COVID-19 era and the governments can support this through the right policy initiatives. The governments can enhance their partnership and collaboration in the digital economy and e-commerce by identifying and leveraging the best practices in India and ASEAN, launching pilot projects, creating joint working groups and, most importantly, removing discriminatory trade barriers.

ENVIRONMENT AND SUSTAINABILITY

27

Untapped Potential in the ASEAN-India Relationship: Climate Change and Green Recovery

Sharon Seah

India's relations with the Association of Southeast Asian Nations (ASEAN) started with the former being a Sectoral Partner in 1992. India became ASEAN's fifth Dialogue Partner three years later. The two sides held their inaugural Summit in 2002 and further elevated ties to a strategic level in 2012 to commemorate the 20th anniversary of ASEAN-India dialogue relations. The ASEAN-India partnership has progressed from functional cooperation in the 1990s to the building of a strong economic foundation with the ASEAN-India Free Trade Area and the ASEAN-India Investment Agreement in 2015. Both sides enjoy dialogue mechanisms across politics, defence, trade, tourism, agriculture and energy. This year, ASEAN and India have reached another milestone in their relationship as they celebrate 30 years of cooperation. As with many relationships, it is natural to progress to an intensification of strategic relations with a view to the future. Hence, it would not be surprising if India were to seek a comprehensive strategic partnership with ASEAN in the future.

Untapped Potential

India's 'Look East' policy was formulated by Prime Minister Narasimha Rao's government in 1991. The objective was to forge political, security and economic cooperation with the countries of Southeast Asia. It was a strategic shift for India and signalled its intent for greater interaction with the Southeast Asian countries and with ASEAN as the premier regional organisation of Southeast Asia. The 'Look East' policy was later complemented by Prime Minister Narendra Modi's 'Act East' policy announced at the 12th ASEAN-India Summit in November 2014. By refining the policy from 'Looking East' to 'Acting East', India saw the strategic imperative to accelerate its engagement with ASEAN and convey the message of focusing on actions and results.

Since 2004, both sides have intensified their engagement using the ASEAN-India Partnership for Peace, Progress and Shared Prosperity as a long-term roadmap. Four Plans of Action to implement the ASEAN-India Partnership for Peace, Progress and Shared Prosperity have been in place, with the latest being the 2021–2025 version. The latest Plan of Action covers three broad areas (Political-Security; Economic; and Socio-cultural Cooperation) and five cross-sectoral areas (the Initiative for ASEAN Integration and narrowing the development gap; connectivity; smart cities; ASEAN institutional strengthening; and sustainable development cooperation).

Apart from these existing areas of cooperation, there are two potential areas in the ASEAN-India relationship that both sides can focus on: climate change and green recovery. Dynamic cooperation in these two areas will deliver the great co-benefits to the ecological and economic environments of India and ASEAN and their peoples and play a pathfinder role in the global management of these problems.

Climate Change

By 2030, India and ASEAN are projected to become the world's third and fourth largest economies respectively. Economic growth and development, while critical and essential for developing countries of the region, would mean a greater depletion of natural resources, higher rates of pollution and greenhouse gas (GHG) emissions. According to the 2018 Climate Watch data, India and ASEAN's share of GHG emissions was 6.84 percent and 5.6 percent respectively in 2018. Together, the two sides made up over 12 per cent of global GHG emissions then. This is not an insignificant number. Both India and Southeast Asia's shares of global GHG emissions are expected to grow as the economies re-open and grow in the post COVID-19 pandemic era. The key is whether both the ASEAN and Indian economies can recover and grow sustainably and inclusively.

Admittedly, ASEAN and India were slow starters in climate action. However, there are the beginnings of an alignment of climate interests between India and ASEAN which, despite their stand on developed countries having to accept the burden of historical responsibility, are increasingly cognisant that no action is not an option. India and ASEAN have demonstrated credible commitment to fulfil their obligations under the 2015 Paris Agreement but their commitments are conditioned on receiving international assistance.

At the time of writing, India has pledged to achieve a net zero target by 2070 at the 26th Conference of Parties (COP26) to the United Nations Framework Convention on Climate Change but it has not submitted its updated Nationally Determined Contributions (NDC). As the world's third biggest emitter of greenhouse gas emissions, India's commitment to net zero has brought optimism and demonstrated leadership for the developing world. However, New Delhi's active role in watering down the term "phase out" to "phase down" coal at the COP26 negotiations was disappointing. Experts argue that this is a necessary move because India's energy security is 70 percent dependent on coal and the industry, it is argued, provides employment and livelihood for millions of Indians. Modi has also pledged to increase India's renewable energy capacity from 100 gigawatts (GW) to 500 GW by 2030. Taken in good faith, India's phase down of coal in tandem with an increase in renewable energy could signal the start of India's transition to a green and just recovery.

Within ASEAN, Singapore, Malaysia, Vietnam and Indonesia have committed to achieve carbon neutrality by 2050 or before. Singapore was the first country to submit its updated NDC and a long-term low emissions development strategy (LT-LEDS) in March 2020 voluntarily. Indonesia and Thailand submitted their LT-LEDS in July and October 2021 respectively. Although the requirement to submit an LT-LEDS is voluntary for developing countries, it is a growing demonstration of Southeast Asia's commitment to long-term plans to achieve the desired outcomes for climate change. Similarly, there is an opportunity for India to explain its long-term energy plans towards a view of phasing out coal with an updated NDC and a long-term low emissions development strategy.

Another piece of the climate change and green recovery puzzle has to do with halting and reversing deforestation. At the recent COP26 meetings, India joined over 140 countries in pledging to halt and reverse deforestation and degradation by 2030. Seven ASEAN member states — Brunei, Indonesia, Malaysia, Myanmar, Philippines, Singapore and Vietnam — have also supported the 'Glasgow Leaders Declaration on Forests and Land Use'.

The conservation of forests and other terrestrial ecosystems is in both ASEAN and India's interests. The two regions hold great stores of forests and peatlands that can act as carbon sinks. Studies have shown that stopping deforestation is far more effective than afforestation or reforestation. Biodiversity resources are economic assets. Indigenous peoples depend on the preservation of forests for their livelihood. India has a draft National Forest Policy that calls for a minimum of one-third of its geographical area to be under forest cover and supports its 2015 NDC target of creating additional carbon sink of 2.5 to 5 $GtCO_2e$ (gigatonnes of carbon dioxide equivalent). Similarly, Indonesia aims to become a net carbon sink by 2050. Its biggest driver of deforestation is commodity-driven deforestation; hence, sustainable peatland management policies and the development of carbon sequestration projects in forestry and agriculture are of interest to Indonesia.

It would make sense for both ASEAN and India to find ways to jointly implement the agreed goals of phasing down coal and the global deforestation pledge. This can be done through knowledge sharing on phasing out of fossil fuels, cooperation in research and development for renewable energy technologies, sustainable forestry management knowledge, redesign of agricultural policies and programmes that can incentivise agriculture, promote food security and benefit the indigenous communities living at the fringe. There are many potential co-benefits arising from cooperation in these areas. For example, the conservation and protection of biodiversity assets are vital to ecosystems functioning and a phase out of coal-fired power plants can lead to a reduction in air pollution which translates to greater public health well-being.

Together towards a Green Recovery

A green recovery is broadly defined as fiscal, monetary and regulatory measures aimed at accelerating economic recovery while incorporating environmentally positive measures that reduce GHG emissions. A green recovery is also expected to enhance the resilience of economies and societies, drive sustainability and boost jobs, income and growth.

Despite the COVID-19 pandemic leading to a global economic slowdown, both regions possess good growth prospects in the long term. India is the world's fifth largest economy and forecasts by the Economist Intelligence Unit put its real gross domestic report growth of seven percent in fiscal year (FY) 2022/23 after an expansion of 9.2 percent in FY2021/22. Meanwhile, the ASEAN economy which, according to the *ASEAN Statistical Yearbook 2021*, has grown at 4.4 percent over the last decade, is expected to return and even exceed this level post-pandemic. Greater economic engagement promises mutual access to markets and labour opportunities.

The ASEAN-India Plan of Action (2021–2025) includes sustainable development under its cross-pillar cooperation section with a focus on achieving United Nations Sustainable Development Goals (UN SDGs), achieving the ASEAN Community Vision 2025 and supporting institutions to facilitate sustainable cooperation development. However, this is too narrow to lead India and ASEAN to their respective pathways to a green and sustainable recovery.

A major transformative framework to guide ASEAN and India in their post-pandemic economic dealings is needed. Existing cooperation in trade and investment, finance, energy, transportation, information and communications technology, tourism, connectivity, smart cities and the blue economy are good starting points for the incorporation of green recovery measures. For instance, can both sides explore the idea of an ASEAN-India digital highway to promote digital trade and economy? This would require substantial investments in digital and cyber infrastructure, along with the upskilling and re-skilling of their respective workforces to participate in the new digital economy. India and several ASEAN member states already enjoy a head-start as a substantial proportion of their populations are information technology savvy and entrepreneurially innovative as well as cyber infrastructure has already been in place. Going digital not only circumvents the difficulties of trading and transacting physically due to the COVID-19 restrictions but also plays a part in reducing GHG emissions. The ASEAN Digital Masterplan 2025, which outlines a vision of what a regional digital economy and society is, also notes that the development of digital services has a role in climate change mitigation.

Conclusion

While the ASEAN-India relationship has indeed grown over the last 30 years, it has often been criticised for its limited scope and relative weakness in comparison to ASEAN's other external partners. However, there are vast stores of untapped potential in the ASEAN-India partnership as this chapter has attempted to show. The COVID-19 pandemic and climate crisis present a rare window of opportunity for the two sides to revitalise the relationship. If India and the ASEAN member states succeed in delivering on their climate pledges, while achieving their UN SDGs and ASEAN Community Vision, the ASEAN-India strategic partnership will serve as a model for other regional partnerships and developing countries of an inclusive and sustainable recovery.

28

Build Resilience and Tap Opportunities for a Greener Future

Arunabha Ghosh and Sanjana Chhabra

The locus of global economic growth has shifted to the emerging economies. Unlike development trajectories of the past, the South and Southeast Asian economies must grow on sustainable pathways. They are in highly vulnerable regions. Moreover, environmental standards are rapidly shifting for international trade and investment. Nor can they follow a heavily state-financed approach to building a greener industrial base because of limited fiscal resources. The Association of Southeast Asian Nations (ASEAN) and India can instead journey together on a different road — one that recognises common challenges and their transboundary impacts, responds to risks and grabs opportunities in a greener economy.

India and ASEAN confront similar environmental challenges, which are centred around land, water, air and climate. Both regions are rich in biodiversity: ASEAN hosts four of the world's 34 biodiversity hotspots while India is one of 17 megadiverse countries. Between 1990 and 2012, most ASEAN member states experienced a decline in forest cover due to the expansion of commercial (rubber and palm oil) plantations. India's forest cover has increased in recent years (24.56

percent of its area in 2019) but there are concerns about the loss of pristine forests being replaced by fast-growing trees, which cannot replace biodiversity. India has committed to restoring 26 million hectares of degraded land by 2030.

The risks associated with water are greater as pressure mounts from growing economies and the imperative of food security. For ASEAN, water demand is expected to increase by one-third by 2025 (against 2005) and double during the latter half of the century, resulting in increased water insecurity. India's total water withdrawal will jump from 949 billion cubic metres (BCM) in 2010 to 1,058 BCM in 2050 — against a finite supply of 1,123 BCM available annually. The quality of water is also threatened with industrial pollution and untreated urban sewage.

As ASEAN and India experience rapid urbanisation, air quality is the primary public health concern. In 2019, 1.67 million deaths were attributable to air pollution in India. Whereas energy-related emissions are the primary driver of air pollution within city limits, both regions deal with particulate matter crossing long distances. Up to 90 percent of transboundary smoke haze in ASEAN is linked to peat fires from commercial plantations. The burning of crop residue in northern India accounts for about 20 percent of PM2.5 pollution in the winter months for cities in the Indo-Gangetic plain.

The climate crisis compounds the risks. In addition to heat stress and inland water stress, the severity of climate shocks is felt along the long coastlines of India and the ASEAN member states. India is one of the most climate vulnerable countries in the world. The frequency of cyclones has increased seven-fold in the Bay of Bengal since 1970. With rapid warming of the Arabian Sea, cyclones are buffeting the western coast as well. Climate change is also impacting ASEAN coasts. For many countries dependent on tourism revenues, marine litter and overfishing are already major challenges. Increasingly, extreme weather events and the decimation of coral reefs will severely impact lives and livelihoods.

The economic development in both regions is threatened by rising environmental risks, whether local (water stress, land degradation) or regional/global (air pollution, climate change). These risks reduce the productivity of natural resources, destroy hard infrastructure and roll back years of development by pushing communities into environment-related deprivation. Environmental risks have financial implications with stranded assets in fossil fuels impacting investors. Further, trade prospects could be dampened with the rising threats of border carbon taxes in Europe, North America and elsewhere.

Can both regions re-imagine an economic future resilient to environmental shocks and be economically dynamic? Opportunities lie in emerging technologies, new channels of investment and potentially millions of jobs. Three pillars could serve as foundations for ASEAN-India cooperation: issues that are transboundary in nature; increase resilience against risks; and create opportunities for exchange of ideas, investment and innovation. We outline five sectors that could derive value from these three pillars.

The first is promoting the energy transition. ASEAN and India are going through multiple energy transitions. Despite early electrification, 45 million people still lack access to energy in Southeast Asia. Despite the rapid electrification of households in recent years, 44 percent of rural households in India remain at the bottom-most tier of energy access. India's energy demand will grow almost three times during the period 2015 to 2040 while ASEAN's will rise 60 percent in the same period. Fossil energy still provides 76 percent and 79 percent of India's and ASEAN's energy needs respectively.

In 2010, India had less than 20 megawatts (MW) of solar power. Now it has more than 114,000 MW of solar, wind, small hydro and biomass-based power, and nearly more than 160,000 MW, including large hydropower. Already 41.5 percent of electricity capacity is non-fossil based. It has set a target of 500,000 MW of renewables by 2030. The ASEAN member states aim to achieve 23 percent of renewable energy by 2025, up from 13.9 percent in 2018.

Both regions can serve each other's interests in renewable energy. India's revolutionary leapfrog to clean electricity brings with it experience in market design, transparent auctions, building large-scale solar parks, upgrading grid infrastructure and creating financial institutions. ASEAN, in turn, has experience in bio-energy, an area of increasing interest to India. India also co-sponsored the International Solar Alliance (ISA) (107 countries have signed the Framework Agreement). Cambodia and Myanmar are members but others should also join. The ISA could support distributed energy programmes for productive uses in rural areas, far-flung islands or as rooftop installations in cities.

Another area of cooperation would be grid integration. The ASEAN Plan of Action for Energy Cooperation (2016–2025) envisions an ASEAN power grid while the ISA is promoting 'One Sun, One World, One Grid'. Integrated grids and cross-border electricity trading could increase energy interdependence and reliability of intermittent renewable energy.

Clean energy gives a massive opportunity for new job creation. More than 330,000 workers will be employed (translating into 1.3 million full-time equivalent jobs) to achieve India's renewable energy targets of 175 gigawatts (GW); more than one million workers would join the workforce with raised targets of 500 GW. Far more jobs are created from distributed energy, which has an employment coefficient seven times that of utility-scale solar. By 2016, renewables supported 611,000 jobs in the ASEAN region with the highest jobs in liquid biofuel production, followed by large hydropower and solar photovoltaics. ASEAN could have 1.7 million to 2.2 million renewables-based jobs by 2030. ASEAN and India could work together on training an army of clean energy workers.

The second is envisioning cleaner and liveable cities. India launched its National Clean Air Programme in 2019, aiming to reduce PM_{10} and $PM_{2.5}$ concentrations by 20 percent to 30 percent by 2024, compared to 2017. The ASEAN Agreement on Transboundary Haze Pollution was signed in 2002. The Sustainable Use of Peatland and Haze Mitigation in ASEAN is another initiative to manage risks of forest fires and transboundary haze.

The two regions could build a clean air platform setting out a vision of clean air for all. By 2030, all major cities with more than 100,000 people should have air quality monitoring coverage and, by 2040, all these cities should meet local air quality standards. They could share experiences on building local enforcement capacity, developing detailed regional airshed plans, creating networks of citizen science monitors and designing emission trading schemes to reduce transboundary air pollution, whether from farms or industrial clusters.

The third is building a circular economy for waste and e-waste. ASEAN and India have relatively lower per capita waste footprints than the developed world. In 2015, India consumed five percent of global plastic but produced nine percent. For Southeast Asia, the shares were equal at eight percent. Plastic waste will clog the cities, impact food systems and endanger other species. India and ASEAN are major e-waste importing regions. E-waste amounts to only two percent of solid waste but 70 percent of hazardous waste globally. Recycling rates in Asia are just 11.7 percent, compared to 42.5 percent in Europe.

Singapore has operated waste-to-energy plants since 1979. By January 2021, India had approved five projects (with 74.7 MW capacity) from municipal solid waste. Thailand's 3R (Reduce, Reuse, Recycle) programme in government offices has removed four billion plastic bags annually. The ASEAN Working Group on Chemicals and Waste is focused on building capacity to implement international conventions concerning hazardous waste.

The opportunity lies in a circular economy. Building on large informal waste recycling capacity, a formalised circular economy can help both regions recover more value while increasing mineral security and creating jobs. Forty-four percent of India's critical minerals could be sourced from e-waste. Effective waste management could create 1.4 million jobs in India.

The fourth is in pooling investment and insurance for nature-based solutions. Across ASEAN, several initiatives for sustainable forest and land management have begun. These include the ASEAN Peatland Forest

Project across Indonesia, Malaysia, the Philippines and Vietnam; the SEApeat Project to reduce deforestation and greenhouse gas emissions; the Heart of Borneo Initiative between Brunei, Indonesia and Malaysia to protect forests on Borneo; national wetland management policies in Malaysia, Myanmar and the Philippines; and community forest management in Vietnam.

India is home to dozens of sustainable agricultural systems and practices, of which at least 16 are most promising. Five — crop rotation, agroforestry, rainwater harvesting, mulching and precision agriculture — have scaled to more than five percent of the net sown area. Crop rotation covers 30 million hectares (Mha) and agroforestry about 25 Mha. India has the largest number of farmers practising natural farming (more than 800,000).

These initiatives can be scaled by pooling investment and insurance for nature-based solutions for environmental restoration and resilience. Pooled projects, such as large-scale agroforestry programmes, create investment opportunities worth billions of dollars. Investing in nature-based solutions requires insurance schemes to help farmers and communities experiment with sustainable practices while protecting against any short-term fluctuations in income. Equally, with natural capital serving as a bulwark against climate shocks, these countries can also reduce economic losses from extreme weather.

The fifth is assessing climate risks and building coastal resilience. ASEAN and India already have an established Project on Enhancing Climate Change Adaptation in Southeast Asia and one on Climate Change Projections and Assessment of Impacts. These programmes can serve as the basis for deeper collaboration on assessing climate risks. These regions need high-resolution climate risk assessments, which go well beyond disaster monitoring and extend to increasing the predictive capabilities of models. Only then can local administrations and communities factor in avoided costs of losses and damage to infrastructure. A Climate Risk Atlas, being developed in India by the Council on Energy, Environment and Water, already shows that three-quarters of all districts are hotspots for extreme climate events. Such modelling capabilities can be shared with the ASEAN member states to identify particularly vulnerable areas.

Building resilience for coastal ecosystems and economies can be a specific area of deepened cooperation. There are numerous country-level and regional initiatives. In the Philippines, 14 coastal municipalities established a network of marine protected areas for fisheries, coral reefs, sea grass beds and mangrove forests. The Coral Triangle Initiative unites Indonesia, Malaysia, Papua New Guinea, the Philippines, the Solomon Islands and Timor-Leste to collectively address the degradation of ocean resources. India's blue economy supports an estimated 95 percent of the country's business through transportation and contributes to around four percent to the country's gross domestic product. India is a member of the Global Ocean Observing System to collect long-term systematic scientific oceanographic data at the national, regional and global levels. It is also involved in the Global Coral Reef Monitoring network. Clearly, there is much on which the two regions can collaborate to boost sustainable development of the coastlines.

As ASEAN and India continue to grow rapidly, they will face their own environmental challenges. The five areas of cooperation listed here go beyond their national boundaries and offer a case for cooperation in dealing with environmental externalities. These interventions can build resilience against risks while creating new markets and employment opportunities. In the 21st century, development has only one pathway — sustainable development. ASEAN and India can pave the road together.

OPEN SKIES

29

ASEAN-India Air Connectivity: Time for a More Liberal Open Skies Policy

Ridha Aditya Nugraha

India has spread its influence across the Association of Southeast Asian Nations (ASEAN) region in the past through the maritime and land trade routes. In the 21st century, such influence could become even more prominent through the air route, ensuring enhanced connectivity between the two regions.

The beginning of this century marked the introduction of low-fare airlines and open skies arrangements between ASEAN and India. The former has proven that AirAsia's famous motto 'Now Everyone Can Fly' — which seemed unrealistic in the early 2000s — is indeed something possible within the region. Open skies arrangements set up the foundation for increased connectivity, removing the limitation on flight capacity, fare, frequency, aircraft type and routes.

Liberalisation is a key change in the aviation business, promoting competition among the airlines and raising the bar for passengers. Airlines are driven to innovate — from products to services — to compete within the market. There are two forms of liberalisation in the aviation sector. The first is on the ground, which is related to foreign direct investment and one that is locked with a single majority ownership clause. The second is in the skies and refers to the freedom of the air. The higher the number, the more liberation it offers; for example, the ultimate Eighth and Ninth Freedoms of the Air allow foreign aircrafts to fly between two domestic points. There are nine levels of Air Freedoms. These include using the air space only to operate domestic flights between airports in a foreign country.

India and the ASEAN member states share a similar history of liberalisation. Both sides initially had a protective approach towards their flag carrier. However, within the last decade, they gradually produced a constrained air service agreement and regulated market and have moved forward towards open skies and privatisation.

The ASEAN member states have started a new round of liberalisation through the introduction of the ASEAN Single Aviation Market instruments in 2009 and 2010, consisting of three agreements:

i. the ASEAN Multilateral Agreement on the Full Liberalisation of Air Freight Services;
ii. the ASEAN Multilateral Agreement on Air Services; and
iii. the ASEAN Multilateral Agreement on the Full Liberalisation of Passenger Air Services.

Any airline designated by an ASEAN member state is allowed to operate both passenger and cargo scheduled services between its home country and a point in an international airport in another member state, and then to a point in an international airport of a third member state without limitations on capacity and route. So far, this multilateral scheme allows only up to the Fifth Freedom of the Air. Any cabotage or the Eighth and Ninth Freedoms of the Air is forbidden. In other words, a foreign aircraft is not allowed to serve a domestic route in any other member state — a contrast from the rules in the European Union.

Having said that, there is progress in the ASEAN open skies landscape. In the past, uncertainty loomed over the first implementation phase of the ASEAN open skies plan because all member states had to first ratify the agreements to ensure that the single aviation market could be enforced within the region. Between 2010 and 2016, several member states opposed the open skies idea to protect their national airlines from being overrun by other wealthier, more competitive foreign airlines. In 2016, these states, namely, Indonesia, Laos and the Philippines, signed a multilateral agreement, signifying the full implementation of a single aviation market. In an effort to address the concerns of some member states, compromises were made — although Indonesia is the largest archipelago among the member states, it only opened five big cities, namely, Jakarta (capital), Denpasar (Bali), Makassar (Sulawesi), Medan (Sumatra) and Surabaya (Java) for inclusion in the single aviation market. This compromise reflected the ASEAN way — ensuring that all the ASEAN member states were on board.

Beyond the freedom of the air, another major driver of aviation integration is the issue of ownership and control. Most ASEAN member states with prominent aviation markets limit foreign ownership of airlines to 49 percent, such as Indonesia, Malaysia, Singapore, Thailand and Vietnam. Even though Cambodia and Laos allow for 100 percent foreign airline investment, there is little interest among investors due to the different stages of development of the aviation industry in these countries. The concept of an ASEAN carrier — a carrier in which much of the ownership is held by the ASEAN member states — has only been discussed at the academic level and there is still a long way to go before such a proposal would be considered by the ASEAN member states.

Along with the various requirements of owning a certain number of aircrafts, the current situation means that significant capital is needed to acquire part of the intra-ASEAN market. Currently, AirAsia, Lion and Vietjet are the three key budget airlines which have the financial power to invest and establish seamless connectivity within the region, namely, flying in Malaysia, Indonesia, the Philippines, Thailand and Vietnam. Singapore has also become an important international destination for these airlines. The three airlines are considered the *de facto* pan-ASEAN airlines. However, due to the costly business model, not all airlines in the ASEAN member states are able to follow their example and seamless connectivity does not apply to all the ASEAN member states for now.

In light of the ASEAN Economic Blueprint 2025, several issues on intra-regional air connectivity need to be addressed. These include ensuring multilateralism prevails over bilateralism, the availability of ASEAN member states' airport slots with fair treatment and the urgency to improve the protection of the passengers. Therefore, it would be prudent for the ASEAN member states to resolve these issues before considering the establishment of more open skies arrangements with other regions, including India.

ASEAN entered into an open skies agreement with China in 2010. This led to greater China-ASEAN connectivity and witnessed the arrival of more Chinese tourists to the region, which positively impacted the economies of the ASEAN member states. However, it should be noted that the agreement allowed Chinese carriers to fly from any point in mainland China to any ASEAN member states, while the airline of the ASEAN member states could only fly to China from their respective home countries and not from any other transit point in the other member states. Fortunately, the situation improved after the ASEAN member states and China ratified the Fifth Freedom of the Air in 2019. Still, there is no guarantee when this multilateral approach will be implemented. Meanwhile, the major Chinese airlines continue to benefit from this arrangement. There is a lesson for ASEAN in this endeavour.

Fostering ASEAN-India connectivity through the open skies within the next decade — specifically, post COVID-19 pandemic — seems realistic and urgent. ASEAN's open skies landscape has become more mature and finds its equilibrium through the ASEAN way. As China and Japan in North Asia — the latter in the last decade — have initiated open skies arrangements through bilateral agreements with the ASEAN member states, it is time to balance this similar connectivity with India and the South Asian region.

India is an ideal open skies partner for ASEAN since the liberalisation progress of both sides is currently on the same page.

Matters relating to the privatisation and permits for private airlines flying international routes in India arose around the same period as those of most of the ASEAN member states. In 2003, India unilaterally initiated a limited open skies arrangement with ASEAN by allowing the latter daily flights to the metro cities and unlimited flights to 18 tourist destinations across the country. These arrangements helped India address the issue of the non-availability of seats on its flights to and from its shore. New Delhi had wanted to explore further open skies arrangements with the ASEAN member states but no time frame was determined. Perhaps now is a perfect time to look into this as the aviation world makes its way out of the COVID-19 pandemic.

Both ASEAN and India have reached a certain understanding on the extent of foreign investment in their respective airline sectors and the freedom of the air. Hence, ASEAN-India open skies should start with establishing the Fifth Freedom of the Air, not limiting to the Third and Fourth Freedoms. This will maximise the strategic location of both partners as gateways for Southeast Asia to Africa and Europe. At the same time, Indian airlines could maximise alternatives for destinations in Australia, New Zealand and East Asia. As these benefits apply to ASEAN and Indian carriers, it will allow for maximum aircraft utilisation to help airlines recover in a post COVID-19 pandemic environment. Furthermore, better planning and the further development of Indian and Southeast Asian airports could make them strong competitors to the Middle East airline hubs, which are currently dominated by Doha, Dubai and Abu Dhabi. Their respective airlines play a significant role in connecting the Middle East to Europe and ASEAN.

The other important but less discussed issue is enhancing passenger protection through ratification of the Montreal Convention of 1999. It ensures that injury to and death of passengers are well compensated. As of today, India and six ASEAN member states have ratified the agreement, leaving Brunei, Cambodia, Laos and Myanmar to do so. This is important for ASEAN's airline industry. Should India-ASEAN open skies become a reality, the convention's ratification should be a condition for the remaining ASEAN member states. Airline liability uniformity is important in enhancing passenger confidence and the relationship between ASEAN and India's airline industries.

The COVID-19 pandemic has witnessed a rise in the number of middle-class citizens in ASEAN and India, thereby enhancing their purchasing power. The post COVID-19 relaxed travel restrictions will see a strong rebound in the travel industry across the world, including India and ASEAN. Both sides can expect a strong return of travellers at the various levels — from backpackers to high-end tourists and for business and leisure. In addition, the movement of the Indian diaspora to ASEAN — specifically to Malaysia, Singapore and Indonesia — which are highly dependent upon air connectivity, is also expected to grow significantly in a post COVID-19 environment. This traffic growth should be matched with the establishment of world-class maintenance, repair and overhaul and ground-handling facilities in the ASEAN and Indian airports.

A positive gesture in the India-ASEAN relationship is the appointment of an Indian Ambassador to ASEAN based in Jakarta. This is a significant development, reflecting the strong ties between India and ASEAN. Among others, this political gesture could offer the Indian and ASEAN establishments an opportunity to progress on the open skies arrangement.

Finally, the last couple of years have been a time of survival for the airline industry in a world confronted by the COVID-19 outbreak. Moving forward, the governments of India and the ASEAN member states will need to work together to ensure that they can maximally capitalise on the opportunities that a more open skies policy would provide to their airlines. Such a landscape would also ensure a less monopolistic airline sector and provide varied travel options and a more competitive ticket pricing for their people. The enhanced ASEAN-India connectivity through the open skies is not merely to provide greater revenue to the airlines and the aviation sector but also to benefit millions of people in India and Southeast Asia on a larger scale.

30

Open Skies: Pathway to Enhanced India-ASEAN Economic Ties

Deeparghya Mukherjee

India and the Association of Southeast Asian Nations (ASEAN) have grown their mutual economic engagement from strength to strength over time. As India seeks to engage with the region better through its 'Act East' policy, economic partnerships between India and ASEAN can be expected to grow and reach new levels in the future. Estimates suggest that India-ASEAN total trade amounted to US$142 billion (merchandise and services) in 2018 and had the potential to double by the year 2025. In the recent past, due to the COVID-19 pandemic, merchandise trade between India and ASEAN settled at US$78 billion in 2021, down from US$97 billion in the pre COVID-19 pandemic period. India expects to increase its exports to ASEAN to US$46 billion in financial year 2022–2023.

Air connectivity is one of the many factors that bring two regions closer to each other. Around 35 percent of the world's trade shipments are by air; a one percent growth in air connectivity results in a six percent growth in trade. Apart from trade and investment, greater air connectivity positively impacts tourist flows across countries. Estimates of the United Nations' World Tourism Organization suggest that the number of international tourist arrivals by air is expected to increase at the annual rate of 3.3 percent till 2030.

Open skies agreements are entered into by countries or regions, facilitating flights by domestic and foreign airlines to operate international flights between the countries and, thereby, opening up access of national airports to foreign airlines. Amongst the benefits of open skies (depending on the level of air freedom — there are nine levels of Air Freedoms, starting from using air space only to operate domestic flights between airports of the foreign country), direct air connectivity eases up travel for business and leisure and allows for the fastest movement of goods and services between two countries. Hence, it is the fastest way to connect people and transport products. Additionally, with increasing tourism and economic relations, there is a fall in the cost of travel and freight movement.

India and ASEAN have facilitated greater economic integration through the ASEAN-India Free Trade Agreement in 2010 and other bilateral agreements between India and the individual ASEAN member states like Singapore and Malaysia. Further, there have been multiple initiatives to improve connectivity between India and the ASEAN member states. Estimates suggest that enhanced connectivity between India and ASEAN could result in cumulative gains higher than five percent of gross domestic product (GDP) for Myanmar, Cambodia, Thailand and Vietnam. It would also help India add two percent to its own GDP.

India-ASEAN Air Connectivity

Earlier, in the early 2000s, the limited open skies agreement eased the way for daily direct flights between Indian metro cities and the ASEAN member states and unlimited flights between 18 Indian tourism destinations and ASEAN cities. The intent to improve connectivity on

Table 30.1: India-ASEAN passenger and freight traffic, 2019

Country	Passengers to India	Passengers from India	Freight to India	Freight from India
Indonesia	2,090	2,904	148	191
Malaysia	1,624,862	1,598,051	18,062	24,637
Myanmar	45,454	43,321	11	384
Singapore	2,333,229	2,433,391	56,971	58,492
Thailand	2,328,661	2,347,712	42,016	35,875
Vietnam	16,447	17,767	251	128

Note: Passengers are reported in numbers and freight is reported in tonnes.
Source: Collated by the author using statistics from the Directorate General of Civil Aviation, India.

both sides had resulted in negotiations to work out the ASEAN-India Air Transport Agreement which is based on the open skies principles covering both passenger and freight traffic. As a result of this and otherwise, India has significantly grown its connectivity with Southeast Asia in the past few years.

The major airlines connecting ASEAN and India include Air India, Indigo, SpiceJet and Vistara from India. The airlines from the ASEAN region which fly into India include Thai Airways, Singapore Airlines, Malaysian Air, Tiger Air, Batik Air, Malindo Air and Air Asia.

Table 30.1 summarises the passenger and freight movements between India and the ASEAN member states in 2019. Clearly, Singapore, Malaysia and Thailand are the countries with the highest passenger and freight movement with India.

Recent Developments

In a report in *The Straits Times* in Singapore on 26 January 2018, Singapore's Prime Minister Lee Hsien Loong stressed the need for greater air connectivity between India and ASEAN. Amongst renewed ties with ASEAN nations, in the 16th India-ASEAN Summit in Bangkok, Thailand, the Singaporean Prime Minister expressed hope that the ASEAN-India Air Transport Agreement would be concluded soon. India and the Philippines agreed to sign a revised air services agreement in December 2020. This is slated to strengthen and improve air connectivity between the two countries. Prior to the onset of the COVID-19 pandemic, flights between the Philippines and India had begun. The air services agreement was signed in September 2021 and is expected to reap mutual benefits in terms of air travel safety and increased number of flights between the two countries.

While the above have been positive developments, India has recently instituted norms which allow foreign carriers to transport cargo from only six designated hub airports of the country. This is in line with the country's *Atmanirbhar Bharat* (Self-reliant India) initiative such that the business of local carriers picks up. At the same time, given the lower ability of domestic carriers to fly cargo to export destinations, this would primarily increase the exporters' cost of transportation of products to the world markets. Undoubtedly, this is a protectionist move that could easily be akin to shooting one's own foot.

Open Skies — Potential Benefits for India and ASEAN

India has a full open skies agreement only with the United States and a limited one with the United Kingdom. There have been recent efforts to enter into agreements with countries outside the 5,000-kilometre radius from New Delhi, the capital of India. The 'Act East' policy and India's growing linkages with Southeast Asia further increase the need to improve air connectivity. The limited open skies policy that India has with the ASEAN member states has led to direct connectivity of the main Indian cities with important cities in ASEAN, including Singapore, Kuala Lumpur in Malaysia, Phuket and Bangkok in Thailand, and Hanoi and Ho Chi Minh City in Vietnam. India's northeastern region has better connectivity with ASEAN.

India's approach to open skies with ASEAN is naturally dependent on other economic and political implications of its engagement with the region. India pulled out of the Regional Comprehensive Economic Partnership in late 2019 and further demonstrates a protectionist trend in most sectors, including civil aviation, in the garb of being *Atmanirbhar*. India has also increased tariffs for a number of items in the successive annual budgets of 2020 and 2021. India and ASEAN are reviewing the terms of the free trade agreement which is currently in force. While it is well recognised that there is high potential for growth in economic linkages between the two regions, India demonstrates a mood to protect domestic airline companies through its recent policy changes. This would, in turn, increase trade costs and reduce the export potential of the exporters. This is enough to emphasise the need for India to work towards a more liberal open skies policy with the ASEAN member states. Fearing competition and protecting domestic companies have not worked in the past and the country does not need to learn the old lessons once again.

On the ASEAN front, many ASEAN member states would want to have closer economic ties with India to balance their exposure to China. This would be greatly facilitated with a more liberal stand by India. China already has had an air transport agreement with ASEAN since 2010 and a more liberal engagement in air connectivity with ASEAN than India. In the post COVID-19 world, as businesses try to diversify their sourcing locations, thereby reducing dependence on any single country, greater air connectivity with ASEAN could become a critical consideration.

Finally, the inevitable privatisation of Air India, the national carrier of India, which is also the Indian airline with maximum international connections, could have several implications. After a significant amount of speculation about possible buyers for Air India, the Tata Group acquired the airline. Talace Pvt Ltd, a wholly owned subsidiary of the Tata Group, now owns the airline. This would, in turn, redefine the space. An existing liberal open skies policy between India and ASEAN could lead to huge benefits from easier and more economical connections with the region either through Singapore or otherwise.

In sum, there are multiple benefits for ASEAN and India to move towards a more liberal open skies policy. As the world recovers from the COVID-19 pandemic and supply chains look towards rearranging to reduce single country dependence, working towards further cooperation in civil aviation could form the base on which greater commercial relations are formed across India and ASEAN. However, the benefits can only be realised with a more liberal temperament from India with respect to international trade and commerce in general and the aviation sector in particular.

HUMAN SECURITY

31

Human Security: The ASEAN Perspective

Kasira Cheeppensook

The Association of Southeast Asian Nations (ASEAN) takes security seriously. The 1967 Bangkok Declaration establishing ASEAN ingrained "security from external interference" in the Association's psyche. Since then, ASEAN's vision of a regional security community — particularly in the context of the ASEAN Political-Security Community Blueprint — has highlighted not only peaceful coexistence but also a community that is "rules-based, people-oriented, people-centred...bound by fundamental principles, shared values and norms, in which our peoples enjoy human rights, fundamental freedoms and social justice." These aspirations are still being translated into practice, with differing views on whether and how ASEAN's notion of a people-oriented and people-centred (security) community could be realised.

ASEAN has also been long familiar with 'comprehensive security'. While the concept broadened the security horizon to include economic, socio-cultural and political aspects *inter alia*, it remained state-centric in the sense that the referent subject as well as the policy target is, in most cases, the state. The state posited itself as the main security provider. This could be problematic when the state fails to take responsibility to protect its citizens, or when it is the source of insecurity for its people through its actions or decision-making processes.

The turning point came in 1997 when ASEAN suffered from the Asian financial crisis which highlighted inadequacies in regional capacity to collectively alleviate mass social sufferings as well as the lack of a conceptual framework guiding programme action. A normative space started opening up for ASEAN to reconsider its way of working, resulting in closer cooperation, a "people-centred" ASEAN vision and a number of programme actions in attempts to realise that vision.

Regarding human-centric norms and experiences, ASEAN is no stranger to the concept of human rights which might arguably be perceived as intertwined closely with human security. ASEAN has formally accommodated the concept in several key political documents, including the legally binding ASEAN Charter which entered into force in December 2008. However, ASEAN's treatment of the concept has been coloured by some reservations regarding differences in historical, political, cultural and religious backgrounds, to name only a few. The ASEAN Human Rights Declaration, adopted in November 2012, reiterated some of these reservations which qualified the universality in human rights application and limited this to state interpretation in domestic implementation.

ASEAN treated the human security concept in a similar manner. ASEAN's pronouncements on human security in its formal documents and meetings have led prominent human rights scholar and activist Sriprapha Petcharamsee (Thailand's representative to the ASEAN Intergovernmental Commission on Human Rights, 2009–2012) to observe in 2013 that "not only is ASEAN still facing challenges in balancing state security and human security, any arguments for strong conceptual links between human security and human rights, which has been recognised and mainstreamed by the UN agencies as well as some Western countries, is still problematic."

Nevertheless, after the Asian financial crisis, statesmen such as Thailand's Foreign Minister Surin Pitsuwan made several efforts to mainstream the concept. At the ASEAN Foreign Ministers' Post-Ministerial Conference (with the ASEAN Dialogue Partners, including India) in 1998, he proposed that ASEAN set up a human security caucus. His proposal met with lukewarm response because of the uncertainty of the concept itself and the actions that it entailed. Over 20 years since Pitsuwan first mooted the idea, that uncertainty still prevails.

ASEAN continued to refer sporadically to human security in a number of statements, including the Chairman's Statement of the 14th ASEAN Regional Forum in 2007 which recognised that "the illicit use of small arms and light weapons posed a serious threat to human security in every part of the world." Though the concept was linked to non-traditional security issues, it is not clear whether human is the main referent subject instead of state-centric security. Assessing the changing norms and security mechanisms in ASEAN, Herman Joseph S Kraft in an article published in 2012 has observed that "even as elements of human security begin to be manifested in ASEAN plans and programmes, however, the concept of human security itself lacks a clear consensus within ASEAN on both what human security means and, consequently, how human security issues should be addressed within Southeast Asia."

Still, there is some optimism about the future of human security in ASEAN. Mely Caballero-Anthony in a 2004 article titled 'Revisioning Human Security in Southeast Asia' viewed human security as "finding a place in the regional security discourses" despite "structural constraints and problems with conceptual clarity", and that "human security is the concept that embodies the security concerns of societies; its argument is from the standpoint of the most vulnerable, who can articulate their security in their own terms, without being excluded and alienated." This might be the case and can even be seen as a development stage in the long process of normative localisation and acceptance. However, similar to the concept of human rights in the region, localisation could detract from the essence of the concept, watering it down and rendering it obscure.

The various programmes and discourses related to human security in ASEAN range from climate change to transnational crimes, such as drugs and human trafficking. The notion that human security is the means through which the most vulnerable could voice out their concerns needs to be balanced against domestic barriers and the structural design of ASEAN's decision-making processes. Some ASEAN member states have laws limiting and controlling the activities of non-government organisations. Although a number of ASEAN organs interact often with the civil society, the space and scope in which non-state actors can participate in or influence policymaking are still largely restricted.

This may affect ASEAN's extra-regional relations with its dialogue and strategic partners, especially in situations where ASEAN faces difficulties in managing regional crises stemming from domestic or internal developments in a member state. Some of these crises clearly have the potential to affect human security regionally, thus blurring the line between ASEAN's non-interference principle and the need for ASEAN's effective involvement to maintain regional peace and security. For example, the current crisis that has escalated in Myanmar after the military coup on 1 February 2021 prompted ASEAN's dialogue partners such as the United States and the European Union to impose a number of targeted sanctions on the military regime. These sanctions highlight human rights violations by the Myanmar military and human security concerns of the Myanmar people as a result of the coup. While recognising ASEAN's central role, these dialogue partners also highlight inclusion — in this case, all key stakeholders — as important in any regional effort to resolve the Myanmar crisis.

Other ASEAN dialogue partners such as India, however, have been largely silent on the Myanmar crisis, though expressing support for the ASEAN response. The human security dimension takes on greater salience when we consider how the clashes between the Myanmar army and the groups resisting the coup can affect India and, by extension, ASEAN-India dialogue relations. India's shared border with

Myanmar is also India's shared border with ASEAN; Myanmar is the land bridge for India's connectivity with and connection to Southeast Asia. Though the Myanmar link was not a feature of discussions when ASEAN-India dialogue relations began first with a Sectoral Dialogue Partnership in 1992 and later a full Dialogue Partnership in 1995, Myanmar's ASEAN membership in 1997 and its bilateral ties with India brought an additional consideration to ASEAN's initiatives for regional connectivity. The ASEAN connectivity dimension is also tied to India's 'Look East' policy which had gone through several iterations over 1991 to 2014, now succeeded by an 'Act East' policy. Both policies underscored India's interest to move from economic engagement to more strategic and security-related cooperation. In terms of economic engagement, Myanmar's overlapping membership in the Bay of Bengal Initiative for Multi-Sectoral Technical Cooperation seemed to promise some potential for ASEAN-India connectivity, mainly in the form of a trilateral highway that would link Moreh, India, with Mae Sot, Thailand, via Myanmar. However, ASEAN and India have not been able to fully explore the range of collaborative activities in non-traditional security areas, including migration and pandemics. Human security concerns do not appear much in the documents related to the ASEAN-India dialogue, apart from mention of the projects related to addressing food security, health and human resource development. There have been some recent changes, however.

The ASEAN-India Summit began in 2002 and became an annual event. The ASEAN-India Dialogue Partnership was then elevated to a Strategic Partnership in 2012. The Strategic Partnership was broad and flexible enough to accommodate a wide range of issues, but this broad flexibility also meant that joint initiatives required skillful manoeuvring and workmanship of those involved. For example, as co-chair of the 23rd ASEAN-India Senior Officials' Meeting in 2021, Thailand highlighted the impact of COVID-19 on development, advancing the idea of "human security transformation through innovation for health and well-beings". The pledge on connectivity rested on the "expedition of the India-Myanmar-Thailand Trilateral Highway project" with possible extensions to Laos, Cambodia and Vietnam.

The underlying importance of trade and investment in the ASEAN-India dialogue and the fact that Myanmar is the only ASEAN member state that shares its border with India set an interesting stage for how the Strategic Partnership could assist ASEAN's efforts to address the current humanitarian crisis in Myanmar. Within the COVID-19 context, India has provided vaccines to Myanmar and has further promised medical supplies to the ASEAN humanitarian initiative for Myanmar. To bolster ASEAN community-building, including ASEAN's vision to become a rules-based, people-centred community, India could also support the implementation of ASEAN's Five-Point Consensus on Myanmar by using its bilateral channels as well as helping to mitigate the humanitarian fallout by ensuring that conduct regarding cross-border influx of refugees falls within international human rights standards. The existing dialogue within the framework of the Strategic Partnership provides an additional venue for communications and normative engagement with all parties involved.

32

Foundations of Good Governance: Enduring Relevance of Human Security

D P K Pillay

India is one of the most diverse countries in the world in almost every category — culture, economy, climate, race, language and religion — and faces threats that cover the entire spectrum of conflict. Since independence, India has made much progress despite its various problems, which include widespread unrest and conflict, unresolved border issues, extreme poverty, high degree of unemployment, recurrent communal and political violence, crimes against women and children, including trafficking, high levels of corruption, reckless exploitation and exhaustion of natural resources, environmental degradation and rapid urbanisation and its associated challenges. India's pace of economic growth, its military might and demographic attributes have led it to rightly demand a place at the superpower high table.

At the same time, its future is beset with many pitfalls and shortcomings. Growth alone cannot help India emerge from poverty and the insecurities that millions of its people face every day. India is home to a third of the world's poorest people and is being outpaced by developing countries on several human development indicators. It is also geographically located in a region of three nuclear armed countries with a history of conflict amongst them.

Indian nationalist Mahatma Gandhi once said, "I shall strive for a constitution which will release India from all thralldom and patronage, and give her, if need be, the right to sin. I shall work for an India in which the poorest shall feel that it is their country, in whose making they have an effective voice; an India in which there shall be no high class and low class of people; an India in which all communities shall live in perfect harmony."

Human Security Approach in Social Upliftment

It is indisputable that a solution to the country's most pressing challenges might lie in the adoption of a human security approach and its operationalisation as inherited from the wisdom of the ancients. India has not sought to make human security a policy goal; instead, it has sought to operationalise the end-state envisioned by the human security advocates through a slew of social and economic security measures that attempt to place people at the centre of concerns.

Despite all the prophesies, India has remained committed to a democratic form of government — one that implies certain assurances and guarantees of freedoms and participation in social, economic and political processes. Though India offers freedom and democratic choice, where it lags is in the delivery of good governance and essential services to its many millions. Good governance is the key to equitable delivery and widespread growth, inclusive development and freedom of choice and opportunity. It has sought to find solutions to the challenges and non-traditional notions of security confronted by the people daily by embarking on several projects, policies and schemes to enhance the capabilities of the people, social opportunities and the economic empowerment of the people. This spans sectors from adult education, sewage and wastewater management to health, food security, child rights and minority welfare; the government has established dedicated ministers and ministries to execute and oversee its many programmes and policies.

The targets for India are greater than for several other countries in terms of population and their attainment is, therefore, no ordinary task. Many Indian programmes are unique in nature and gigantic in execution — the *Rashtriya Swasthya Bima Yojana* (a government-run health insurance programme for the Indian poor), the Mahatma Gandhi National Rural Employment Guarantee Act (MNREGA), the *Aadhaar* (biometric identification system) enrollment exercise and the *Jan Dhan Yojana* (financial inclusion programme) are but a few examples. Among the world-class systems in place are the Delhi Metro rail network as well as other urban systems that have helped displace polluting vehicles while providing cheap transportation to the masses. The green revolution made India self-sufficient in food grains and milk from being a donor dependent country until the 1970s. Similarly, in many states like Kerala, healthcare and education are comparable to those in the developed countries.

Human Security in Policymaking and Implementation

The plethora of social welfare schemes intended to benefit the people and underprivileged groups have resulted in some success but have failed to make a significant difference to the lives of the poorest. Corruption, gender inequality, a lack of decent work and political, religious and caste-based violence continue to hinder the development projects and affect the enjoyment of rights guaranteed by the constitution. One of the key reasons for the failure is that these myriad schemes function in silos without regard to inter-linkages. What is missing is the vision — both political and economic — that could bring together these plans and schemes under one umbrella. A human security approach could take the impact of these schemes further by identifying the needs and vulnerabilities of the people and measuring the final impact of the schemes to improve the overall well-being.

A government scheme, for example, might aim to admit a child in school, but does it also ensure that the education imparted is adequate and effective to attain employment? Having the child attend school is a welfare measure. Ensuring that the child gets an education that will lead to gainful employment is a human security approach. Linking the mid-day meal scheme for the children with school attendance has increased enrolment and improved sanitation and hygiene standards. However, what this enrolment has achieved is debatable because the attendance levels achieved in schools have not been matched by higher quality educational attainments as the standards of teaching and the facilities available in many schools are poor. An overarching and holistic vision must define an end-state, wherein school enrolments, coupled with nutrition and sanitation, will result in a healthy, skilled and secure workforce ready for the job market. Thus, instead of merely an education ministry target for an increase in school enrolment, a coordinated effort must involve targets for skills-building, health indicators, sanitation goals and job worthiness of the pupils enrolled.

Another example is in the implementation of the MNREGA, which seeks to provide guaranteed employment for a minimum of 100 days. A human security framework would enable an understanding of everyday challenges and long-term needs, in addition to mere employment for 100 days. This large available workforce can then be used to achieve community or regional targets, such as planned efforts for rainwater harvesting, thereby increasing the availability of fresh water and raising of water tables. It could also be part of an overall, coordinated plan to achieve rural connectivity within a certain period.

A third example is the multiplicity of identity cards held or required by Indian citizens. In addition to being cumbersome, this is also a security risk, as there have been instances of misuse of the cards for fraud and illegal activities. At great expense to the exchequer, the Unique Identification Development Authority of India (UIDAI) created the *Aadhaar* card, which has the holder's biometric details and thus cannot be duplicated. At the time of conceiving this project, a visionary approach would have ensured that all parameters necessary for the issue of a 'Below Poverty Line' card, a 'Scheduled Caste/Tribe' certificate, a 'Backward Caste' certificate, a ration card, a voter identity card and a Personal Account Number (PAN) card issued by the Income Tax Department would be captured in the *Aadhaar* card. A single card should be able to serve multiple purposes. Obtaining a PAN card or a voter identity card is not an easy process, especially for the poor or for migrants who do not have a permanent address and, therefore, no proper proof of residence. The number of *Aadhaar* cards issued in India is a record of sorts; no other country has carried out an exercise of this scale for the provision of identity and social security to its citizens.

A human security approach would have helped adopt a comprehensive solution to the need for identity, with security as well as access to public services. It would have identified these problems and found a permanent solution to the need for multiple processes, procedures and cards to access government services. The UIDAI is, therefore, a unique exercise but a wasted opportunity to ease the difficulties faced by the underprivileged and migrants in obtaining some form of identity.

The desired end-state of a human security approach is to ensure that India becomes an equitable society where all citizens enjoy equal protection and opportunities without the need for quotas and reservations. This requires that marginalised people are mainstreamed, and inclusion is an accepted norm. Inclusion is not achieved by way of handouts and limitless reservations. The emphasis should be on providing opportunities and choices through a systematic development of capabilities. If outcomes were more important than statistics, a human security approach would be a handy tool to understand contemporary challenges and find solutions that are holistic, achievable and sustainable.

Conclusion

It must be admitted that operating with a human security approach is more difficult than a conventional traditional security approach because it involves a change in thinking where 'people empowerment' becomes important. Toward this end, policymakers must emerge from their silos to implement welfare, development and security initiatives that involve all organs of the government in a coordinated manner. Real security can only be achieved if the potential or root causes of insecurity are addressed through a robust, visionary and long-term approach to human development. This can be done by using the human security approach and making people central to any intervention — responding to their insecurities instead of the security of the state.

The essence of human security can be found in one of Gandhi's last notes, "Whenever you are in doubt, apply the following test. Recall the face of the poorest and the weakest person you may have seen, and ask yourself, if the step you contemplate is going to be of any use to them. Will they gain anything by it and give them control over their life and destiny? Then your doubts and yourself melt away." Gandhi's thoughts were expressed not in the language of nationalism and religious or community identities but were also woven around the individual and the universality of basic human concerns. Bringing that individual — shorn of the trappings of religion, caste, class, gender and other forms of identity — to the centre of the security and development agenda would be a tribute to that vision.

Section V
CONCLUSION

33

Dynamics of ASEAN-India Relations

Ong Keng Yong

Relations between the Association of Southeast Asian Nations (ASEAN) and India have not measured up to expectations despite steady progression over the years. The most severe disappointment came with the decision of the present Narendra Modi government not to join the Regional Comprehensive Economic Partnership (RCEP) after years of negotiations. As perceived by ASEAN, it is a purely political choice at the expense of long-term strategic ties and economic growth trajectory with its Southeast Asian neighbours.

The end of the Cold War catalysed major changes to the ASEAN-India relationship. Prior to the early 1990s, forging both economic and political ties with ASEAN did not align with India's geo-political calculations. India did not see ASEAN as economically significant vis-à-vis India's own aspirations. In this vein, India maintained its protectionist economic policies towards the individual ASEAN member states and mostly disregarded the goals of the nascent ASEAN Free Trade Area, the precursor to the envisioned ASEAN Economic Community. Moreover, India and ASEAN also diverged ideologically during the Cold War as India had a close strategic relationship with the Soviet Union while ASEAN took an anti-communist stance.

The post-Cold War era saw India shifting its engagement with ASEAN. Credit was given to Prime Minister Narasimha Rao who developed a 'Look East' vision from his perception of a gradual strategic convergence of interests between India and ASEAN. Despite making considerable strides in the following decades — starting with a Sectoral Partnership with ASEAN in 1992 which blossomed into a full Dialogue Partnership in 1995, elevation to a Summit Partnership in 2002, and peaking at the Strategic Partnership level in 2012 — there has been a sense of cynicism on both sides pertaining to the current state and future of ASEAN-India relations.

Today, there are few in India rooting for closer ASEAN-India cooperation. Domestic concerns in India dominate the narrative on the prospects of the relationship which is shaped largely by exigencies and opportunities that may arise from time to time. India's economic ties with ASEAN have much to achieve, given the limitations of India's export sector and the government prioritising domestic manufacturing. Therefore, India may not value ASEAN as a huge export market, unlike other major and regional powers. Although Modi regularly megaphoned an 'Act East' policy based on the 'Look East' vision, aimed at boosting India's visibility and profile in ASEAN/Southeast Asia, India's priorities remain South Asia and the Indian Ocean.

Strategically, ASEAN seems unlikely to be on India's radar, even in the aftermath of a coup by Myanmar's military (*Tatmadaw*) deposing a democratically elected government. Though New Delhi did not invite a representative of the State Administration Council military regime to the Special ASEAN-India Foreign Ministers Meeting in June 2022, it has not consulted with ASEAN to address the unstable situation in neighbouring Myanmar, which is strategically important to India. Perhaps India's geo-political calculus deems it necessary to avoid antagonising the *Tatmadaw*, in view of the complexities of ethnic separatist insurgencies in India's northeast and western Myanmar.

New Delhi also appears reluctant to consult with ASEAN on the concept of the Indo-Pacific, as advocated by the United States (US),

Japan and other European countries. Whether this is due to India's seeking out a rather hegemonic influence over the Indian Ocean, owing to its geo-strategic location as the 'natural centre of gravity' in the Indian Ocean region or the lack of faith in ASEAN's capability and capacity, the need to engage each other is critical in an age of intense power competition and rivalry between China and the US. Indian strategic thinking seems to consider the Indian Ocean as 'India's Ocean'; hence, extra-regional consultations on the Indian Ocean is an insult to India's dominance over what many in New Delhi believe is its own backyard.

Experts in and out of the region have pointed out that there are constraints to India's bid for a major role in the Indian Ocean. They see the significant military presence of the US in the Indian Ocean and the adjacent seas in Arabia, East Africa and Southeast Asia as becoming more prominent rather than fading quietly into the horizon. New Delhi's fairly lacklustre relations with the regional powers in these areas, and India's traditional instincts against close security cooperation with other states are regarded as outdated. Perhaps the chief constraint comes from China's efforts in the Indian Ocean which has poked a big hole in India's preconceived notion of Indian dominance in the Indian Ocean.

While India has expressed the desire to play a big role in international organisations, it does not stem so much from a belief in multilateralism than from a pursuit of global power credentials. The country's reluctance to move concretely on specific initiatives in multilateral platforms, which are seen as particularly important to the nations on the rim of the Indian Ocean and the surrounding seas, is glaring. New Delhi is viewed as more interested in taking its dues from the Western countries that have long dominated international organisations. With ASEAN-led multilateralism, India's interest remains inadequate as it continues to favour bilateral partnerships to advance national interests.

However, India has been shaky even with bilateral endeavours and is yet to prove itself as a constructive and reliable partner in such undertakings. There seems insufficient focus on the strategic and longer-term considerations. Indeed, many experts in ASEAN see an Indian preoccupation with Pakistan and that country's relations with China and other regional states. The initially limited Indian involvement in the multilateral efforts to contain the COVID-19 pandemic was viewed unfavourably in some quarters as India is one of the world's largest producers of vaccines against infectious diseases. (Today, India exports large quantities to countries needing the vaccines.)

Regardless of whether India backtracks on its commitments to ASEAN (especially on the RCEP) and the individual member states in the Southeast Asian grouping, it has decided on ASEAN not being as strategically important as studying the value of the Quadrilateral Security Dialogue (also called the Quad). The more the four Quad countries — the US, Australia, Japan and India — manage to concretely structure the Quad, the less critical will 'ASEAN centrality' be. However, the big question is whether India is actually comfortable enough with the Quad to further substantiate this concept of a security mechanism in the Indian Ocean and the contiguous neighbourhood.

A fundamental concern is India's hierarchical attitude vis-à-vis its relations with other countries and a preference for "strategic autonomy" which invariably excludes the major powers from the Indian Ocean. As such, aligning India's strategic policies with those of its Quad partners in the region will be a problem. However, if the Quad becomes more substantive to Indian strategic perception and calculations, then where does ASEAN centrality stand? Many regional experts share one strand of thought: New Delhi sees strategic ties as a zero-sum game. It has not yet reconciled to the notion of a win-win situation in engaging ASEAN as a collective as well as engaging individual ASEAN member states on their own merit, notably Indonesia, Myanmar and Thailand, which are key states on the eastern rim of the Indian Ocean.

It will not be easy for India to accept any sort of intervention by its Quad partners in the Indian Ocean because India sees itself as superior, being the largest democracy in the world. Going forward, these kinds of formulations will not work. Singapore tried to draw India into the economic orbit of the East Asian market to which India responded with hesitancy and eventual resistance, stressing that the country is economically not ready to be a part of any East Asian economic integration. India is not willing to be involved on other people's terms as Indian elites see their country as a global power with a "natural" mandate to exercise dominance over the Indian Ocean, owing to a geography which places India in the centre of the Indian Ocean.

However, the efficacy of this Indian Ocean centre-point is dubious. In theory, India can play the role of a strategic fulcrum in the region, particularly with an assertive China. Yet, the defining characteristic of such a role is the ability to balance conflicting interests of multiple powers. From its strategic standpoint, however, India must be the dominating and overriding factor in Indian Ocean affairs. On the other hand, major powers like the US and China will not accept that, even though Washington has publicly stated that India is a key security provider in the region and the US is willing to cooperate with India to maintain peace and stability in the Indian Ocean.

For experts in and beyond ASEAN, it is important that India plays a significant role in the maintenance of regional security and economic progress without describing it in contentious terms. Apart from economic prospects, in the socio-cultural arena, there has been so much Indian influence in Southeast Asia over the centuries. The Indian culture and philosophy have a strong following around the world and its digital competency is well recognised. If India can keep itself open and welcoming in terms of the economy, social connectivity and development, that would be attractive enough for ASEAN to bank on India for the contemporary Southeast Asian blend of open regionalism.

Looking ahead, the base-line of the future of India revolves around its regional influence in the Indian Ocean. If there can be a bit more strategic balance in the Indian political and economic approach towards the member nations of ASEAN, and if India focuses on its touted democratic and demographic dividends, much mutual benefit can come out of it. Many in ASEAN believe that India's potential is enormous. The raw material for the country's growth and regional strength is there. The challenge is to use it judiciously.

34

India and ASEAN: The Past and the Future

P Kumaran

India and the Association of Southeast Asian Nations (ASEAN) region have enjoyed strong cultural and trade links for over a millennium. In 1992, the relationship was suddenly turbo-charged with a series of policy initiatives, leading to India's first-ever Comprehensive Economic Cooperation Agreement (with Singapore), several bilateral free trade agreements (FTA) and the India-ASEAN FTA. Growing ties with ASEAN were initially described in India as the 'Look East' policy. This was upgraded to the 'Act East' policy in 2014, the evolution reflecting greater attention to physical and virtual connectivity projects and expanding security content. From Dialogue Partners in 1992, we have now become Strategic Partners, this year marking 30 years of our engagement.

Our trade and investment flows have multiplied several times. Consequently, ASEAN is today India's fourth largest trading partner and accounts for more than a tenth of our total trade. In turn, India is ASEAN's seventh largest trading partner, with bilateral trade at over US$86 billion. Investment flows are also substantial both ways, with ASEAN accounting for approximately 18 percent of investment flows into India and over 20 percent of India's outbound investments since 2000. Singapore is the principal hub of both inward and outward investments.

As businesses on both sides started expanding mutually, connectivity became both a driver and an outcome. Air links have expanded rapidly, and we are extending highways and multi-modal links deep into continental Southeast Asia with new urgency. Indeed, over the last 25 years, inter-penetration and travel between India and ASEAN have been so extensive that most Indians now think of this region as part of their neighbourhood. Growing connectivity and the sense of proximity it has created have also put India among the fastest growing sources of tourists for Southeast Asia. The six million-strong Indian diaspora in the region — rooted in diversity and brimming with dynamism — constitutes an extraordinary human bond between us.

ASEAN represents the commercial, physical and cultural crossroads of Asia. It brings together a number of extra-regional players through various mechanisms such as the ASEAN Regional Forum, East Asia Summit, and ASEAN Defence Ministers' Meeting-Plus (ADMM-Plus). ASEAN is also a region of immense economic opportunities and includes most of India's significant emerging partners. What happens in the South China Sea, the Western Pacific or the Straits of Malacca has profound implications for India's security and prosperity. Involvement with ASEAN has indeed heightened India's maritime consciousness, motivating it to pursue its maritime interests with greater vigour.

Engagement with ASEAN is one of the key vectors of India's 'Act East' policy, and of our broader engagement in the Indo-Pacific region, as the ASEAN region represents one of our largest markets, a participant in our key value chains, a source of remittances and a valued technology partner. We have excellent political ties, marked by warmth, respect and goodwill. We also have expanding defence and security cooperation. ASEAN is a 650-million strong population with a demographic that is similar to that of India, a 35-percent youth population and an economy of over US$3 trillion. There is a tremendous growth in urbanisation and digitalisation. All these present a big opportunity for India.

India-ASEAN relations are also remarkably free from contestations and claims. We have a common vision for the future, built on a commitment to inclusion and integration, belief in sovereign equality of all nations irrespective of size and support for free and open pathways of commerce and engagement. India's own thinking about regionalism was impacted by ASEAN, as it now consciously seeks to ensure that its neighbours also benefit from its growth and prosperity.

ASEAN, as a project, has been a great stabiliser in the region and has the potential to be a great influencer. However, it faces a new power equilibrium and rivalries, greater political and geo-strategic unpredictability, geo-economic upheavals and multiple issues relating to rules and norms, posing new challenges to its autonomy, unity, cohesiveness and resilience.

Creating a stable balance in Asia is one of India's top-most priorities, as we believe that only a multipolar Asia can lead to a multipolar world. ASEAN thus perceives value in engaging India and leveraging its ability to shape a multipolar and balanced Asia.

India's 1991 crisis and the economic reforms it triggered made India look towards the model of economic growth adopted by successful Asian economies. What started as an economic correction in India increasingly factored in political developments and ended up more as a strategic initiative. The original agenda of trade, investments and economic links steadily grew into something much larger. It also went beyond ASEAN to cover Japan, Korea and China. In more recent years, this outreach has expanded further to include Australia and the Pacific islands.

As India grew economically, its dependence on maritime trade routes and the open sea lanes of communication became vital for its national interests. This, along with changing power equations in the region, motivated India to expand its security links with ASEAN by joining various fora such as the ASEAN Regional Forum, East Asia Summit and ADMM-Plus. The relationship has now moved well beyond the economic and cultural dimensions, with numerous institutionalised dialogue mechanisms at various levels.

The security and stability of the Indo-Pacific region will be an inevitable component of international security in the 21st century. India's expanding presence in the Indian Ocean region, and the Indo-Pacific in general, is of overriding security consequence. India's first integrated maritime outlook, summarised by the evocative acronym SAGAR (Security and Growth for All in the Region), was released in 2015. This approach involves advancing cooperation and using our capabilities for the larger good, apart from deepening economic and security cooperation with our maritime neighbours.

ASEAN now occupies a central place in the security architecture of the Indo-Pacific region, from the Indian perspective. India collaborates with ASEAN on humanitarian assistance and disaster relief initiatives, is a part of the Regional Cooperation Agreement on Combating Piracy and Armed Robbery against Ships in Asia (ReCAAP) and participates in various cooperation mechanisms in the Straits of Malacca and Singapore. Our regional engagement is also strengthened by a broad range of bilateral defence and security relationships with all ASEAN member states. India also started participating more regularly in military exercises and joint training engagements to promote greater understanding and inter-operability.

There is still considerable scope for India to expand cooperation with ASEAN and other key powers to enhance net security in the region. Prominent areas of interest include capacity-building programmes, connectivity, counter-terrorism, cybersecurity, maritime security and helping build a multilateral rules-based order in the region. There are also opportunities to work together to develop infrastructure, affordable vaccines and life-saving medicines, apart from cooperation in the blue economy, be it in areas such as tackling plastic debris in oceans, hydrological surveys, marine pollution and illegal, unreported and unregulated fishing. There is also merit in strengthening e-commerce and payment system links, as this could help micro, small and medium-sized enterprises (MSME) on both sides.

The 'Act East' policy and greater maritime activities are already helping revive India's east coast ports that were extinguished during the colonial period. Their revival, along with the development of connecting ports in Bangladesh and Myanmar, coupled with completion of the Kaladan multimodal project and the India-Myanmar-Thailand Trilateral Highway, will significantly augment connectivity between the South Asian Association for Regional Cooperation and ASEAN.

Over the years, ASEAN has hugely benefited from investment-led participation in the global value chains (GVCs) and regional value chains. India aims to do the same in the coming years by promoting large investments in the manufacturing sector. As the idea of supply chain resilience gathers momentum, India also hopes to benefit from some of the relocation of supply chains in the Asian region. The Production Linked Incentive scheme, announced by the Indian government in a number of carefully selected sectors, and the relentless push to enhance ease of doing business are big steps, powered by the belief that a credible 'Make in India' programme will also contribute to resilient global supply chains, given India's strengths in information technology, start-ups, pharmaceuticals, human capital and culture. Younger demographics and a greater sense of self-assurance will continue to propel India's march forward in the coming decades.

The criticality of the Indian Ocean to global trade and development will continue to increase as Asia rises. This will be both an opportunity and a challenge, and India is preparing to fully shoulder its responsibilities. As such, it has entered into a number of white shipping agreements, arrangements for exclusive economic zone surveillance cooperation, anti-piracy patrols, growing cooperation under the Indian Ocean Naval Symposium framework and collaboration under the Indian Ocean Rim Association umbrella. The development of the Andaman and Nicobar Islands would also be a significant game-changer.

India views the Indo-Pacific as a geographic and strategic expanse, with ASEAN as a bridge connecting the two great oceans. Prime Minister Narendra Modi articulated India's Indo-Pacific approach at the Shangri-La Dialogue in Singapore in 2018. His vision was one of a free, open and inclusive region with Southeast Asia at its centre, underpinned by a shared belief in a common rules-based order applied to all states individually and to the global commons, freedom of navigation, unimpeded commerce and peaceful settlement of disputes. In essence, this was a call for an Asia of cooperation rather than of rivalry.

India's approach towards the Indo-Pacific region is further elaborated in its Indo-Pacific Oceans Initiative (IPOI), which emphasises mutual respect, dialogue, cooperation, peace and prosperity (represented by the Hindi acronym '5S'). It also includes promoting a rules-based international order; keeping the seas, space and airways free and open; the region secure from terrorism; cyberspace free from disruption and conflict; keeping economies open and engagement transparent; and sharing resources, markets and prosperity. All our bilateral and plurilateral initiatives in the region are within the framework of our commitment to these broad principles. Like the ASEAN Outlook on the Indo-Pacific, the IPOI emphasises ASEAN centrality, a rules-based framework and abiding respect for sovereignty.

It is often felt that the lack of foreign direct investment (FDI)-linked intra-industry manufacturing trade between India and ASEAN appears to be a limiting factor in GVC linkages. Early completion of the ASEAN-India Trade in Goods Agreement review and addressing outstanding issues in a substantive manner, as part of the review process, can help reach the full potential of our trade. On the other hand, the digitalisation of agriculture and MSMEs on both sides promises to open new opportunities to enhance trade.

India should look at greater integration in service sector value-chains with ASEAN, as the latter's share of India's service exports is less than five percent. Market access for Indian service-providers in key modes and sub-sectors is still subject to restrictions arising from a lack of mutual recognition, commercial presence conditions and visa/immigration requirements. These regulatory and other barriers need to be addressed. Outward FDI by Indian service companies could help reduce the extent of the problem, as has already happened in some cases. India should also make efforts to enter the ASEAN manufacturing market by exploring the possibility of providing services content in ASEAN's manufacturing value chains, thus taking advantage of the growing trend of 'servicification' in the manufacturing industries and offering 'solutions' that conveniently bundle products and services in a manner that delivers greater value to clients.

India's northeastern region is an important pivot in enabling its 'Act East' policy, but its strategic potential has not been realised yet. Links with Southeast Asia will accelerate its progress. In turn, a connected and growing northeast will be a stronger bridge to ASEAN. There is a need to enhance its economic and trade linkages with ASEAN, taking advantage of the emerging opportunities and gearing up the northeast in terms of human resources, public health and intra-regional connectivity (perhaps involving Bangladesh) with railways, highways and waterways and streamlining of cross-border trade.

India is today making a determined effort to modernise infrastructure, expand manufacturing, enhance the quality of human resources, deepen the formalisation of the economy and remove impediments to economic efficiency. There is a lot that India has learned and continues to learn from the ASEAN region. India's consistent effort has been to expand its engagement and reinforce key dimensions like security, connectivity and doing more business. However, to be productive and effective over time, our approaches towards engagement require continuous refreshing and adaptation.

About the Editors

Professor Tommy Koh is a Professor of Law at the National University of Singapore and an Ambassador-at-Large at the Ministry of Foreign Affairs. He is the Co-Chairman of the China-Singapore Forum and the Japan-Singapore Symposium. He served as the founding Co-Chairman of the India-Singapore Strategic Dialogue for 10 years.

Mr Hernaikh Singh is Deputy Director at the Institute of South Asian Studies in the National University of Singapore. He has more than 30 years of experience in Singapore government and non-government organisations, business sector and academia. He holds a Master's degree in Arts (Southeast Asian Studies) from NUS. For his outstanding academic achievements, he was awarded the Dr Benjamin Batson Gold Medal. He graduated with a Bachelor of Arts (Honours) degree from the same university.

Ms Moe Thuzar focuses on Myanmar and ASEAN (regional governance issues with particular focus on the areas under the ASEAN Socio-Cultural Community). She was with the ASEAN Studies Centre at ISEAS, starting from its establishment in 2008 to August 2019. Prior to joining the Centre, she headed the ASEAN Secretariat's Human Development Unit, which coordinated ASEAN cooperation in labour, youth, social welfare, education, women's affairs, poverty reduction and rural development and civil service matters. At ISEAS, Ms Thuzar is also co-coordinator of the ISEAS' Myanmar Studies.

About the Authors

Dr S Jaishankar is currently the External Affairs Minister of India. In a four-decade diplomatic career, he served as the Foreign Secretary as well as India's Ambassador to the United States, China, Singapore and the Czech Republic. He was also President (Global Corporate Affairs) at Tata Sons Pvt Ltd and a Distinguished Visiting Research Fellow at the Institute of South Asian Studies in the National University of Singapore.

Dr Vivian Balakrishnan is Singapore's Minister for Foreign Affairs. He previously served as the Minister-in-charge of the Smart Nation Initiative; Minister for the Environment and Water Resources; Minister for Community Development, Youth and Sports; Second Minister for Trade and Industry; Minister-in-charge of Entrepreneurship; Second Minister for Information, Communications and the Arts; and Minister of State for National Development. Before becoming a Member of Parliament in 2001, he was the Chief Executive Officer of Singapore General Hospital. He became the Medical Director of Singapore National Eye Centre in 1999. He studied Medicine at the National University of Singapore after being awarded the President's Scholarship in 1980.

Dato Lim Jock Hoi is the Secretary-General of ASEAN. He was previously the Permanent Secretary of the Ministry of Foreign Affairs and Ministry of Trade, Brunei Darussalam, and was Brunei

Darussalam's Senior Official in the ASEAN Economic Community Pillar, the Asia-Pacific Economic Cooperation and the Asia-Europe Meeting. He served on the High-Level Task Force on ASEAN Economic Integration (HLTF-EI) and was the HLTF-EI Chair in 2017. He was also Chairman of the Governing Board of the Economic Research Institute for ASEAN and East Asia. He was conferred 'The Most Honourable Order of Seri Paduka Mahkota Brunei' award by His Majesty Sultan Hassanal Bolkiah Mu'izzaddin Waddaulah in 2007.

Section I: History

Ms Nalina Gopal is an independent curator and researcher in Singapore where she runs a historical research and museum consultancy, Antāti. She was, until earlier this year, a curator at the Indian Heritage Centre (IHC) and oversaw its curatorial team. She has curated several landmark exhibitions drawing out the diversity and material heritage of Indians in Singapore and Southeast Asia. Her recent co-edited book is *Sojourners to Settlers: Tamils in Southeast Asia and Singapore*, a Singapore bicentennial commemorative publication of the IHC and Institute of Policy Studies.

Professor S D Muni is Professor Emeritus at Jawaharlal Nehru University, New Delhi, and an Honorary Fellow at the Institute of South Asian Studies in the National University of Singapore and National Institute of Security Studies, Sri Lanka. He is also a former ambassador and special envoy of the Indian Government. He has published widely; his latest book, co-authored with Rahul Mishra, is *India's Eastward Engagement: From Antiquity to Act East Policy* (SAGE International Publishers, 2019).

Section II: Areas of Convergence

Mr Manu Bhaskaran is a Partner of the Centennial Group, a strategic advisory firm headquartered in Washington, D.C. As the Founding

Chief Executive Officer of its Singapore subsidiary, Centennial Asia Advisors, he coordinates the Asian business of the Group which provides independent economic research on Asian political and macro-economic trends. He is an Adjunct Senior Fellow at the Institute of Policy Studies in the National University of Singapore.

Dr Amitendu Palit is a Senior Research Fellow and Research Lead (Trade and Economics) at the Institute of South Asian Studies in the National University of Singapore. He specialises in international trade and investment policies, geo-economics, Asian connectivity, regional political economy and the Indian economy. Earlier, he worked for several years in the finance, industry and civil supplies ministries in India.

Dr Francis Mark A Quimba is a Research Fellow at the Philippine Institute for Development Studies and Director of the Philippine APEC Study Center Network. He has worked on several research topics, including agriculture, trade and rural development. His current research interest is in the innovation activities of local firms. He has participated in roundtable discussions on issues of trade, industrial development, innovation and e-commerce.

Dr Rahul Sen is a Senior Lecturer at the School of Economics in the Faculty of Business, Economics and Law in Auckland University of Technology, New Zealand. He is also a Fellow at the New Zealand-India Research Institute in Victoria University, Wellington, New Zealand. He was previously Fellow at the ISEAS-Yusof Ishak Institute, Singapore, from 2003 to 2007.

Mr Karan Singh Thakral is the Executive Director of the Thakral Group, a Singaporean business operating in real estate, retail, manufacturing, technology, logistics and distribution, with offices in 30 countries. He has led the group's Indian operations for four decades and has led and served in several government and industry bodies focused on India. He has also served as Singapore's Non-Resident Ambassador to Denmark and Sri Lanka. He has a keen interest in India-ASEAN relations.

Dr Naushad Forbes is the Co-Chairman of Forbes Marshall, India's leading steam engineering and control instrumentation firm. He is also the Chairman of Ananta Aspen Centre, Bharatiya Yuva Shakti Trust and Centre for Technology, Innovation and Economic Research in India. He was an occasional lecturer at Stanford University (1987–2004) and sits on the boards of several educational institutions and public companies. An active member of the Confederation of Indian Industry (CII), he was President of CII in 2016–2017.

Dr Sinderpal Singh is a Senior Fellow and Assistant Director at the Institute of Defence and Strategic Studies (IDSS) and concurrently Coordinator of the South Asia Programme, IDSS, at the S. Rajaratnam School of International Studies in Nanyang Technological University, Singapore. He has published articles in several international journals and his single-authored book is entitled *India in South Asia: Domestic Identity Politics and Foreign Policy from Nehru to the BJP* (Routledge 2013).

Dr T C A Raghavan is India's former High Commissioner to Pakistan and Singapore. He is currently Director General, Indian Council of World Affairs, New Delhi, India. He is the author of several books, including *Attendant Lords: Bairam Khan and Abdur Rahim, Courtiers and Poets in Mughal India* (HarperCollins, 2018), *The People Next Door: The Curious History of India's Relations with Pakistan* (HarperCollins, 2017) and *History Men: Jadunath Sarkar, G S Sardesai, Raghubir Sinh and Their Quest for India's Past* (Collins India, 2019).

Dr Myo Thant is an economist with the Asian Development Bank (ADB). Earlier, he taught in New York University and worked at the United Nations. At ADB, he develops new forms of regional economic cooperation such as the growth triangles and economic corridors, especially in the Greater Mekong Subregion. He is also an authority on the economic analysis of global public health issues such as HIV/AIDS.

Dr Prabir De is a Professor at the Research and Information System for Developing Countries, New Delhi, where he coordinates the ASEAN-India Centre. He works in the field of international economics and has research interests in international trade and development. He has a PhD in Economics from the Jadavpur University, Kolkata. He has contributed several research papers in international journals and written books on trade and development.

Associate Professor Sophana Srichampa is Chair for the Centre for Bharat Studies at the Research Institute for Languages and Cultures of Asia in Mahidol University, Thailand. Her research background is on the social, religious, linguistic and cultural issues of the ethnic, diasporic and migrant worker groups in Thailand and Southeast Asia. She also focuses on Indian studies, connectivity through the trilateral highway and people-to-people collaboration.

Dr Rajeev Ranjan Chaturvedy is the Founder of Lilawati Memorial Library in Kaimur district of Bihar and Associate Professor in the interdisciplinary School of Historical Studies and School of International Relations at Nalanda University, Bihar, India. He is the Coordinator of the Centre for Bay of Bengal Studies and the Centre for Conflict Resolution & Peace Studies at Nalanda University.

Ms Tan Ming Hui is an Associate Research Fellow in the Policy Studies Group at the S. Rajaratnam School of International Studies in Nanyang Technological University, Singapore. She previously worked as an Associate Librarian at the National Library Board (Singapore). Her research interests include Japan's foreign policy and the international relations of Northeast Asia.

Ms Nazia Hussain is a Senior Analyst in the Centre for Multilateralism Studies at the S. Rajaratnam School of International Studies in Nanyang

Technological University, Singapore. Earlier, she interned at the Centre for Humanitarian Dialogue, Singapore. Her research interests include Indian Ocean security, Sino-Indian relations, ASEAN and regional security and insurgency in Northeast India and its trans-national linkages.

Dr Shankari Sundararaman is a Professor of Southeast Asian Studies at the Centre for Indo-Pacific Studies in Jawaharlal Nehru University, New Delhi, India. She has been a Visiting Fellow at the Asia-Pacific College of Diplomacy at the Australian National University and the Centre for Strategic and International Studies in Jakarta, Indonesia.

Section III: Areas of Differences

Ms Sulaimah Mahmood is Senior Director, ASEAN & Southeast Asia Oceania (Trade Division), at the Ministry of Trade and Industry, Singapore. She was involved with the administration of the Generalised System of Preferences Scheme and in overseeing trade relations with the United States, Europe and the World Trade Organization. She was posted to the Asia-Pacific Economic Cooperation Secretariat (1996–1998) as Special Assistant to the Chair of Committee on Trade and Investment and as Director of the Subcommittee on Customs Procedures.

Ambassador Sudhir T Devare is a former Indian diplomat. He was Ambassador to South Korea, Ukraine, Armenia, Georgia and Indonesia. He also served as Secretary (Permanent) in the Indian Ministry of External Affairs and was closely associated with the implementation of India's 'Look East' policy. He was a Senior Visiting Research Fellow, Institute of Southeast Asian Studies, Singapore; Fellow, Weatherhead Center, Harvard University, Cambridge, United States; and Director General, Indian Council of World Affairs.

Mr Kavi Chongkittavorn is a Senior Fellow at the Institute of Security and International Studies in Chulalongkorn University, Thailand. He was editor-in-chief of *Myanmar Times* (2017), after a three-decade long stint with *The Nation*, an English daily in Thailand, from 1984–2013 as a reporter, editor, managing editor and editorial writer. He was special assistant to the ASEAN Secretary General in 1994–1995. He is now a columnist for *The Bangkok Post*.

Ms Moe Thuzar is an ISEAS-Yusof Ishak Institute Fellow and co-coordinator of the ISEAS Myanmar Studies Programme. She was previously a lead researcher at the ASEAN Studies Centre at ISEAS. She joined ISEAS in 2008 after 10 years at the ASEAN Secretariat, heading the Human Development Unit in her last three years there. She has contributed to several compendia and volumes on ASEAN and Myanmar.

Ambassador Shivshankar Menon is a Visiting Professor at Ashoka University, India; Chair of the Ashoka Centre for China Studies; and Distinguished Visiting Research Fellow at the Institute of South Asian Studies in the National University of Singapore. He was previously India's National Security Advisor and Foreign Secretary, and India's Ambassador/High Commissioner to China, Pakistan, Sri Lanka and Israel. He has published *Choices: Inside the Making of Indian Foreign Policy* (Brookings Institution Press, 2016) and *India and Asian Geopolitics; The Past, Present* (Brookings Institution Press, 2021).

Ms Hoang Thi Ha is a Senior Fellow and Co-coordinator of the Regional Strategic and Political Studies Programme at the ISEAS-Yusof Ishak Institute, Singapore. Before the current position, she was a Lead Researcher at the ASEAN Studies Centre at ISEAS and Head of the Political Cooperation Division in the ASEAN Secretariat. Her research interests include major powers in Southeast Asia, South China

Sea disputes, ASEAN in the Indo-Pacific discourse and ASEAN's institutional building.

Professor C Raja Mohan is a Visiting Research Professor at the Institute of South Asian Studies (ISAS) in the National University of Singapore and a Senior Fellow at the Asia Society Policy Institute, New Delhi, India. Earlier, he served as the Director of ISAS. He has been associated with several Indian think tanks, including Carnegie India and the Observer Research Foundation. He has published widely on India's foreign policy and Asia's geopolitics.

Section IV: Looking to the Future

Dr Limin Hee is the Director of Research at Singapore's Centre for Liveable Cities, a nexus and knowledge centre for liveable and sustainable cities, where she focuses on research strategies, content development and international collaborations. She played similar leading research roles at the National University of Singapore School of Design and Environment, the Centre for Sustainable Asian Cities and the Asia Research Institute.

Mr Aaron Maniam is currently Deputy Secretary (Industry and Information) at Singapore's Ministry of Communications and Information, overseeing various aspects of domestic and international digitalisation policy. He previously served in various government roles, including as founding Head of the Centre for Strategic Futures and First Secretary at Singapore's Embassy in Washington, D.C. He is a 'World Cities Summit Young Global Leader'.

Dr Pushpa Pathak is currently a Senior Visiting Fellow at the Centre for Policy Research, New Delhi, India. She works on urban development issues. She has a PhD degree in Regional Development from Jawaharlal Nehru University, New Delhi. She participated in the Special Program in Urban and Regional Studies at the Massachusetts Institute of Technology, Cambridge, United States.

Dr Marie-Hélène Zérah is a senior researcher at the Institute of Research for Development, Paris, France. She is presently on a senior visiting fellowship at the Centre for Policy Research, New Delhi, India. She is currently working on the role of small towns in India, urban energy transformation and the governance of smart cities. She has published on issues of right to the city and urban democracy.

Dr Jayant Menon joined the ISEAS-Yusof Ishak Institute, Singapore, in 2020 as a Visiting Senior Fellow to continue his work on trade and development in the Asian region, following his early retirement from the Asian Development Bank, where he was Lead Economist in the Office of the Chief Economist. He holds adjunct appointments with the Australian National University, University of Nottingham and the Institute for Democracy and Economic Affairs, Malaysia.

Dr Arpita Mukherjee is a Professor at the Indian Council for Research on International Economic Relations, New Delhi, India. She has over 25 years of experience in policy oriented research, working closely with the governments in India and abroad. She specialises in trade, investment and trade agreements. She has over 80 publications and is a member of government committees and policy panels.

Ms Sharon Seah is a Senior Fellow and Coordinator at the ASEAN Studies Centre and the Climate Change in Southeast Asia Programme at the ISEAS-Yusof Ishak Institute, Singapore. Her research interests are in the ASEAN rule of law, multilateralism, climate change and the environment.

Dr Arunabha Ghosh has been the founder Chief Executive Officer of the Council on Energy, Environment and Water, New Delhi, India, since

2010, and a public policy professional, adviser, author, columnist and institution builder. He was invited by France to advise on the COP21 negotiations and helped conceptualise and design the International Solar Alliance. He co-founded the Clean Energy Access Network and was nominated to the United Nations Committee for Development Policy in 2018.

Ms Sanjana Chhabra is a Research Analyst at the Council on Energy, Environment and Water, New Delhi, India and she works with the Chief Executive Officer. Her current research includes hydrogen, energy access and energy transition. She has previously worked at ICF and the National Council of Applied Economic Research as a researcher. She was a sportsperson and represented India in many international shooting events.

Mr Ridha Aditya Nugraha developed the Air and Space Law Studies at the International Business Law Programme in Universitas Prasetiya Mulya, Indonesia. In 2019 and 2020, he was engaged as an ASEAN Passenger Protection Support Expert at the EU-EASA ARISE Plus Civil Aviation Project in ASEAN. Before joining the academia, he worked with a Jakarta-based law firm, a Dutch low-fare airline and a Danish international consulting firm.

Dr Deeparghya Mukherjee is an Associate Professor of Economics at the Indian Institute of Management, Nagpur, India, and a Visiting Research Fellow at the Institute of South Asian Studies in the National University of Singapore. His research interests include international trade and economic relations with a focus on South and Southeast Asia. His recent edited volume is *Economic Integration in Asia: Key Prospects and Challenges with the RCEP* (Routledge, 2019).

Dr Kasira Cheeppensook is an Assistant Professor in the Department of International Relations in the Faculty of Political Science, Chulalongkorn University, Thailand. She is currently the Director of Political Science

Doctoral Programme and Deputy Director of the Centre for Social and Development Studies. Her research interests include ASEAN, normative transition and human security.

Colonel (Dr) D P K Pillay is a Fellow at Manohar Parrikar Institute for Defence Studies and Analyses, New Delhi, India. He served as a Defence Specialist in the National Security Council Secretariat; Planning Officer in the International Cooperation Wing of the Ministry of Defence; and Military Advisor with the International Committee of the Red Cross. In 2019, he was nominated amongst the 'Researchers who Change the World' for his paper on food security.

Section V: Conclusion

Ambassador Ong Keng Yong is the Executive Deputy Chairman of the S. Rajaratnam School of International Studies in Nanyang Technological University, Singapore. He was previously High Commissioner of Singapore to India and, later, Secretary-General of ASEAN. He co-chairs the India-Singapore Strategic Dialogue with his Indian counterpart.

Mr P Kumaran has been India's High Commissioner to Singapore since July 2020. Previously, he was Ambassador (Qatar), Deputy High Commissioner (Sri Lanka), Counsellor (United States and Pakistan), First Secretary (Belgium), Second Secretary (Libya) and Third Secretary (Egypt). He also served as Deputy Secretary (Europe West) and Joint Secretary (Consular, Passport and Visa Division) in India's Ministry of External Affairs. Ambassador Kumaran has a BTech in Electronics and Communication from the Indian Institute of Technology-Madras (Chennai).

Index

A
Aadhaar (biometric identification system), 211, 267
Abe, Shinzo, 182
accommodation, 152
accountability, 212
'Act East' policy, 12–14, 28, 43, 50, 63, 64, 73, 79, 131, 132, 151, 174, 251, 263, 280, 283
Aditya Birla Group, 57
Aditya Birla, 57
adult education, 266
agribusiness, 40
agriculture, 68, 69
AIFTA *see* ASEAN-India Free Trade Agreement (AIFTA)
AirAsia, 245
air connectivity, 251
Air India, 255
air pollution, 231, 236
air quality, 236
Airtel India, 49
Akbaruddin, Syed, 176
ancient monuments, 134
Andaman and Nicobar Islands development, 283

AOIP *see* ASEAN Outlook on the Indo-Pacific (AOIP)
Arabian Sea littoral, 81, 82
architectural monuments, 106
area-based development, 200
ARF *see* ASEAN Regional Forum (ARF)
artificial intelligence (AI), 76
ASCN *see* ASEAN Smart Cities Network (ASCN)
ASEAN Agreement on E-commerce, 210
ASEAN Agreement on Transboundary Haze Pollution, 238
ASEAN-centric regional architecture, 28
ASEAN-China interaction, 158
ASEAN-China Summit, 161
ASEAN Community Vision, 12, 232, 233
ASEAN Defence Ministers' Meeting-Plus (ADMM-Plus), 12, 64, 74, 80, 174, 280
ASEAN Economic Blueprint 2025, 248

ASEAN Five-Point Consensus, 160
ASEAN Foreign Ministers' Post-Ministerial Conference, 261
ASEAN Human Rights Declaration, 260
ASEAN-India Air Transport Agreement, 253
ASEAN-India Business Council, 55
ASEAN-India business ties
    business opportunities, 57
    challenges and potential, 58–60
    past to present, 56–58
ASEAN-India Centre in New Delhi, 12
ASEAN-India Commemorative Summit, 219
ASEAN-India connectivity
    aviation connectivity, 99
    digital connectivity, 99, 100
    energy products, 100, 101
    maritime connectivity, 98, 99
    rail connectivity, 97
    roads and highways, 95–97
    trade facilitation, 100
ASEAN-India cooperation, 98
ASEAN-India Development Partnership Programme, 125
ASEAN-India Dialogue Relations, 80, 126
    dynamics of, 273–278
ASEAN-India digital highway, 232
ASEAN-India economic engagement, 22
ASEAN-India Free Trade Agreement (AIFTA), 20, 252
ASEAN-India Free Trade Area, 227
ASEAN-India Friendship Year, 13, 121
ASEAN-India Investment Agreement, 227
ASEAN-India Maritime Transport Cooperation Agreement, 98
ASEAN-India Network of Think Tanks Roundtable, 124
ASEAN-India Partnership for Peace, Progress and Shared Prosperity, 227, 228
ASEAN-India Plan of Action (2021–2025), 232
ASEAN-India relationship, 22
ASEAN India Space Cooperation, 219
ASEAN-India Special Foreign Ministers Meeting, 219
ASEAN-India strategic partnership, 98
ASEAN-India Students Exchange Programme, 133
ASEAN-India Summit, 263
ASEAN-India Trade in Goods Agreement, 43, 209
ASEAN-India Trade in Services and Investment Agreement (AITSIA), 20, 43, 46, 47
ASEAN-India trade relations, 36, 64
    direct investment flows, 21
    economic relationship, 21
    expanded economic ties, 20
    extensive economic relationship, 20
    FDI equity inflow, 46
    India and China's flows, 24
    Philippines, 36, 37
    satisfactory outcome, 24
    Singapore, 36
    substantial economic relationship, 20

Index 303

supply chain reconfiguration, 26
Thailand, 36
total goods trade, 22
tourist flows growth, 21, 22
Vietnam, 36
ASEAN Investment Report 2020–2021, 47
ASEAN-led East Asian regional order, 74
ASEAN Maritime Forum, 64, 98
ASEAN Outlook on the Indo-Pacific (AOIP), 74, 173, 178, 183
ASEAN Peatland Forest Project, 240
ASEAN Plan of Action for Energy Cooperation (2016–2025), 238
ASEAN Plus One agreements, 145
ASEAN Plus One FTAs, 142, 146
ASEAN Political-Security Community Blueprint, 259
ASEAN region *see* Association of Southeast Asian Nations (ASEAN)
ASEAN Regional Forum (ARF), 12, 28, 64, 74, 80, 157, 174, 280, 282
ASEAN Secretariat data, 46, 47
ASEAN Single Aviation Market, 246
ASEAN Smart Cities Network (ASCN), 195
ASEAN Socio-Cultural Community Blueprint (Secretariat), 130
ASEAN Statistical Yearbook 2021, 231
ASEAN+3 (ASEAN plus China, Japan and Korea) Summit, 12
'ASEAN Way', 75, 77
ASEAN Working Group on Chemicals and Waste, 239
Asia-Europe Meeting, 12
Asian civilisation, 163
Asian Development Bank (ADB), 66, 88, 96
Asian financial crisis, 260
1982 Asian Games, 57
Asian Highway (AH) system, 90
Asian Relations Conference in Delhi, 165
Asia-Pacific Economic Cooperation, 151, 174, 186
Asia-Pacific region, 13, 175, 181
Association of Southeast Asian Nations (ASEAN), 9, 142, 149, 192
  economic cooperation, 11
  full-time diplomatic mission, 12
  institutional integration, 11
  investments into India, 45
  membership, 9, 10
  non-communist countries, 10
  services trade, 36
  trade and economic agreements with, 44
  trade and investment partners, 44
Atmanirbhar Bharat (Self-reliant India), 44, 154, 254
Australia, 28, 154, 177
automobile industry, 47

B
'Backward Caste' certificate, 269
Bali Concord II, 130
Basic Exchange Cooperation Agreement, 176
Bay of Bengal Initiative for Multi-Sectoral Technical and Economic Cooperation (BIMSTEC), 64, 80, 81, 88, 125, 263
B2B collaborations, 220
'Below Poverty Line' card, 269

Bhaumakavya, 6
Biden, Joe, 184
bilateral agreements, 20
bilateral investment treaty, 38, 47, 64, 65
bilateralism, 248
biodiversity, 230, 231, 236
bio-energy, 238
bioinformatics, 50
Blue Economy, 49, 50, 98, 241
border crisis, 168
BPO operations, 49
British Indian Army, 164
British military engagement, 164
broad-based institution, 175
Buddhism, 106, 107, 132
Buddhist tourism circuit, 123
Bush, George, 184
business cooperation, 65
business landscape, 59, 60
business linkages, 63
business-to-business channels, 27

C
Caballero-Anthony, Mely, 261
Cambodia, 26, 80
Cambodian conflict, 11
capacity-building projects, 133
carbon neutrality, 230
caste-based violence, 267
CECA *see* Comprehensive Economic Cooperation Agreements (CECA)
Chagla, Mohammadali Carim, 9
Chan, Chun Sing, 147
Chaudhury, Dipanjan Roy, 133
Cheena Bhavan (Sino-Indian cultural studies), 165
Chiang, Kai Shek, 165
child attend school, 268

China, 11, 19, 28, 80, 151
    ASEAN and India's relations with, 157–162
    ASEAN's Dialogue Partners, 157
    border crisis, 168
    economic influence, 158
    military action, 167
    military power, 185
    nationalism, 165
    national movement, 184
    occupation of Tibet in 1950, 166
    people-to-people exchanges, 158
    perceived geopolitical reality, 158
    regional political influence, 158
    relationship, 22
    revisionist power, 159
    strategic influence, 158
    Western imperialism, 164
China-ASEAN connectivity, 248
Chryse Chersonesos, 4
Churchill, Winston, 165
City Data Officer, 203
city's urban planning systems, 191
civilisational heritage, 132
civilisational linkages, 116
Clark Airport construction project, 39
clean energy, 238
climate change, 101, 185, 192, 228–231, 236, 262
Climate Change Projections and Assessment of Impacts, 240
climate crisis, 236
Climate Risk Atlas, 240
2018 Climate Watch data, 229
clinical trial market, 50
CLMV (Cambodia, Laos, Myanmar and Vietnam) countries, 67, 68, 99, 219

Index   305

closer economic integration, 142
coastal ecosystems, 241
coastal tourism opportunities, 50
COC *see* Code of Conduct (COC)
Code of Conduct (COC), 76, 159, 160
Cold War, 9–11, 80, 273
colonialism, 106, 164
Commemorative Summit with ASEAN, 12
commerce, connectivity and culture (3 'Cs'), 131
Common Era (CE), 3
communication technology, 69
community building, 130
competitive application process, 200
competitiveness, 59
complementarity, 56
complex balance of power, 175
Comprehensive and Progressive Agreement for Trans-Pacific Partnership, 177
Comprehensive Economic Cooperation Agreement (CECA), 27, 150, 279
Comprehensive Economic Partnership Agreement, 134, 142
Comprehensive Progressive Trans-Pacific Partnership, 151
comprehensive security, 259
comprehensive strategic partners, 158
computer programming, 37
Confederation of Indian Industry, 56, 144
1962 conflict, 166
connectivity, 65, 178
    land connectivity, 88–93
    maritime connectivity, 87

    people-to-people connectivity, 65, 67
    physical connectivity, 87, 88
consultancy, 37
consumer markets, 63
contemporary "Asian identity", 182
conventional energy, 67, 68
cooperation, 13, 68, 160
cooperative developmental idea, 9
corruption, 267
Council on Energy, Environment and Water, 240
counter-terrorism, 184
COVID-19 pandemic, 32, 44, 45, 47, 64, 69, 82, 84, 123, 141, 144, 151, 158, 168, 203
    air connectivity, 251
    cities' 'smartness', 196
    Fourth Industrial Revolution, 217
    global economic slowdown, 231
    social distancing, 217
    vaccine exports, 13
    vaccine support, 178
    work-from-home, 210, 217
crop diversification, 68, 69
cross-border
    business opportunities, 56
    clearance ecosystem, 100
    connectivity project, 96
    digital payment, 224
    economic activity, 88
    electricity exchange, 100, 101
    electricity trading, 238
    e-payments, 60
    fibre optic networks, 99
    investments, 70
cross-civilisational linkages, 121
cross-pillar cooperation section, 232

cross-regional connectivity, 66
cultural diplomacy, 132
cultural diversity, 130
cultural exchanges
    and creativity, 114
    cultural embrace, 111
    cultural influence, 113
cultural integration, 112
culture industry, 116
cutting-edge fields, 60
cybersecurity infrastructure, 76, 194, 232
cynicism, 74

D
Dalai Lama, 167
Data and the City (Kitchin), 202
data-driven smart urbanism, 202–204
Data Maturity Assessment Framework, 203
data protection, 194
DataSmart Cities Strategy, 203
data trends, 44
Datuk Ali bin Abdullah, 10
decision-making process, 151, 260, 262
Delhi Metro rail network, 267
Department of Science and Technology, 220
devaraja (god-king), 107
development cooperation, 13
Dewa Baruna, 6
Dialogue Partner in December 1976, 10
digital
    connectivity, 99
    economy, 44, 49, 60, 69, 210, 217
        adopt technology, 221

        B2B collaborations, 220
        digital infrastructure, 211
        distributional impacts, 210, 211
        G2G collaboration, 218–220
        infrastructure and connectivity, 221
        online financial services, 221
        recommendations, 222–224
    environment, 193
    financial inclusion, 224
    future, 126
    identification system, 211
    intelligence, 191
    payments, 69
    technology, 115
    villages, 219
    watches, 57
Digital Economy Partnership Agreements, 70
digital turn, 203
dignity/*samman*, 132
diplomacy, 129
direct investment flows, 21
domestic and foreign airlines, 252
domestic environment, 57
domestic political agenda, 174
domestic product, 44, 58
drug manufacturing, 50
dynamic experimentation, 192
dynamic industry sectors, 64

E
EAMF *see* Expanded ASEAN Maritime Forum (EAMF)
EAS *see* East Asia Summit (EAS)
East Asia Free Trade Agreement, 142
East Asian 'Tiger' economies, 81

Index   307

East Asia Summit (EAS), 12, 28, 64, 74, 81, 157, 174, 280
Eastern Indian Ocean region, 81
East-West Economic Corridor (EWEC), 89, 96
e-commerce, 49, 210, 211
    adopt technology, 221
    B2B collaborations, 220
    digital infrastructure, 211
    distributional impacts, 210, 211
    G2G collaboration, 218–220
    infrastructure and connectivity, 221
    market, 218
    negotiations, 220
    online financial services, 221
    provisions, 146
    recommendations, 222–224
economic and security ties, 131
economic community, 130
economic complementarities, 27
economic cooperation, 11, 76, 83, 177, 228
economic engagement, 12, 19
economic integration, 154
economic liberalisation, 63, 74
economic partnership, 19
Economic Research Institute for ASEAN and East Asia, 96
The Economic Times, 133
Economist Intelligence Unit, 231
educational exchange programmes, 124
e-governance, 217
Eighth and Ninth Freedoms of the Air, 246
electricity, 100
electronic goods, 57
Eminent Persons' Lectures Series, 67
end-to-end digital trade, 70
energy security, 68
energy transition, 237
English Language Training and Entrepreneurship Development Centres, 67
Enhanced Trade Partnership, 154
enthusiasm, 157
entrepreneurship, 59, 64
European Union (EU), 130
e-waste, 239
exclusive economic zone surveillance cooperation, 283
Expanded ASEAN Maritime Forum (EAMF), 12
expanded economic ties, 20
Experts Group meetings, 146
Export Import Data Bank of India, 28

F
FDI *see* foreign direct investment (FDI)
federal system, 59
Federation of Indian Chambers of Commerce and Industry, 56
films and dramas, 109, 110
financial and insurance services, 47, 67
financial technology, 60
food price volatility, 69
food security, 68, 69, 236
foreign airlines, 56
foreign direct investment (FDI), 22, 35, 45, 51, 153, 246
foreign investors, 70
foreign policy, 74
forestry management, 230, 231
Four Plans of Action, 228

Fourth Industrial Revolution (4IR), 210, 211, 213, 217
free trade agreement (FTA), 13, 27, 64, 82, 83, 142, 149, 209, 279
full-time diplomatic mission, 12
functional cooperation, 227

G
Gandhi, Mahatma, 165, 166, 266
　human security, 270
　non-violent means, 166
Gandhi, Indira, 9
Ganga Mekong Cooperation, 80
Garuda, 113
GDP *see* gross domestic product (GDP)
gender inequality, 267
geo-political calculus, 274
geo-political challenges, 25
geo-political strategy, 74
G2G collaboration, 218–220
'Glasgow Leaders Declaration on Forests and Land Use', 230
global
　collaboration, 26
　competitiveness, 25
　economic growth, 235
　economy, 149
　financial crisis, 82
　governance, 161
Global Coral Reef Monitoring network, 241
Global Ocean Observing System, 241
Global Smart City Index, 191
Global Times, 168
global value chains (GVCs), 25, 283
GMR Group, 39
Goh, Evelyn, 175

good governance, foundations of, 59, 265–270
Goods and Services Tax bill in 2017, 59
Government Technology Agency, 197
'Greater East Asia Co-prosperity Sphere', 182
Greater Mekong Subregion (GMS) programme, 88, 89
greenhouse gas (GHG) emissions, 229
green recovery, 231–232
grid integration, 238
gross domestic product (GDP), 68, 217, 252
Guiding Principles and Objectives for Negotiating the RCEP, 152
Gujral, I K, 12

H
harmonising trade, 66
'Hawkers Go Digital' programme, 195
healthcare industry, 50
higher education, 106, 107
high touch smart city, 193–195
Hikayat Hang Tuah, 5
Hikayat Raja Muda, 5
Hikayat Sang Boma, 6
Hindu and Buddhist sites, 108
Hinduism, 106, 132
Hindustan Times, 134
home appliances, 57
horticulture, 68
hospitality, 47
Housing and Development Board (HDB) planners, 192
Huang, Xilian, 158

human rights concept, 161, 260
human security, 259–264
　　drugs and human trafficking, 262
　　human rights concept, 260
　　human rights violations, 262
　　policymaking and implementation, 267–269
　　relevance of, 265–270
　　social upliftment, 266, 267
Hundred Days of Reform, 164
hydro energy, 68, 238

I
ICCCs *see* Integrated Command and Control Centres (ICCCs)
ICT *see* information and communications technology (ICT)
ICT-led services, 47
IMDA *see* Infocomm Media and Development Authority (IMDA)
Imphal-Moreh 111-kilometre railway line project, 97
income inequality, 211
India
　　'Act East' policy, 13, 14
　　blue economy, 241
　　border crisis, 168
　　civilisational heritage, 132
　　Commemorative Summit with ASEAN, 12
　　communist supporter, 10
　　1962 conflict, 166
　　1991 crisis and economic reforms, 281
　　Dialogue Partner in December 1976, 10, 11
　　economic prosperity and security, 9
　　economic relations with ASEAN, 27
　　emerging challenges, 13, 14
　　Indo-Pacific strategy, 175
　　institutional integration, 11
　　investments in ASEAN, 47, 48
　　'Look East' policy, 11
　　nuclear weapons free zone, 10
　　Pakistan influence, 10
　　pharmaceuticals and healthcare products, 50
　　pre COVID-19 pandemic trade, 64
　　religious traditions of, 106
　　renewable energy, 238
　　strategic autonomy, 183–186
　　support for the Sri Lankan, 10
　　total water withdrawal, 236
　　on Vietnam, 13
　　Western imperialism, 164
　　World War II, 165
　　see also individual entries
India-ASEAN
　　air connectivity, 252
　　bilateral engagement, 221
　　connectivity, 131
　　film festival, 110
　　interface, 80, 82
　　rail land bridge, 92
　　relationship, 28, 73, 81, 131
　　services, 31
　　trade, 29, 177
　　see also ASEAN-India trade relations
India-ASEAN CECA, 30, 31
India-ASEAN Commemorative Summit, 80
India-ASEAN cultural linkages
　　films and dramas, 109, 110

310   Index

  Hindu and Buddhist sites, 108
  Ramayana epic, 107, 108
  religious linkages, 106, 107
  textiles, 108, 109
India-ASEAN FTA, 279
India-ASEAN summit in 2002, 12
India-China
  1962 border war, 75
  exchanges, 164
  gaps, 166
  relations, 167, 168, 184
  trade in 2021, 168
India-Myanmar border, 88
India-Myanmar Coordinated Patrol, 98
India-Myanmar-Thailand-Hanoi train link, 92, 97
India-Myanmar-Thailand-Malaysia-Singapore rail link, 97
India-Myanmar-Thailand Trilateral Highway, 66, 90, 131, 178, 264
Indian
  bilateral investment treaty, 38
  direct investment, 21
  economy, 44, 47
  foreign direct investment, 22
  foreign policy, 184
  massive trade deficit, 24
  national movement, 163
  political and business establishment, 24
  political ideas, 106
  supply chain reconfiguration, 26
  total goods trade, 23
  see also India
Indian Council of Social Science Research fellowships, 133
Indian Institutes of Technology (IITs), 124, 133

Indian Ministry of Commerce and Industry, 44, 64
Indian Ministry of Tourism, 40
Indian Ocean, 3, 10, 25, 49, 275–277, 283
Indian Ocean Rim Association umbrella, 49, 64, 283
Indian smart cities
  area-based development, 200
  data-driven smart urbanism, 202–204
  infrastructure development, 200–202
  local area development, 200
  urban governance, 200–202
Indian Technical and Economic Cooperation Programme, 133
Indian textiles and raw materials, 56
Indian Urban Data Exchange and an Urban Observatory, 203
India-Pakistan issues, 81
India-Singapore Comprehensive Economic Cooperation Agreement, 20, 152, 214
India-Singapore Entrepreneurship Bridge, 219
India-Singapore-Thailand Trilateral exercise, 76
India's Ministry of External Affairs, 123
India's Ministry of Tourism, 123
India's Northeast Frontier Railway, 97
Indo-Gangetic plain, 236
Indonesia, 10, 13, 35, 44, 47, 49, 65, 230
  multilateral agreement, 247
  people-to-people connectivity, 67
Indo-Pacific Oceans Initiative (IPOI), 13, 64, 284

Indo-Pacific region, 13, 14, 49, 160
  fluid geographies, 182, 183
  geo-economic imperatives, 14
  India and ASEAN, 186
  India's strategic autonomy, 183–186
  India's vision of, 174
  political concerns, 182
Indo-Pacific strategy, 174, 175
Infocomm Media and Development Authority (IMDA), 194
information and communications technology (ICT), 46, 68, 69, 199, 218
information technology (IT), 37, 38, 69, 99, 150
infrastructure development, 39, 47, 76, 200–202
infrastructure gaps, 223
Institute for Management Development, 191
institutional connectivity, 65, 66
insurance service, 67
Integrated Command and Control Centres (ICCCs), 202
intercultural communications, 115
international collaboration, 195, 196
International Monetary Fund, 47
International Solar Alliance (ISA), 238
Internet of Things (IoT) software, 49
intra-RCEP investments, 153
intra-regional air connectivity, 248
intra-regional supply chains, 146
investment flows, 280
investment promotion, 70
investment relations, 35
  wholesale and retail trade services, 37
investor-friendly policies, 44
4IR *see* Fourth Industrial Revolution (4IR)
ISA *see* International Solar Alliance (ISA)
ISEAS-Yusof Ishak Institute's ASEAN Studies Centre, 158
Islam, 132

J
Jaishankar, S, 176
Jan Dhan Yojana (financial inclusion programme), 267
Japan, 28, 153, 177
Jeepney Modernization Programme of the Philippines Department of Transportation, 40
Jensen, Robert, 212
Jiribam-Imphal-Moreh route, 97
job-creating enterprises, 153
Joint Working Group on Financial Technology, 219
Journey to the West, 164

K
Kaladan Multimodal Transit Transport (KMTT) project, 66, 95, 96, 131
Kalinga, 5
Kanchi, 5
Kang, Youwei, 164
Kashmir dispute, 184
Kazhagam, 5
Keling/Kling, 5
Khattar, Sat Pal, 58
kingdom of glory, 5
Kitchin, Rob, 202
knowledge sharing, 195, 196
Korea, 28

Kraft, Herman Joseph S., 261
Kumaran, Shambhu, 38

L
land bridge challenges and motivations, 88, 89
land connectivity, 88–93
    governance and institutions, 92, 93
    land bridge challenges and motivations, 88, 89
    rail transport, 91, 92
    road transport, 90, 91
Land Transport Authority, 193
Laos, multilateral agreement, 247
Latin American economies, 182
learning city, 196
Lee, Hsien Loong, 14, 126
Lee, Kuan Yew, 11, 57
liberalisation, 245
'Licence Raj', 57
Lim, Hng Kiang, 147
linear fashion, 80
Line of Actual Control, 167, 168
liquid biofuel production, 238
local area development, 200
local entrepreneurs, 70
logistics, 41
long-held protectionism, 174
long-term low emissions development strategy (LT-LEDS), 230
'Look East' policy, 11, 12, 27, 28, 43, 44, 57, 63, 73, 79, 80, 81, 131, 209, 228
Lopez, Ramon, 38
low-carbon growth path, 101
low-fare airlines, 245
low wage growth rates, 211
Lowy Institute's 'Asia Power Index 2021', 176
LT-LEDS *see* long-term low emissions development strategy (LT-LEDS)
lucrative market, 69

M
Mactan-Cebu Airport, 39
Mahabharata, 106
Mahatma Gandhi National Rural Employment Guarantee Act (MNREGA), 267, 268
Mahayana Buddhism, 5
Mahindra Motors, 39, 40
'Make in India' in 2014, 59
Malaysia, 35, 44, 45, 49, 56, 65
    people-to-people connectivity, 67
Mani Maykhala, 4
Manimekalai, 5
Manimekhala, 5
manufacturing competitiveness, 24, 39
Mao, Zedong, 166
maritime connectivity, 87
maritime cooperation, 178
maritime security ties, 98
maritime transport, 178
market equity capitalisation, 47
medical tourism, 67
Meiktila-Kyaingtong-Tachileik, 90
Mekong-Ganga Cooperation (MGC) initiative, 64, 88
Mekong-India Economic Corridor (MIEC), 96
membership, 9, 10, 153
micro, small and medium-sized enterprises (MSME), 283

mid-day meal scheme, 268
middle class, 60
military realm, 76
Ministry of Electronics and Information Technology, 219
Ministry of Housing and Urban Affairs (MoHUA), 202, 203
Ministry of Human Resource Development, 133
Ministry of Information and Communications, 219
Misri, Vikram, 175
Mission Management Unit, 203
mobile phones, 212
Modi, Narendra, 14, 41, 59, 73, 75, 132, 143, 168, 185, 228, 273
    Indo-Pacific region, 174
    Shangri-La Dialogue speech, 174
Mohamad, Mahathir, 11
MoHUA *see* Ministry of Housing and Urban Affairs (MoHUA)
Monetary Authority of Singapore (MAS), 145
Monius, Anne, 5
motivations, 89
Mountbatten, Lord Louis, 182
MRAs *see* mutual recognition agreements (MRAs)
MSME *see* micro, small and medium-sized enterprises (MSME)
MSMEs sector, 212
Mukherjee, Bhaswati, 132
multifaceted relationship, 63
multilateral connection, 65
multilateralism, 175, 248
multinational enterprises (MNEs), 48
Municipal Services Office, 193
mutual recognition agreements (MRAs), 214

Myanmar, 14, 66, 69
    human rights violations, 262
    State Administration Council regime, 161
    topography, 89
    violence, cycle of, 160
Myanmar crisis, 161, 262
Myanmar-Thai border, 88

N
Nalanda University, 124
Nang Mekhala, 4
Nanyang Technological University, 193
National Clean Air Programme in 2019, 238
National Committee for Trade Facilitation (NCTF), 100
National Cyber Security Masterplan, 194
National Institute of Urban Affairs, 203
National Investment Promotion and Facilitation Agency, India, 43
nationalism, 166
Nationally Determined Contributions (NDC), 229
National Parks Board, 197
national rural broadband networks, 219
national security aides, 183
National Urban Digital Mission, 203
National Urban Learning Platform, 203
'natural centre of gravity', 275
natural resources, 229
negotiation process, 143
Nehru, Jawaharlal, 164, 165
'Neighbourhood First' policies, 121
NephroPlus (India), 50

New Zealand, 28
next generation, 126
Neytal, 6
9th Association of Southeast Asian Nations (ASEAN) Summit, 130
non-alignment and strategic autonomy, 183
non-communist countries, 10
non-Congress government in New Delhi (1977–1980), 10
non-government organisations, 262
non-government players, 132
non-Indian manufactured goods, 56
non-interference principle, 262
non-political representative, 161
non-tariff barriers, 66
northeast region, 66
North-South Economic Corridor, 96
'Now Everyone Can Fly', 245
Nuclear Suppliers Group, 185
nuclear weapons, 75
nuclear weapons free zone, 10

O
Obama, Barack, 184
'omni-enmeshment' strategy, 175
OneService mobile application, 193
online financial services, 221
open skies agreement, 245
   developments, 253
   domestic and foreign airlines, 252
   India-ASEAN air connectivity, 252
   potential benefits for, 254
"open, stable, secure and prosperous Indo-Pacific" vision, 173
Opium War of 1840, 164
Osborne, Milton, 122
overlapping membership, 131, 263

P
Pacific and Master Plan on ASEAN Connectivity, 96
Pakistan, 11, 80, 184
Pakistan influence, 10
Pali language, 106
Pali-Sanskrit vocabulary, 106
Pambagyo, Pak Iman, 145
pan-Asianism, 165, 182
pan-Asian project, 164
pan-city initiatives, 200
2015 Paris Agreement, 229
participating countries (RPCs), 141, 143
Patel, Sardar Vallabhbhai, 166
Pattinapalai, 4, 6
Payne, Gregory, 132
"people-centred" ASEAN vision, 260
people empowerment, 270
People's Liberation Army (PLA), 166
People's Republic of China, 166
people-to-people connectivity, 65, 67, 129
   community building, 130
   economic community, 130
   multi-pronged approach, 129
   optimising existing mechanisms, 133
   politico-security community, 130
   socio-cultural community, 130
   weakest links, 131
people-to-people ties
   education and think tanks, 124, 125
   in sub-regions, 125
   tourism, ASEAN-India neighbourhood, 123
perceived geopolitical reality, 158

Personal Account Number (PAN) card, 269
Personal Data Protection Commission, 194
Petcharamsee, Sriprapha, 260
pharmaceuticals and healthcare products, 39, 50
"phase out" to "phase down" coal, 229
Philippine Department of Tourism, 40
Philippines, 36, 37, 158, 241
    coastal ecosystems, 241
    multilateral agreement, 247
Philippines-India Agreement on Air Services, 41
physical connectivity, 65, 87, 88
physical infrastructure, 64
pilgrimages, 106
Pilipinas Taj Autogroup Inc., 39
Pillai, Gopinath, 58
pilot project, 219
Pitsuwan, Surin, 260
PLA *see* People's Liberation Army (PLA)
Plan of Action forward, 222
Plan of Action to Implement the ASEAN-India Partnership for Peace, Progress and Shared Prosperity (2021–2025), 218
plastic waste, 239
Plaza Accords in 1985, 25
PLI *see* Production Linked Incentives (PLI)
pluralism epistemology, 111
PMCs *see* Project Management Consultants (PMCs)
political cooperation, 228
political economy, 89
political relationship, 80

politico-security community, 130
Pollock, Sheldon, 5
pollution, 229
positive narrative, 81
post-Cold War period, 73, 79, 274
post COVID-19 world, 43–51
post-free trade agreements, 43
post-Independence business ties, 56
post-pandemic economic dealings, 232
post-World War II, 184
pragmatic cultural policy, 115
pre COVID-19 pandemic trade, 64
primary public health, 236
private investment opportunities, 47
private sector, 193
Production Linked Incentives (PLI), 44
professional services, 47
Project Development Fund, 99
Project Management Consultants (PMCs), 200, 201
Project on Enhancing Climate Change Adaptation in Southeast Asia, 240
public diplomacy, 129, 132

Q
Qing empire, 165
Quad-Plus members, 76
Quadrilateral Security Dialogue (Quad), 14, 74, 76, 176, 181, 276
Quarterly Journal of Economics, 212
Quick Impact Projects, 133

R
rail connectivity, 97
Rail India Technical and Economic Service Ltd., 97

rail transport, 91, 92
Rajendra Chola I, 5, 6
Ramayana, 4, 105–108, 122
Ram, Sumant Bharat, 58
Ram, Vinay Bharat, 58
Rao, Narashima, 11, 57, 73, 121, 209, 228, 274
Rashtriya Swasthya Bima Yojana (a government-run health insurance programme for the Indian poor), 267
ration card, 269
RCEP *see* Regional Comprehensive Economic Partnership (RCEP)
RCEP Trade Negotiating Committee, 142
real estate development, 47, 58
Real Estate Regulation and Development Act in 2016, 59
Regional Comprehensive Economic Partnership (RCEP), 13, 24, 28, 35, 75, 82, 131, 174, 209, 221, 254, 273
   2006, 142
   2019, 143, 144
   2020, 144, 145
   benefits of, 145, 146
   2012, launch of, 142, 143
   long-term interest, 144
regional connectivity, 56
regional cooperation, 11
Regional Cooperation Agreement on Combating Piracy and Armed Robbery against Ships in Asia (ReCAAP), 282
regional economic cooperation for development, 10
regional geography, 182
regional high-capacity fibre-optic network, 219
regionalism, 175
regional security community, 259
regional trade architecture, 142
regulatory cooperation, 222
religious and cultural engagements, 20
religious linkages, 106, 107
renewable energy, 40, 67, 68, 238
Republic of India, 166
responsibility, 229, 259
restrictive institutional arrangements, 66
Rigveda, 105
road transport, 90, 91
Rohingya issue in Myanmar, 81
Royal Care Dialysis (Philippines), 50
3R (Reduce, Reuse, Recycle) programme, 239
Russia, 181

S
SAGAR (Security and Growth for All in the Region), 282
samriddhi, co-prosperity, 132
Samudra Manthan, 113
samvaad, dialogue and negotiation, 132
Sangam era, Tamil literature, 4
Sang Nila Utama story, 6
sanskriti evam sabhyata, civilisational and cultural links, 132
Sanskrit language, 5, 106
satisfactory outcome, 24
SCAFs *see* Smart Cities Advisory Forums (SCAFs)
'Scheduled Caste/Tribe' certificate, 269
SCM *see* Smart City Mission (SCM)
SEApeat Project, 240
seaward trade, 56

Sectoral Dialogue Partner, 11, 20, 79, 80, 95
'Security and Growth for All in the Region' policy, 98
security cooperation, 131, 228
security-related issues, 12
security threats, 81
Sejarah Melayu, 5
'Seniors Go Digital' programme, 195
17th India-ASEAN Summit, 14
74th Constitutional Amendment Act 1992, 201
2018 Shangri-La Dialogue in Singapore, 173
sharing economy, 212
shipping agreements, 283
Sikhism, 106
Silapadikaram, 4
Silk Road, 164
Singapore, 13, 22, 29, 35, 45, 47, 49, 65, 230
    city-to-city mutual learning, 195
    climate change, 230
    cybersecurity infrastructure, 194
    data protection, 194
    electronic goods, 57
    exports and imports, 36
    infrastructure and leads, 192
    people-to-people connectivity, 67
    trading partner, 36
Singapore Stone, 5
Singapore University of Technology & Design, 191
Sino-US partnership, 184
16th India-ASEAN Summit in Bangkok, 253
skilled labour, 213
small- and medium-enterprises (SMEs), 146, 217
smart cities, 196
Smart Cities Advisory Forums (SCAFs), 200
Smart City Mission (SCM), 199
Smart Nation Sensor Platform, 193
Smart Nation vision, 191
smartphones, 212
smart technologies, 193
SME exporters and start-ups, 223
SMEs *see* small- and medium-enterprises (SMEs)
social distancing, 217
socialist revolution, 166
social media, 114
social welfare schemes, 267
socio-cultural community, 130, 134
soft power diplomacy, 132
software services, 69
solar and wind energy, 68
solar photovoltaics, 238
South Asian Business Group of the Singapore Business Federation, 55
South China Sea, 3, 14, 25, 76, 159
Southeast Asia, 56, 80, 105, 106, 132
    cultural linkages, 132
    economic complementarities, 27
    regional connectivity, 4, 20, 56
    tourism sector, 135
    Treaty of Amity and Cooperation, 157
Southeast Asia: An Introductory History (Osborne), 122
Southeast Asian society, 132
1995 Southeast Asia Nuclear Weapons Free Zone, 157
Southern Economic Corridor, 96
Soviet Union, 10, 11, 57, 80, 184

'spaghetti bowl' effect, 142
Special Economic Zones, 201
special purpose vehicles (SPVs), 200, 201
SPVs *see* special purpose vehicles (SPVs)
Sri Lanka, 5
Sri Thendayuthapani Temple, Singapore, 3
State Administration Council regime, 161
'State of Southeast Asia 2022' survey, 158, 159, 178
Straits of Malacca, 3
The Straits Times, 253
strategic engagement, 28
Strategic Investment Research Unit (SIRU), 43
strategic partnership, 43, 121, 263
    blue economy, 49, 50
    digital technologies, 49
    sectoral opportunities for, 47, 48
student exchange, 67
sub-regional cooperation, 64
substantial economic relationship, 20
Sulalat al-salāṭīn, 5
supply chains, 26, 88
suruksha, regional and global security, 132
sustainable agricultural systems, 240
sustainable development, 178
Sustainable Use of Peatland and Haze Mitigation in ASEAN, 238
Suvarnabhumi, 4

T
TAC *see* Treaty of Amity and Cooperation (TAC)
Tagore, Rabindranath, 164, 165
Talace Pvt Ltd., 255

Tamil legends, 5
Tamil pantheon, 6
Tamu-Mandalay-Meiktila-Myawaddy, 90
tariff barriers, 21
Tata Communications, 49, 220
Tata Group, 57
Tata Motors, 39, 40
Tech Mahindra (India), 49
telecommunications service, 67
televisions, 57
'test-and-learn' approach, 193
textiles, 108, 109
Thailand, 13, 14, 29, 36, 45, 230
    3R (Reduce, Reuse, Recycle) programme, 239
Thakral Group, 55
Thakral, Kartar Singh, 57
13th Philippines-India Joint Working Group on Trade and Investments in September 2020, 38
think-tank collaborations, 124
Tibetan refugee influx, 167
Tolkappiyam, 6
topography, 89
tourism sector, 40, 67, 116, 123, 135
tourist flows growth, 21, 22
TraceTogether, 196, 197
Tracks 1.5 and 2.0 conferences, 13
trade
    connectivity, 178
    deficit, 143
    facilitation, 66
    imbalance, 150
    and investment partners, 44
    liberalisation, 24, 88
traffic control, 196
transformative framework, 232
trans-regional mythic motif, 6

Treaty of Amity and Cooperation (TAC), 12, 157, 158
Trilateral Highway Motor Vehicle Agreement (T-MVA), 95, 96
Trump, Donald, 183
Trusted Data Sharing Framework, 194
12th ASEAN-India Summit in November 2014, 228
26th Conference of Parties (COP26), 229, 230

U
UIDAI *see* Unique Identification Development Authority of India (UIDAI)
unemployment, 211, 213
Unicommerce India, 49
Unique Identification Development Authority of India (UIDAI), 268
United Kingdom, 47
2021 United Nations Climate Change Conference, 101
United Nations Economic and Social Commission for Asia, 96
United Nations Framework Convention on Climate Change, 229
United Nations International Trade Statistics Database, 177
United Nations Security Council, 185
United Nations Sustainable Development Goals (UN SDGs), 232
United Nations' World Tourism Organization, 252
United States (US), 25, 173, 181
    Basic Exchange Cooperation Agreement, 176
    India's trade with, 177

urban development, 191
urban governance, 200–202
urban infrastructure development, 202
Urban Redevelopment Authority, 197
urban sewage, 236
US-China relations, 75
US-China strategic rivalry, 175
Ushahidi, 212
utility-scale solar, 238

V
vaccine development, 50
vaccine manufacturing supply chain, 50
Vedic arithmetic, 107
Vedic God Varuna, 6
videocassette recorder sets, 57
Vientiane Action Plan, 130
Vietnam, 10, 26, 29, 36, 49
    United States (US) war, 10
Vietnam War, 9
violence, cycle of, 160
Vishwabharati University, 165
Vision Statement, 12
Volvo, 193
voter identity card, 269

W
Wang, Yi, 159, 160
waste-to-energy plants, 239
water demand, 236
Western imperialism, 164
whole-of-society approach, 192, 193
wholesale and retail trade services, 37, 47
win-win partnership, 69
work-from-home, 210, 217
working-age population, 64

World Cities Summit, 195
World Sanskrit Conference, 107
World Trade Organization (WTO), 25
World Trade Organization Agreement on Trade Facilitation, 100
World War II, 165, 182
WTO *see* World Trade Organization (WTO)

X
Xi, Jinping, 168
Xuan Zang, 164

Z
Zone of Peace, Freedom and Neutrality (ZOPFAN), 10

www.ingramcontent.com/pod-product-compliance
Lightning Source LLC
Chambersburg PA
CBHW050527300426
44113CB00012B/1987